Shotguns On Review
38 Guns Tried & Tested

Bruce Buck

A SHOOTING SPORTSMAN BOOK

www.shootingsportsman.com

Copyright © 2011 by Bruce Buck
Photographs copyright as credited
All rights reserved
Used by permission

ISBN 978-1-60893-002-9

Designed by Lynda H. Mills

Printed in China

5   4   3   2   1

Library of Congress Cataloging-in-Publication Information

A SHOOTING SPORTSMAN BOOK

www.shootingsportsman.com

Distributed to the trade by National Book Network

Dedicated to

Richard "Schmoker" Schmitt

1942~2007

One of the good guys

Contents

Introduction
— 1 —

On Reviewing Guns
—5 —

Arrieta Model 06 .410
— 16 —

AyA 4/53 Cabela's Classic
— 20 —

B. Rizzini Round Body Game Gun
— 25 —

Baserri Mari HR Hunter
— 30 —

Beretta A400 Xplor Unico
— 34 —

Beretta Silver Pigeon V 28-Gauge
— 39 —

Beretta SV10 Perennia III
— 44 —

Blaser F3 Competition Sporting
— 49 —

Browning Citori Superlight Feather
— 55 —

Browning Superposed
— 61 —

Caesar Guerini Apex Field
— 65 —

Caesar Guerini Ellipse EVO
— 70 —

Caesar Guerini Magnus Light and Woodlander
— 74 —

CSMC A-10 American
— 78 —

CSMC RBL Launch Edition
— 85 —

CSMC RBL 28-Gauge
— 93 —

FAMARS Dove Gun
— 97 —

Fausti Dea Round Body
— 103 —

Franchi Veloce
— 108 —

Grulla 217RB
— 112 —

Huglu Side-by-Side
— 116 —

Ithaca Model 37 Featherlight 28
— 121 —

Kimber Valier
— 126 —

Kimber Marias
— 131 —

Kolar Sporter
— 137 —

Krieghoff Essencia
— 142 —

McKay Brown
— 148 —

Merkel 2116ELC
— 152 —

Perazzi MX8/20 28-Gauge
—157 —

Remington 105 CTi
—162 —

Remington Model 332
—168 —

Robertson Side-by-Side
—171 —

Ruger Gold Label
—176 —

Smith & Wesson Elite Gold
—182 —

Verney-Carron Azur Eloge .410
—189 —

Webley & Scott Boxlock
—193 —

Winchester Model 42
—199 —

Zoli Z Expedition
—203 —

Sources
—208 —

Introduction

Let's serve the guests pheasant." That's what started it. The year was 1972. I had just waded through law school and then business school and was based in the Big Apple. The girl I was dating was known for her dinner parties, so I thought nothing of it. In search of pheasant, I hailed a cab, crossed Park, then Fifth, went over to the West Side and then down Broadway to Balduccis, at that time home of New York City's more exotic foods. While placing my order, I saw one of my friends rooting though the pâtés and triple crèmes. We got to talking, and I told him why I was shopping.

"Bruce, you don't *buy* pheasant," he said. "You *hunt* them. Come with me this weekend and I'll show you. But first you'll need a shotgun." I'd never owned or even fired a shotgun, but it sounded like fun. Any excuse for new gear.

The next stop was Abercrombie & Fitch, where a polite but bemused salesman heard my request for a "pheasant gun to supply a dinner party of eight." Without even cracking a smile, he produced an 870 20-gauge, and I was off and running. That weekend we went to a Connecticut pheasant club where, much to my astonishment, I actually connected with a bird or two while my pal gleefully shot the rest.

You'd think that would have started it, but it didn't. The gun went into the back of the closet behind the fly-fishing gear. Then about six months later my friend called with an invitation to go

skeet shooting. It was fun. I also went to a couple of preserves to provide more birds for those dinners.

But it wasn't serious—yet. New York City and real day-to-day life had other priorities. But that all changed. One weekend I was down at New Jersey's Fort Dix shooting American-style skeet with some of the locals. I'd just entered my first NSSA shoot and shot what seemed to me was a good score. My bubble burst when one of my squad mates told me not to be disheartened. He was sure that with more experience I'd get better.

While manfully practicing away, I glanced down the line of skeet fields and saw a group of shooters all the way at the end. I asked who they were and why they weren't up here shooting with us. I was told that they were International Skeet shooters and that we didn't have much to do with them. Being curious, I trotted down to have a look.

The International guys invited me to try it out. I was told to start my gun with the butt at my hip, sort of like what I did when I tried to shoot pheasants. There would be a variable delay, so I might have to wait a second for the bird to come out. And it would come out faster, so I had to be ready for that. I hunkered down and called.

It seemed as though the ground actually shook when that old Winchester trap heaved out that International-speed bird. The target was so fast that, without even thinking, I yanked up the gun and fired. And the clay broke! I couldn't believe it. I was hooked. Low gun, fast birds. This was sport! The fact that I didn't hit much after that really didn't matter.

At that time, in the early '70s, the US Olympic, Pan-American and World Championship teams were decided at a once-a-year, winner-take-all, five-day US team trial. If you held a good International Skeet average, you got an invitation to the trial. If you placed first or second at that event in an Olympic year, you were on the US Olympic team. There was actually a chance, no matter how remote, that a weekend warrior could get hot and make the team. Today there is a series of trials throughout the year that pretty much precludes a civilian who has to work for a living from seriously attempting to make the team. But back then it was possible.

Because the average Joe actually had some vague hope of making a national team, International Skeet (IntSk) was a pretty popular sport. Far more so than now. That first year I went to numerous weekend competitions in the Northeast. And it was at one of these shoots that the second chapter began.

I met a Canadian couple, Bob and Jane McCaldon, who were serious about International Skeet but even more so about hunting ruffed grouse. Would I like to come up to Ontario that fall and join them for a week of chasing grouse and woodcock? I happily agreed, not knowing anything about what I was getting into. I'd never seen a grouse or a woodcock, not even in Central Park.

Oh, did I mention that Bob and Jane were marathoners and triathletes? I was pretty good at walking on city sidewalks and hailing cabs, but beating the bushes and walking uphill all day was new to me. At the end of the first day, Bob and Jane had gotten a couple of grouse. I had been scared witless by a few, my legs ached, the arm carrying my gun had stretched a foot, and I definitely needed a restorative libation. It sure wasn't anything like shooting preserve pheasants.

Fast forward. I divided my free time between IntSk competition and seasonal upland hunting. I got a little better at both. After some years I was even invited to coach IntSk at the US Olympic Training Center for a couple of summers. Those who can't do, teach, right?

After 16 years, four unsuccessful Olympic trials and something approaching a half-million rounds of ammo, it began to dawn on me that I simply wasn't good enough to beat the best on a regular basis. Close didn't count. It was time to hang it up. Besides, a new game called sporting clays was just opening up, and that looked like fun instead of work.

I also had the chance to do a bit of traveling on wingshooting trips. Some of the guys in the gun club I joined loved to wingshoot all over the place. They were kind enough to invite me. I went to different spots in the US, then to Honduras and Colombia for doves, and finally to Scotland a couple of times for driven grouse. I loved the trips and particularly liked the idea that no one kept score—other than the barkeep with the drink tab.

Writing about it all snuck up on me. Sporting clays in the US pretty much started in 1986. By the end of that year Al Anglace and some others had started the Connecticut Travelers, a sporting clays club in the Northeast. In a fit of something or other, I volunteered to write the club's newsletter, *Reload!* Had I but known . . . .

I was having fun scribbling the little shotgun advice columns. While I probably shouldn't have been giving shooting advice to anyone, I rationalized that, since I probably had done everything wrong possible, what was left had to be right. In a fit of hubris, I began sending the newsletter to the editors of shooting magazines just in case they were interested in what the Connecticut Travelers were up to.

This went on for years. And years. It was totally ignored. In the mid-'90s I did a couple of little pieces for Kenny Gagnon's *Modern Skeet and Clays* Magazine. It was fun, but I really didn't think much about it. Then it started.

In 1989 I moved from New York City to Connecticut and had more time on my hands. One day in 1994 I was shooting at a local gun club and talking to Roland Leong, a fellow gun nut and shooting pal. He asked me why I didn't put all of my old newsletter gun-advice columns, written under my pen name, the Technoid, onto an Internet site that he would set up and run. It would be great fun. We thought that the name *Shotgun Report* was cute, so we registered it, set up a site and started filling it with my old Technoid *Reload!* junk. As readers e-mailed questions, Roland and I would dream up answers and post them to the site, www.ShotgunReport.com. Surprisingly, it got to be pretty popular, and it remains so to this day, 17 years later. It has to be one of the longest-running shotgun sites on the Internet. It all goes to show that bad advice is better than no advice at all.

In the spring of 1997 Neil Chadwick and Debbie Phillips started *Clay Pigeon*, a newspaper-style monthly devoted to sporting clays. Neil was—and is—recognized as one of the best target setters in the Northeast. We had gotten to know each other as I shot his courses.

They were looking for content and asked me if I could do something for *Clay Pigeon* similar to what I was writing in *Reload!* and on *Shotgun Report*. I happily contributed an Ask the Technoid column to answer readers' questions.

When it rains, it pours. A bit later that year I got a letter from Ralph Stuart, editor of *Shooting Sportsman* Magazine. He said that he had been reading my newsletters and was wondering if I might be interested in doing the magazine's book review column. I told him that I hadn't reviewed any books since Miss Parker's fourth-grade class, but if he would send me a book as a test, I'd give it a try. He could decide if he liked what I wrote, and I could decide if I liked doing it. To my surprise, it worked out, and I became the magazine's book reviewer.

So there I was, writing for *Clay Pigeon*, *Shooting Sportsman*, *Shot-* *gun Report* and *Reload!* all at once. Who woulda thunk it? What had started as a hobby was now taking some serious time with very real monthly deadlines.

But there were some benefits, too. As happens for gun writers, junkets here and there materialized. Now I had an excuse to shoot more. It was my job. It was research. I even tried that line on my wife, much to her amusement.

In 1999 my *Clay Pigeon* writing grew to include gun reviews. I really liked writing those. I've always been a gear head and just loved an excuse to try out different shotguns. Five years later *Clay Pigeon* was absorbed by Mike Brunton's *Clay Shooting USA*, and I transferred my Ask the Technoid column there. In 2002 Vic Venters, who had replaced Michael McIntosh writing gun reviews for *Shooting Sportsman*, was called to other duties, and I moved from reviewing books to reviewing guns.

Shooting Sportsman also sponsors a couple of annual bird hunts called Readers & Writers Adventures. I began to host some of those. It was a privilege having the opportunity to meet the readers, a number of whom have become personal friends over the years.

In 2005 my wife and I moved from Connecticut to Florida, and I took retirement seriously. I'd had more than 20 shooting venues within two hours' drive of my New England home. Florida doesn't offer quite that number near our house, but there is plenty to keep me busy. It's nice to be able to shoot in comfort year-round, too. There's even an Olympic bunker up the road. I wear my golf spikes when I shoot there so that I don't slip on my tears.

Today I don't shoot the insane amount of shells that I did when trying out for the US team, but I run something between 10,000 and 15,000 annually, testing guns and shells, tinkering with stuff, shooting clays and taking a bunch of annual trips in search of the real thing.

Some of my favorite annual busman's holidays are to the Vintage

Cup, the Southern Side by Side, the SHOT Show and the SCI Convention. These shows give me the chance to look over everything that's new in shotguns and spend some time chatting with the guys who make and market them as well as the men who shoot them. I also have had the opportunity to visit gun factories in the US, Spain, England, Germany and Italy. Watching the guns being made is always an eye-opener. We take so much for granted when we hold the finished product in our hands.

And that's where it stands today, 40 years later. Life is good when your avocation becomes a vocation. Suchadeal! You couldn't ask for more fun.

On Reviewing Guns

We are all gun reviewers. Every time you borrow a friend's shotgun, look at a new or used one in the store or even peruse an ad, you are mentally reviewing that gun. I just do it in a slightly more formal structure, but it is really no different. With an eye toward giving you insight into the process, I'll go through what I look for when reviewing a gun for a magazine or when vetting a gun that I am considering buying.

I usually start with the receiver, because that's what most people concentrate on. I first look for design similarities with actions I am familiar with. You can definitely learn a lot from studying the parts diagram. Is it an Anson & Deeley-style boxlock? A Holland & Holland-style sidelock? If so, I know that the design is solid. Ditto any over/unders from Beretta, Perazzi or Browning (Belgian or Japanese). These are proven beyond any doubt. Sometimes I'm not sure how something will work out, so I ask around among my gunsmith acquaintances or friends in the industry. One particular new company had what looked like a weak stamped ejector trip arm, so I mentioned it. Turns out that the part works just fine and has proven durable. Unsurprisingly, the company's gun designers knew more than I did.

Sometimes an action design's main benefit is more cosmetic. The triggerplate action, which places the parts more centrally, makes it easier to produce an action with a nicely rounded underbody and

more comfortable field carry. That's if the makers wish to exploit the feature. They don't always. Some O/U triggerplate guns, like those from Perazzi, FAMARS and Zoli, have detachable triggers. They are great for yanking out and showing your friends. But as a practical matter, if the stock is easily removable, they aren't big assets to repair management, and they do add a little width and weight to the receiver.

It's possible to have an excellent design and lousy assembly or inferior parts. I once peeked inside an older mid-grade Spanish sidelock, one with the traditional H&H seven-pin action. The metal in that particular '60s gun was soft, and the inside was a mess. But it was a well-designed mess. Today's Spanish guns of a similar class have perfectly fine metal hardness. Hint: Before you buy any used gun, insist on being able to look inside the action.

Sometimes you can't get the interior tour. Your only hope then is to go by the design of the gun, the reputation of the maker, how the action feels as it is dry fired, and what you can see on the outside. Mistakes and poor fitment of metal on the outside can be a guide. If what you can see outside is bad, imagine what they are trying to hide inside.

Features often give you some indication of the quality of the gun. Sidelock side-by-sides, if they are better quality, usually come fitted with intercepting sears. This is a second sear, in addition to the primary one, that engages a second notch at the rear of the hammer. If the gun is inadvertently dropped hard enough to jar the primary sear from the hammer, the intercepting sear will act as a safety and prevent the hammer from dropping. If the trigger is pulled normally, both sears are pulled from the notches to let the hammer fall. Even some of the better boxlock side-by-sides have intercepting sears. Intercepting sears are a nice feature, involve a little more time and cost, and could come in very, very handy.

I always make a point of running a magnet over the gun. Occasionally it turns up a surprise. One Italian O/U had a steel receiver but aluminum forend iron, probably to control weight. I wasn't too happy about the gun hinging half on steel and half on aluminum. Aluminum really isn't bad; it just depends on where it is used.

Ejectors are one of the main problem areas of any two-barrel shotgun. Early Beretta 680-series guns had problems there, as did the Belgian Brownings from the '70s and later with the new-style fracture-prone ejectors. I try to test the ejector function using cheap steel-base hulls, because the steel expands when fired but doesn't contract the way brass does. Steel-base hulls can stick in tight chambers. If there is going to be an ejector problem, it more likely will happen first with the steel-base shells. I look for ejectors that toss the hulls well clear of the gun, but I don't want them to be so strong that they pelt people standing a dozen feet away. The harder they eject, the sooner they wear out or break. On my own guns, like the Superposeds with fragile ejector arms, I cut off a coil or two from the ejector springs to lower the wear. Works like a charm.

Triggers are personal up to a point. I measure pull weights with a trigger gauge. Hopefully they come out something around four pounds, more or less, sort of. Three to six pounds is a usable range, depending on the weight and use of the gun. Field guns can take a slightly heavy pull in order to prevent a stumble causing an inadvertent shot, but you know you are in trouble when the trigger pull is more than the weight of the gun. The precision of the shot and the more controllable circumstances of target shooting make lighter pulls practical. More important than trigger-pull weight is freedom from creep, slop and over-travel. There is nothing worse than a crumby trigger with what seems like a two-stage pull.

Trigger tuning is definitely an area where manufacturers try to save money, as that is generally a hand-labor process. Just about any trigger that isn't crippled by a bad design can be made good with some file time. It's just a matter of how long someone is paid to work on the gun.

Some makers claim that with modern CNC and EDM machinery they can cut their trigger sears to a correct pull without handwork. Perhaps, but I've seen more failures in this area than successes. As long as the design of the trigger is decent, it should be repairable. A poor trigger pull will generally just cost the owner some time with a decent gunsmith.

There is often discussion about inertia versus mechanical triggers. The former require the recoil of the first shot to move the inertia block to the rear and swing it over to engage the other sear. Many mechanical triggers have spring-loaded inertia blocks that will select the second sear when the trigger is pulled the first time. In theory, if you get a dud shell, the mechanical trigger will still deliver the second shot and the inertia trigger won't. I have Belgian Brownings set up both ways and have never been able to notice the slightest difference in real-life performance.

Double or single triggers? I'm happy with either. I have O/Us and side-by-sides set up both ways. I like the instant choke selection of double triggers but, to be frank, I often select the top barrel of a single-trigger O/U by simply firing the lower barrel first. Works like a charm. And it's amazing how often that "too-open" first-barrel choke decks the bird.

On sidelock side-by-side guns, especially the Spanish ones, it's best to get double triggers. Single triggers on those guns are tricky. The English have made them work by pouring on the man-hours, but when a sidelock side-by-side is built to a sane price, double triggers are the safer bet. That said, there are many boxlock-action side-by-sides with fine single triggers.

Double triggers have their downsides. The second shot isn't quite as fast. It's plenty fast for the real world of hunting, but it's hard to get a lightning-fast *controlled* double tap with two triggers. Your hand may not move when switching from the front to the rear trigger, but your grip definitely will relax ever so slightly. This is happening just as you are taking the recoil from the first shot. Couldn't happen at a worse time.

Most single-trigger guns are selective in that you can push a button or move the selective safety to activate the other barrel for the first shot. I'm sure that there is someone out there who can do that while a bird is in the air, and I doff my cap to you, sir. I sure can't. Most single-trigger O/Us have the barrel selector built into the safety. I simply never have the presence of mind to slide the toggle over as I move the safety forward.

Automatic safeties are always problematic. Field guns sometimes have them, but target guns never do. I don't like them, and here's why. I practice on clay targets a lot with my field guns. It really pays off in the fall. An auto safety drives me loony when I shoot clays. When I hunt, I constantly check the safety by feel, so I'm not worried about inadvertently leaving it live. On the plus side, many auto safeties are a piece of cake to convert to manual, so all is not lost.

All actions have some sort of locking system. That's what actions do. Is one better than another? I don't really know. Each system has its devotees. In my experience everything loosens up sooner or later, but modern guns are so good that most of us will never live to see that. I have a Webley & Scott double that is almost 90 years old. It's still tight, but it hasn't been shot that much compared to a target gun. When it does come off face, it will be a bit of a job, as the hinge pin on that gun is not replaceable. The hook will have to be dovetailed or TIG'd. The makers of many modern O/Us simply inventory locking bolts in several increasing sizes. When the old one wears, a new and larger one is quickly substituted. When I visited Battista Rizzini's Italian plant, he told me that he could completely rebuild a 100,000-round gun in a half-hour. With Browning Superposeds, it is often easier just to add a bit of length to the locking bolt by TIG welding rather than replace and refit it. When you read about a gun, it is nice to have this pointed out so that you will know what you—or your heirs—will be in for down the road.

Kersten crossbolts on O/Us and Greener crossbolts on side-by-sides have always seemed to me to be more complicated than necessary, but they obviously work and work well. I just don't like them because the crossbolts get caught on my hunting clothing when I carry the gun open and in my right hand. That's my problem, but it may not be yours.

We all worry about locking systems because we think that we will keep the gun longer or run more shells through it than will actually be the case. There aren't many hunting guns of any quality that you will wear out in a lifetime afield. Target shooting is different, and there you probably will need to do some rebuilding every 50,000 to 100,000 rounds. I had a Browning Superposed through which I personally put 106,000 rounds before it started to get a little loose. Another FN Superposed was still snug at 80,000. A couple of my Remington 1100s were junk (cracked receivers) by 35,000, but I didn't know then the secret of keeping a fresh mainspring in the gun. Autoloaders with weak mainsprings will beat themselves to death. If I had known that back then, they would have lived a lot longer.

So when I comment on a gun's action, I'm really not as concerned with longevity as I am with technical design just for the sake of it. There are so many different approaches, and with modern metallurgy they all seem to work pretty well.

Speaking of locks, it is always wise to note how the forend locks onto the barrels. There are two basic designs: the Anson pushbutton and the Deeley latch. Generally we see the Anson pushbutton on side-by-sides and the Deeley lever on O/Us. In both cases this allows the designer to use a minimalist forend if he prefers. When an Anson button is used on an O/U, it often results in a deeper forend than necessary. Whereas a Deeley latch on a side-by-side often requires that the forearm be made longer than necessary. In both cases the front end of the forearm can be less graceful than it should be. Not always, but it happens often enough that I make a point of mentioning it.

Barrels are different. Barrels are not really a design issue. They are more a function of execution. I don't care whether the barrels are joined by a separate monoblock piece into which the tubes are inserted, are of one piece as with the demi-block or chopper-lump system, are joined with a separate dovetail plate incorporating the lumps or something else. All methods applied with modern techniques and metals are strong. Chopper-lump jointure is more time-consuming and traditional and has the vague reputation of being able to place the barrels closer together than when using a monoblock for easier barrel regulation and supposedly more strength, but you couldn't prove it by me. Browning's Japanese O/Us went to monoblocks after using demi-blocks for years and nothing suffered.

To me, the barrels, not the action, are the heart of the gun. That's because they establish the all-important balance. Balance is everything. Durability and fit are of less concern. Just about all modern actions are strong. Most gunstocks can be bent or cut to fit most shooters. But balance and moment of inertia (the ability to change direction) are key. Yes, with subtle addition of weights fore and aft, balance can be fine tuned, but for the most part it is built in by the barrels.

The problem for a reviewer is that balance isn't a finite term. It's one of personal preference. What you like and what I like might be different. And the word "balance" doesn't really cover the situation. For example, imagine a broomstick and two bricks. Put a brick on each end of the broomstick and the "gun" will weigh a certain amount, balance in the middle and be slow to start swinging and slow to stop swinging. This would be called a high moment of inertia and might be what you want for long crossing clays or pass-shooting waterfowl. Now take the same broomstick and the same two bricks and put the bricks together in the middle. Same overall weight. Same central teeter-totter balance point, but now the "gun" is fast to start and fast to stop with a low moment of inertia. This might be just the thing for fast, close shots at grouse and quail. The balance point is the same on both examples, but the handling performance is very different. Just saying that a gun is "centrally balanced" doesn't mean very much.

Generally, I prefer a gun to have a central weight bias if it is heavy, but the weight should move forward as the gun gets lighter to avoid whippiness. A neutrally balanced seven-pound gun is fine, but one that is six pounds or less can be a handful for sure.

That's why I look at barrels so carefully. Thin barrels are light but expensive to make due to closer tolerances. Thick barrels are heavy and cheaper to make. Cheap guns tend to have heavy barrels. In a light sub-gauge gun that needs a little weight up front, that might work to your advantage, but it won't in a heavier gun.

It's also important to realize where the weight in the barrels is. Some modern screw-choke guns can add as much as two ounces of extra weight right at the muzzle. Try waving one of those guns around with and without the chokes in to really understand what adding screw chokes has done to the handling. That's why fixed-choke guns generally seem to feel better. Manufacturers could use Briley or Teague thin-wall chokes, which don't add any weight, but they cost a lot more than just jugging the muzzles and threading for thick and inexpensive add-on chokes. It often comes down to cost.

Gun balance is also influenced by the length of the barrels. The current trend is toward longer barrels, but that may just be fashion, like Churchill's espousal of the 25-inch length in the 1920s. Since one looks pretty much down the rib of a shotgun—well, you actually look at the bird, not the rib, but you know what I mean—visual length isn't a major player. But barrel length definitely affects balance. Pick your barrel length based on how the gun balances, not on any current fashion trend. Most 12-gauge guns pick up about $1^1/2$ ounces for every two inches of extra barrel length. And that weight is all up front.

A lot can also be done in fine-tuning barrel balance by the selection of the top and side ribs. In the '90s I ordered a long-barreled sub-gauge Perazzi for doves in South America. Perazzi not only let me choose the overall weight of the barrels but also offered many rib options that would let me move the balance of the barrels forward or aft. I wanted a slight-forward weight bias, so I chose solid side ribs from the tip of the forend forward but ribless under the forend. I could have picked ventilated side ribs for slightly lower weight or a design without side ribs and only a barrel hanger like Krieghoff's. Choices are confusing but nice.

This brings up one of the problems of reviewing a gun with a long option list like that Perazzi. Since you can basically order what you want in barrel length, balance, ribs, decoration, stock fit and even actions, any review is problematic. The best that can be done is to point out what the options are and what effect they will have so that you can make an informed choice.

The barrels not only affect balance but also deliver the shot to the target. I test each review gun for barrel convergence and point of impact vis-à-vis the rib. Barrel convergence is the ability of both barrels to shoot to the same place. You'd think that they would always do that, but that's not so. One American manufacturer told me that it considers an eight-inch pattern separation at 40 yards to be acceptable. Since effective working patterns are seldom more than 24 inches wide, you would be giving up one-third of your pattern. I've had name-brand O/Us and side-by-sides that were wildly off, some barrels throwing one pattern a full 30 inches away from the other. It's almost as if the tubes were cross-eyed.

So I make sure to test for convergence when I review a gun or consider a used-gun purchase for myself. If one maker's sample is bad, that certainly doesn't mean that all of the guns the company makes are like that, but it pays to check. The companies that make double rifles in addition to shotguns generally do a better job, but there is never a guarantee. Always, always check convergence.

Unless you already own the gun and shoot it well. If that's the case, then don't tempt fate by asking too many questions. Then it's like going to the doctor when you feel fine. All you can do is break even or lose.

If convergence is off and you already own the gun, if it has fixed chokes you might be able to save it by having the chokes reground on a bias. I did that to a Parker Reproduction 28-gauge that was way off in convergence, and the gunsmith was able to bring the impacts back together, though at the loss of some choke constriction. If it's a screw-choke gun, Briley often can make eccentric chokes to correct the problem.

I also check each gun for point of impact (POI). That is where the gun shoots (assuming both barrels shoot to the same place) when you are looking flat down the rib. Hopefully, POI isn't left or right of center. That's a mess and probably means a mis-laid rib. Everyone has a preference as to vertical height of POI, and my job is only to report what it is, not what it should be. I've tried some lightweight sub-gauge side-by-sides that shot very flat—actually under the line of sight when looking flat along the rib. I don't know if that is how they were set up or whether light-barreled side-by-sides experience downflip on firing, but a low-shooting gun can be a real problem, as it forces you to cover, and thus obscure, your target. You end up shooting blind.

As a personal preference, I like to set up my O/Us, pumps and autoloaders to shoot dead on 50/50 (that's half the pattern above the target and half below) when my cheek is pushed hard into the stock so that I look flat down the rib. Set up this way, when I use normal moderate cheek pressure, I see a little bit of rib and my guns shoot just a little bit high. If I get a dropping bird and have to cheek hard, I can never "lose" the bird as my eye drops below the level of the rib. I like to see just a little more rib on my side-by-sides, because I think that side-bys shoot a touch lower and need more height built in.

Others like their guns set up differently, and I have no problem with that. It's just important to remember that a gun's point of impact in relation to sighting down the rib will determine how you set up the stock height. Never assume that what you see is what you get until you test where the patterns go in relation to the rib.

While on the subject of barrels, my reviews usually state the interior barrel dimensions. These include the length of the chamber, the length of the chamber forcing cone, the barrel bore interior diameter and the choke dimensions. Although I include this stuff, I'm not at all sure it matters. No one has yet proven to me that overbored or back-bored barrels or long or short forcing cones matter a whit. There is all sorts of advertising hype about it, but I haven't seen any solid proof that .740"-ID 12-gauge barrels pattern differently than .725"-ID ones. Ditto with long or short forcing cones. There's a lot of theory, but I haven't seen rock-solid proof one way or the other.

I don't test pattern percentages when I review guns, because patterns are affected as much by the choice of shell as by choke. I usually mention what the choke dimensions are so that you can draw your own conclusions, but I don't spend my time tinkering with every possible shell/choke combination. Life is too short. If some gun has a choke that measures far from the accepted standard for its designation, I'll mention it, but that's all. Analyzing a million patterns is fun, right? I wouldn't deprive you of that joy.

If you are going to get into deep pattern analysis, you should consider Andrew Jones's "Shotgun-Insight," at www.shotgun-insight.com. It is a computer program that allows you to enter a digital photograph of a paper shotgun pattern. The program then counts the pellets and analyzes the results. Definitely less work for mother. I also strongly recommend Jones's book, *Sporting Shotgun Performance*, for some of the most detailed pattern-performance analysis I have ever read. It takes off where Journée, Burrard, Brindle, Brister and the others left things.

With the action and barrels out of the way, the next part of the gun I look at is the wood. Configuration comes first. One of the reasons I like autoloaders so much is that today the better brands come with shim-adjustable stocks. Unlike what some of the makers think, all shotgunners are not size 42-Regular. The eccentric shims that come with many of today's autoloaders allow adjustment of the stock up and down, left and right. Different recoil pads account for lengthening and shortening. This is marvelously convenient and will allow you to adjust the gun for a perfect fit.

In an O/U or side-by-side life is not as simple. Due to the way the stocks mate with the backs of the receivers, stock-adjustment shims are not applicable. The alternative is an adjustable stock, but that can add significant unnecessary weight to a field gun. Besides, we all know that if something is adjustable, it can become unadjusted at the most inopportune time. For a target gun, with your car and tool kit parked a few hundred feet from the field, it may not matter. With a field gun, a loose adjustable-stock comb is something else again.

Stock fit depends on physiognomy and shooting style. Certain brands tend to cater to certain sizes and styles. For example, some American makers lean toward short, low stocks. These are best suited to someone with a full face, short neck and erect-head shooting style. Longer, higher stocks tend to work best for thinner-faced, longer-necked shooters who might crawl their stocks a bit more. It was interesting to see that the Japanese Browning Citori O/Us had relatively high stocks until the 525 model in 2002. Then the stocks became lower, which Browning said would better suit American shotgunners. Beretta's standard field guns are made with longer, higher stocks for the European market and lower stocks for American consumers.

In a review I'll always mention a gun's stock dimensions. If you aren't sure what works best for you, simply measure a gun that you shoot well and compare the numbers to the dimensions of the review gun.

Pistol grips also have a lot to do with gun comfort. Most field guns have relaxed pistol grips, or no pistol grips at all if they have English stocks. Target stocks go from relaxed grips to large vertical grips. In theory the large vertical grips force a low right elbow. Good for people who tuck in tight when they shoot. Bad for those who hold their elbows wide to keep from arcing as they pivot on a crossing bird. In reviewing such a gun, I don't say what is best. My job is just to point out what there is and what the consequences of picking one grip or the other are.

Like stocks, forends are very personal. If you shoot with your left hand well to the rear, the forend almost doesn't matter. But if you hold your left hand well forward, the forend assumes a more important role. I've always considered the splinter forend on English doubles and the small O/U Merkel game forend to be the classics. I also understand a slightly bulkier forend for target shooting. What I don't understand is the point of the Schnabel forend.

As a practical matter, the Schnabel has a number of disadvantages. The thin ridge is fragile and easily damaged in the field. Early Berettas once had a terrible problem with Schnabels being damaged in shipment due to improper packing. It's also a "finger dinger" if you shoot with your left hand well out and extend your forefinger. In O/Us that use Anson pushbutton releases, it often forces awkward incorporation of the Anson button.

But the aesthetics of this Hapsburg Lip are what really get me. The design was purloined from those busy Rube Goldberg German and Austrian rifles, not shotguns. The vertical lip of the Schnabel is completely out of sync with the rounded lines of a nice shotgun. It denies a smooth transition from receiver to barrel. It's a gewgaw that serves no purpose. And it's ugly. Really, really ugly. There! I feel much better now.

Checkering always gets a paragraph or two. Today mechanical—mostly laser—checkering is just about universal in moderate- to mid-priced guns. Fancy guns still get the handwork. Hand checkering takes time and costs more, but it can produce more intricate patterns at this point in time. Machine checkering is perfectly adequate for most purposes and is getting better by the day. Beware of checkering that is too fine. It may be artsy, but it will not provide the slip-free grip that you should expect from slightly coarser and more-functional checkering.

And speaking of wood, frankly the higher the X-rating, the more I like it. I'm a sucker for fancy wood. It doesn't make the gun shoot better any more than truffles are more nutritious than mushrooms, but it sure is easy on the eyes. Yes, your heart breaks when you ding it or scratch it on barbed wire or when plunging down a talus slope, but there is a price for everything. Unfortunately, no two pieces of natural walnut are the same, so you may or may not get wood like that on the review gun. Don't think that just because it's a review gun it got the best wood. Sometimes yes. Sometimes no. I'm occasionally amazed at what arrives in the UPS truck.

And all pretty wood isn't structurally equal, either. The more involved the grain is, the more likely the wood is to have cracks and knotholes. If a review gun costs extra for nice wood, I check it carefully for these blemishes. I also would hope that the highly stressed area at the head of the stock has a relatively solid, straight grain to preclude future cracking. Since wood varies from gun to gun, make sure that you examine this before committing to a purchase.

Stock finish is another important aspect of any gun review. It appears to be the European custom to leave the walnut grain slightly unfilled. It's an American custom for assembly-line guns to have a finish more suitable for a bowling pin than a firearm. Fortunately, there are exceptions to both. They are duly praised when they occur and damned when they don't. I make sure to pull the stock off of a test gun to see if the inside of the head is coated with finish to protect from punkiness due to overzealous oiling. Some makers take this extra step. Some don't. But it deserves to be pointed out. If you purchase a gun without this protective interior coating, a few coats of thinned TruOil will set things right. That said, I've been told by my betters that some best-gun craftsmen prefer that the wood facing sidelock locks should not be sealed, as this allows it to breathe and not hold moisture against the metal. I'm not so certain. The last thing that you want is moisture-swollen wood in that area. It's a Hobson's choice for sure.

Wood-to-metal fit is another indicator of quality that is always mentioned. With modern computer-driven pantographs doing the cutting, most guns don't have a problem here unless the wood wasn't properly aged and it shrank. If a stock isn't headed up properly, there is a good chance that it will develop a crack as you use it—and you don't want that.

Proud wood is something that I look for too, though I'm not really sure how proud it can get before there is no pride. Manufacturers usually maintain that they leave stock wood a little higher than the action metal it joins to allow for wood shrinkage over time or for refinishing. I don't mind a little of this if it's not too much, but I do notice that the really well-made guns have wood that is flush to the metal. I think that what you really are seeing is something that is carefully handmade versus something machine-made with some increased tolerance just in case.

The exterior finish of the shotgun metal is more of a cosmetic issue unless it is screwed up. Real rust bluing involves numerous cardings, or sandings, between salt baths. If shortcuts are taken, you'll be able to see some of those carding striations running along the barrel. Hot bluing isn't as labor intensive as rust bluing, but the temperatures used in hot bluing generally preclude the use of conventional soft solder and require brazing or higher-temperature solder. High-temperature solder can warp thin barrels. Hence the tendency of high-quality thin-walled barrels to use low-temperature rust bluing and more-fragile soft solder. Heavier barrels can get away with the durable high-temperature soldering, but then you have nicely blued heavy barrels. Can't win for losing.

The above is a pretty general statement, and many makers with modern machinery are cutting down on the downsides of the two processes, but generally it's true, and that's why I point out the type of bluing and rib attachment in a review.

I also check very carefully for solder blushes, gaps and over-runs along the ribs. This is mostly a cosmetic issue, but gaps in the solder line could mean loose ribs later on. Today at least one maker is attaching the ribs by laser welding. That should prevent any problems down the road.

Engraving is art, and as such it is strictly *de gustibus non est disputandum* ("Of taste there is no dispute"). My job isn't to state whether the engraving is in good taste or not but simply to point out whether it is done by machine, hand or a combination thereof and whether it is of a good quality of execution. Of course, sometimes I can't resist whining about some egregious artistic blunder, but you are free to ignore it and trust in your own good taste.

Laser engraving has come a long way in the past 10 years, and it currently is advancing at an astonishing pace. I don't know if it will ever equal hand engraving, but it may. Some of the laser-cut hand-chased patterns that the studio Bottega Giovanelli is turning out for a number of Italian makers are surprisingly good.

And then there is case coloring. I often find case coloring particularly attractive in that it can pretty much hide, or at least diminish, bad engraving. Originally, case coloring was a fortuitous byproduct of case hardening. The part to be hardened was surrounded with charcoal, bone and other carbonizing substances, heated in an oven, and then quenched. The process transferred carbon to the outer layer of the part, producing a hardened surface and, as a byproduct, the pretty rose, straw, blue and red colors. The hard-metal outer surface was resistant to wear, while the inner surface remained slightly ductile with a low brittleness. As steel alloys improved, hardening requirements changed, but the attractive case coloring was still desirable.

Chemical hardening, often using sodium cyanide salts at high temperature, is a common hardening practice today. It's more easily controlled than the carburizing pack and produces its own type of case colors.

Both the charcoal/bone and cyanide case colors are manipulated by closely guarded trade-secret recipes that allow a wide color variety. Generally I like the bone/charcoal colors a bit better, but your taste may differ. Much of it really depends on the way the process is employed rather than which process is selected. I believe that the Spanish and Italians mostly use chemical case coloring because of

some quirk in their laws, while the Americans, English and Germans can use both methods.

Both types of case coloring are fragile and wear off relatively quickly, especially in areas where the gun's metal is rubbed during use or subjected to direct sunlight. This can be forestalled by a protective application of clear lacquer. Krieghoff uses a kind of automotive clear coat on its Essencia case colors and claims it is very long lived. I've used clear nail polish on some case-colored guns with pretty good results.

I've never been a big fan of silver receivers, but that's just me. You may have done better in Art Appreciation 101 than I did. Chrome (ugh!), French gray (OK), silver nitrite (durable) or just a clear coat are all seen today. Silver receivers do sometimes show engraving to better advantage than case coloring, but that's always a risk requiring that the engraving be worth showing. When in doubt, it's hard to go wrong with an engraved blued receiver.

The hardest part of the gun review to write is about the shooting. A gun's shooting dynamics are so subjective. Mechanical aspects of the gun either work, work poorly or don't work. The shooting performance of a gun is different. Different guns shoot differently for different people.

Recoil is a good example. It's difficult to say that one gun is a kicker while another isn't. Every shooter you loan the gun to will have his own opinion based on how the gun fits him and on how he holds it when he shoots. Mr. Newton's laws never change, but the people applying those laws certainly do. All guns of the same weight using the same shells have the same recoil. No way around that. It's just how that recoil is delivered that makes one gun seem to be softer than another.

No recoil device, such as the common hydraulic or spring-operated compression buttplate, can actually lower recoil in the mathematical sense. It can, however, space out that recoil over a longer period of time so that you get more of a push than a poke. This longer recoil time is why gas-operated semi-autos seem to kick less, too. Either way, it seems as though there is less kick, even if there really isn't.

So, with this in mind, I make a habit of loaning review guns to a variety of shooters, both new and experienced. I listen carefully to what they say. If they agree with my opinion, I print it. If they disagree with me, I ignore them. Well, not exactly . . . .

Gun balance and handling are other vague areas. American engineer Don Amos has done a marvelous job attempting to quantify the nuances of handling by measuring guns' moments of inertia with a turntable and timer. He generates MOI numbers both when the gun is mounted to the shoulder and when it is unmounted in the hands. These numbers can be compared to those generated by a broad range of previously measured guns. MOI numbers don't tell us what is good or bad, just which other guns produced the same results. I don't use MOI numbers in my reviews, as most readers don't have the comparison list, but perhaps I should.

When possible, I will take a review gun hunting if it is a field version. But to be frank, I can learn a lot more on a skeet field about how a gun handles. Since skeet offers repeatable and known targets, it is a good way to compare one gun to another or to look for certain characteristics. The variables that crop up with live birds are eliminated, so you end up testing the gun, not the skill of the shooter.

In all, describing how a gun shoots is somewhat like describing a wine. You have to use a lot of adjectives. Descriptors like "bad" and "good" are easily understood. It's the nuancing that muddies the waters.

A review always mentions the items that come packed with the gun. These might include the gun case, chokes, choke wrench, balancing-weight set, small tools and a warrantee. Industry warrantees vary from one year to the lifetime of the original owner and his named heir (Smith & Wesson's Elite Gold). A long warrantee may sound good, but it's the service of the company that counts. There is no point in sending off a gun for a small guaranteed repair and having it take the best part of a year in the repair shop. A friend of mine bought an expensive Italian gun from a small maker. It had a lifetime guarantee, but he had to send it back to Italy several times for service, which was never performed properly. For this reason I try to comment on the service reputation of a manufacturer when I do a review.

And then there is price. In the reviews included here, I've made the prices as up-to-date as possible. A gun that I reviewed eight years ago may still be in production and current in all respects, but one thing has certainly changed: the price. Gun prices have escalated almost as much as gas prices. A Spanish sidelock I tested in 2003 has exactly doubled in price by 2011. Same gun, different money. Most European makers have increased their prices, but the amounts vary. The Beretta 391 Sporter was $1,000 in 2001. Ten years later it costs 45-percent more for the same gun. The financial turmoil of a few years ago severely affected the sporting-shotgun market. In the US sales of black rifles and pistols soared for political reasons, but sporting-shotgun sales plummeted as fast as discretionary spending did. The strong euro merely accentuated the problem.

With the increase in price obviously comes a reassessment of the relative value of the gun. While I attempt to point out the pluses and minuses of all guns equally, I expect more from an expensive gun. Inflation has moved a number of guns from what were once good deals to what are now average ones.

I often get asked what I do with a gun that shows mechanical problems during testing. That's a problem with gun reviewing. I sometimes get an early production version that hasn't been entirely vetted yet. Besides that, I'm simply receiving a sample of one; the next gun out of the shop could be different. If the gun has an obvious mechanical assembly error, I request a second gun. One maker had to send me three guns before I got one that was right. If the gun has a design issue, I comment on it and hope that the maker will address it sooner rather than later. At least you are forewarned . . . .

And finally, the nuts and bolts of reviewing a gun are one thing. The business world in which the guns are supplied is another. Contrary to popular opinion, reviewers generally don't get free guns or anything like that. In fact, a lot of times I have to plead with a manufacturer to get a gun to review. You'd be amazed. The PR people at the gun companies definitely remember whether or not you said nice things about their products. My editors at *Shooting Sportsman* have received more than one howling complaint of biased unfairness and blind stupidity on my part.

One time I requested a review gun from a certain importer. The company's PR guy said he would be happy to send me one and, if I gave the gun a good review, I could keep it as my reward. My self-important righteous indignation bubbled up, and I promised myself that I would give the gun a scathing review. That would teach him to try to buy me. Unfortunately, when the gun arrived it turned out to be pretty good. What to do? Hoist by my own petard! In the end I gave the gun the good review it deserved and then returned it to the importer. I have since avoided reviewing that company's guns.

Generally, my reviews tend to be positive. That's because, with a limited number of reviews to do a year, I pick guns that I think will interest readers. Good guns are more interesting than bad guns. Unless, of course, the bad guns are monumental disasters by major companies that I can have some fun with. But by and large I want to share the good stuff with those who are kind enough to lend me an ear.

So that is what I try to cover when I review a gun. The following 38 reviews are the results. I hope you find them informative.

Arrieta Model 06 .410

No, I haven't been seduced by the pipsqueak pipe or fallen prey to the idiot stick. Well, there *is* my Winchester Model 42 problem, but I am recovering nicely. This review of the Arrieta side-by-side Model 06 in .410 was more fortuitous than intentional. Jack Jansma made me an offer I couldn't refuse. Jansma, a well-respected longtime gun dealer and shooting-trip organizer, is one of the main US importers of the Spanish-made Arrieta shotgun.

Arrieta's line basically consists of two versions of the Holland & Holland sidelock classic side-by-side in 13 grades. One version has the traditional flat-sided bar and sidelock, while a more recent Round Action version uses the same action internals but with edges that have been cosmetically rounded for a softer look and more comfortable one-hand field carry. Other Spanish makers like AyA, Grulla and Garbi make similar rounded models. Arrieta's round-action usually has a slight swelling where the forward nose of the sidelock merges into the action bar, just aft of the slightly narrower knuckle.

Jansma told me that Arrieta had a third version of its H&H action that was cosmetically a copy of the Boss rounded-action. It was the Arrieta Model 06. Jansma had received a set of five in 12, 16, 20, 28 and .410. One customer immediately bought the middle three. Another dealer wanted the 12. Would I like to look at the .410? Yes, thank you.

The original Boss rounded-action side-by-side exterior is equally rounded along the entire length of the action bar and through the knuckle. There is no smooth swollen bump where the line of the knuckle merges with the bar just under the sidelock plate. This constant, smooth Boss curvature is what the Arrieta 06 copies so nicely and what sets it apart from the company's usual round-action models. That and the Boss-style engraving. This isn't the first time the Boss look has been used in Spain. Upscale Spanish maker Arrizabalaga also produced a gun with that exterior style.

Of course, none of these are true round-actions like the trigger-plate Dicksons and McKay Browns. The Arrieta rounding is cosmetic, though it involves a bit more than just grinding off the sharp edges.

All Arrietas have H&H-style internals, so the 06 action is proven stuff. It's a bar-action sidelock with the leaf springs facing forward. Lockup is by Purdey double underbolts with a Scott spindle and toplever. It has disk-set strikers for easy firing-pin removal from the face of the breech, if you happen to have the little two-pronged tool. The fences have proper gas vents in case of a shell malfunction. The locks on our 06 were not hand-detachable, but they were on the 12-bore 06 from the same set. Your choice. The receiver on our sample was a true .410 size.

Internally, the locks utilize intercepting sears to forestall accidental discharge if the gun is dropped or jarred. Interestingly, on our test gun the intercep-tors were coil-spring powered. In photos of the 12-gauge I saw, they appeared to be leaf-spring actu-ated. That's the dif-ference between a five-pin and a seven-pin Arrieta action. On five-pin guns intercepting-sear coil springs are contained under the sidelock's bridle and don't re-quire locating pins. On seven-pin guns sear leaf springs are outside the bridle and require the two extra pins. Perhaps the small .410 receiver hadn't the space for the seven-pin arrangement. There is no difference in function. The mainsprings are all leaf type, almost certainly EDM cut. All the interior bits were nicely engine turned. With the exception of some machining marks on one of the hammers, the work was clean.

Since all Arrieta guns are handmade the old-fashioned way, most

options are available if you order one. An ordered gun will take six to 12 months, depending on how busy the company is. Our test gun had an automatic safety, but I'm sure you could arrange for a manual. Arrieta's Website (www.arrietashotguns.com) lists the Model 06 as available with assisted opening. I assume this would be the H&H-pattern spring-assist set under the barrels as used by oth-er Spanish makers. Our .410 did not have this feature, nor would I consider it really appropriate in this gauge.

Our gun came with double triggers. The front blade was artic-ulated. A non-selec-tive single trigger is available if you must. Trigger pulls on the front and rear both averaged about 4½ pounds. The front was crisp, but the rear had a little creep. The usual Southgate ejec-tors handled the expulsion chores.

The outside of the receiver has the aforementioned rounded Boss configuration. The 100-per-cent-coverage, minute rose & scroll hand engraving is also in the Boss pattern and of very nice quality. The action is case colored. Jansma said that the coloring was by chemical cyanide rather than bone and charcoal. It is not gaudy but appears subtle and attrac-tive—far nicer than some other chemical efforts I've seen.

All Arrieta barrels are true old-fashioned chopper-lump construc-tion, something some Italian makers charge a good bit more for.

The Model 06 has Boss-style engraving and is rounded along the entire length of the action bar and through the knuckle.

Jansma is a fan of 29" barrels on this Arrieta, and I agree. At 2 pounds 3 ounces the barrels are about two-thirds the weight of 12-gauge barrels, and they certainly appear to be in proper proportion and balance for the gun. The chokes were fixed Improved Cylinder and Modified, but you can order what you wish. The 3" chambers are appropriate for a .410 with at least modest hunting pretenses. The forcing cones appear conventionally abrupt, but I think that the .410 is one cartridge that could benefit from a more gradual taper. All Arrieta barrels are chrome lined.

The rib is the classic swamped, unetched English game style, so attractive and appropriate on a gun like this. Solder joints all appeared correct and blemish-free. The rust bluing was semi-bright, and the surface was smooth without any ripples. The muzzle bore a classic brass bead. In all, these look like good barrels.

One of the nice things about Arrieta is that custom stock dimensions are included free on an ordered gun. With that in mind, there is no point in discussing the fit of our 06 sample, other than to say that, like most of the more expensive side-by-sides, it was stocked longer and higher than cheaper guns. For some reason makers of many production-line side-by-sides feel that the usual over/under dimensions will work on a side-by-side. They don't. Side-by-side guns should be stocked

All Arrietas feature Holland & Holland-style sidelock actions. One difference with the Model 06 in .410 (versus other gauges) is that the intercepting sears are coil-spring operated, explaining why the gun has five-pin locks instead of seven.

a touch higher than O/Us to account for barrel flip. Double-trigger guns also should be stocked a bit longer than single-trigger guns.

Our 06 had a classic English stock with no drop points, as befit its smooth rounded action. The oval wrist provided a good grip without excessive bulk. The forend was a very modest beavertail, which was advantageous in giving just a little bit of extra purchase on the narrow .410 barrels. Wood-to-metal fit was generally very nice but not perfect, with one side of the rear of the forend prouder than the other. The butt sported nicely engraved case-colored heel and toe plates, but the checkering there was a little clumsy compared to the good checkering on the grip and forend. If you looked carefully, you could just see the outline of the stock-hollowing plug, showing the extra effort Arrieta took to balance the gun.

I would rate the walnut at about 75 percent up the scale between plain and stupefying. The grain was well laid out, being straight and strong through the more fragile wrist and forend, with nicer figure at the butt. The traditional oil finish was nicely done, while the rich brown stain complemented the wood grain. The bottom of the stock sported a gold-colored oval for initials or family crest. I was surprised that the Anson button at the front of the forend was set in plain wood and not surrounded by a more upscale engraved metal escutcheon. The inside of the forend was properly but plainly finished. The interior of the stock wood under the sidelocks was a little rougher than I would like on a gun of this price.

And speaking of price, Arrieta's 2011 list price for the Model 06 is $17,200, plus 10 percent for gauges smaller than 16. That brings our test gun to an MSRP of almost $19,000. The least-expensive Arrieta H&H sidelock is the Model 557 at $4,950. The popular midrange rounded-action 871 starts at $7,250. Why the considerable extra money for the 06?

The answer is time. The better-than-average wood and deluxe, all-leather case add to the cost, but what makes the difference is man-hours. Paul Chapman, director of gunsmithing at Arrieta importer Griffin & Howe, told me he believes that all Arrietas are functionally well made but that the higher-grade guns reflect the increased time and effort on the details. This certainly reflects Jansma's experience with the guns. He felt it was a matter of degree, not of kind. Dale Tate of Tate Gunmakers took me through our sample gun. He pointed out the areas where the extra handwork was obvious in engraving, metal and wood fit, bluing, and general slickness of parts. He felt it was quite nicely made. So too did *Shooting Sportsman* Editor at Large Silvio Calabi and Senior Editor Vic Venters.

That's a pretty knowledgeable cheering section.

As would be hoped, our Arrieta 06 functioned correctly during our shooting tests. There were no failures of any kind. Barrel convergence was correct. Chokes patterned appropriately for their designations. Ejectors were well timed and popped those solid-gold AA .410 hulls a modest four feet.

The handling and balance of the gun were marvelous. Really nice. The overall weight of 5 pounds 15 ounces was heavy enough to feel like a real gun. The balance point was just aft of the hinge, but the 29" barrels increased the moment of inertia enough to keep the gun from being twitchy. With many lightweight double-trigger guns, I bobble slightly when shifting my finger to the rear trigger, but not with this one. It was steady and deadly on clays. Some guns are real shooters, and this was one of them. I would have no hesitation taking on preserve quail with this gun.

You are the best judge as to whether the extra engraving, nicer wood, classic Boss receiver shaping, subtle barrel striking, balancing, and careful hand-fitting of parts make the extra cost of the 06 worth it compared to Arrieta's proven, popular and very functional 500 or 800 series guns. Either way, Arrietas are definitely good guns. Hippies from the '60s might say they are "boss."

AyA 4/53 Cabela's Classic

The Basque gunmaking firm of Aguirre y Aranzabal was founded in 1917 by Miguel Aguirre and Nicolas Aranzabal. Ninety years later it has survived two world wars, a civil war, political unrest and an abortive gunmaker collectivization. It has gone from a small producer to a large manufacturer and back to a small producer, with about 20 workers. Over time AyA has built about 600,000 guns, but now annual production is around 700. Today's emphasis is on handcraftsmanship. Almost all production is side-by-sides with substantial English influence. AyA's most popular guns are the Holland & Holland-pattern sidelocks Numbers 1 and 2 and the boxlock No. 4 series.

The No. 4 boxlock side-by-side has been in the AyA lineup since 1960. The 4/53 is an upgrade of the No. 4 and is built to a higher standard. Our test gun, a 20-gauge 4/53 Classic built for Cabela's Gun Library, was a heavily engraved 4/53. Cabela's sells the standard case-colored unengraved 4/53 for $3,199. The 4/53 Classic is $3,899. The extra $700 includes 100-percent-coverage engraving, 29" barrels instead of the standard 28" barrels and a better wood finish.

The heart of the AyA 4/53 Classic is the Anson & Deeley boxlock action. With the basic design originating at Westley Richards more than 130 years ago, it is so tried and true that only the execution, not the design, bears comment.

The interior of the action is purposeful but not pretentious. On our gun little was polished, and there were numerous machine marks. That said, everything fit and worked properly. I saw no evidence of the "soft" metal or shoddy construction that was common at one time in Spanish guns of this level. The 4/53 is a moderate, practical gun, and the interior work is appropriate to it.

It was interesting to compare the workings of the AyA with those of the Turkish-made Smith & Wesson Gold Elite. The AyA shows obvious handwork and handfitting, with only the most basic high-tech machining. AyA does use a couple of CNCs to machine its receivers, and the company also makes receivers for other makers, but the emphasis is on handwork and the flexibility it permits. The S&W's bits and pieces are cleaner, as befits more CNC production, but the gun has a more machine-made look. Both guns are nice but in different ways.

The 4/53's receiver is forged from a single piece of steel. Leaf springs drive the hammers. The firing pins are disk-set in the face of the standing breech for ease of removal. That's just as well, because pulling the stock off of this type of gun requires the removal of five fitted screws and a lot of fiddling. Lockup is by the usual double underbolt, with the forward lump penetrating through the floor of the receiver.

The outside of the receiver is busy and severe at the same time. The receiver has 16 —repeat, 16—slotted screw heads showing. Each side shows the cover screw for the replaceable hinge plus three transverse action screws, each with its own setscrew. The bottom of the action has the usual triggerplate and bottom plate screws. The screws on the sides were not quite perfectly indexed.

The Cabela's special-edition 4/53 Classic features 29" barrels and 100-percent-coverage engraving, with pleasing wood in classic English proportions.

The severity of the receiver comes from its square cross-section, lacking even the slightest rounding of the lower edges of the action. The sides of the rear of the action where the stock heads up are also absolutely straight. The highest AyA boxlock grade No. 4 Deluxe has the rear of the receiver scalloped for a more interesting appearance.

The 4/53 comes with proper double triggers. Ours had nicely weighted pulls of 3¾ pounds each, but the rear trigger had more

creep than it should have. The front trigger is not articulated, a feature that one finds on higher-grade guns. The tang safety is automatic, with a non-slip button and a nice "clicky" feel.

The gun has standard Southgate ejectors, which worked perfectly. Empties were tossed about 10 feet. The timing was correct, as the empties flew out together.

The most durable action and ergonomic wood won't make up for a pair of cross-eyed, porcine sewer pipes. Not to worry, though. The barrels on the 4/53 Classic are so right that they make the gun.

It has always seemed to me that mid-priced Spanish guns have slightly heavier barrels than the English guns they emulate. The Spanish barrels are legendary for their strength, and this might be part of the reason.

A little heavier isn't necessarily a bad thing, especially in a sub-gauge. The 4/53's obvious English counterpart is the Webley & Scott A&D boxlock. I had one in 20 gauge with 26" barrels. It was a marvelous gun but a little too fast for my taste. The 29" barrels on the 4/53 Classic are a perfect length for this 20-gauge, as they put a little more weight forward. In the AyA No. 4 lineup 29" barrels are an extra-cost option, so their inclusion in the price of the Cabela's gun is a plus.

The barrels are of true chopper-lump construction. Some consider this a premium feature. Makers who do offer monoblock and chopper-lump barrels usually charge more for the latter. Tom Bryant, manager of Cabela's online Gun Library, told me that the barrels are joined by brazing, except for soft solder at the regulation point, and that the ribs are silver-brazed also. This should be more durable than traditional soft-soldering. The barrels are rust-blued to a nice, ripple-free modest gloss on the outside. On the inside the bores are polished but not chromed.

The top rib is in the swamped English game style, with the concave top remaining smooth and blued the same as the barrel. It simply disappears when you are shooting the gun. Tucked between the barrels, it is invisible from the side and is a major contributor to the gun's svelte profile. I realize that there are those who want raised ribs, vented ribs or matte ribs on their side-by-sides; they will have to look elsewhere. Not surprisingly, the AyA has a simple small steel bead at the muzzle.

In keeping with the traditional chopper-lumps, swamped rib and rust bluing, the AyA 4/53 Classic has fixed chokes. Ours were marked IC (four stars in the Spanish system) and Modified (three stars). The IC choke was .005" constriction on a .623" bore. It was 4½" long with a 2" parallel. The Modified choke was .011" on the same .623" bore and also measured 4½" long with a 1½" parallel. The nominal bore diameter for a 20 is .615", so this gun's bores were slightly oversize. The choke constrictions are a touch more open than normal for the designations but just about perfect for the practical 20- and 30-yard shots you expect from an upland 20. The advantage to these fixed chokes over screw chokes is that they can be made long enough to slowly squeeze the load and then stabilize it with an adequate parallel. This should result in less shot damage and a more uniform pattern. Typical 20-gauge screw chokes are much shorter and must make design compromises. This gun is chambered for 2¾" shells only, not 3". AyA does not recommend the use of steel shot.

Like so much else on the 4/53, the wood is pure English. Our test gun had an archetypical English stock. Those lines just seem to complement the beauty of a side-by-side. I won't get into the possible right-hand-control benefits of a Prince of Wales stock, as we all have our opinions there, but few would deny the beauty of the classic straight wrist of the English stock.

The wrist of the AyA stock is dainty—one of the smallest in circumference I can remember holding. It greatly contributes to the lithe feel of the gun. Still, it provides adequate purchase because it is oval, not round. It also has the slightest hint of a diamond cross-section for further grip enhancement. You can't see it, but you can just barely feel it. This diamond wrist was popular on English guns of the 1920s.

The nose of the comb is adequately pronounced. This keeps the first joint of the thumb well below the line of sight as well as enables the slender wrist. The butt is checkered for ease of mounting and that classic look.

The dimensions of our test stock were 14⅞" x 1 17/32" x 2⅝", with a modest amount of right-hand cast-off. Pitch was a little less than usual at 1½" stand off. Cataloged dimensions for Cabela's stocked guns seem to run at 14⅞" x 1½" x 2¼", so our stock was a little bit lower than normal. Custom dimensions are available, but this will cost an extra $450 and will take nine months. You might be better off buying the gun off the shelf and then getting it bent for $200 or so.

The stock attaches by the traditional vertical bolt through the wrist, not by a drawbolt like the S&W, RBL and most O/Us. I could find no visual evidence of stock hollowing and plugging in the butt checkering to alter balance. The stock appears to be solid.

Like the stock, our forend was classic English. It was a petite splinter, with an Anson push-button release properly set into an inletted escutcheon in the tip. The high-set Anson button allows the front of the forend to tuck up under the barrels for a very clean line, unlike the Kimber, S&W, RBL and lower-grade Merkel efforts. The AyA forend fit properly with no slop. The central bolt holding the forend iron to the wood was also nicely set off by an engraved escutcheon.

The AyA 4/53 is hand-checkered finely enough to look good yet remain functional. There were some blunt diamonds at the edges, but overall it was quite good. The pattern is, yet again, simple and classic. It wraps fully around the underside of the wrist for a better grip. A wrap-around pattern requires considerable skill to execute. Farther back there's a silver-colored metal oval for initials.

The walnut on our sample had decent but not remarkable figure. It was certainly better than average. I was told that the 4/53 Classic doesn't come with especially upgraded wood but that all the 4/53s Cabela's has been seeing lately have had nice wood. You can get a feel for the wood grade by visiting the Cabela's Gun Library Website (www.cabelas.com/gun-library.shtml) and looking at the AyA 4/53s for sale. Some of the samples shown have very nice wood, indeed.

Cabela's does get an upgraded oil finish on its 4/53 Classics, and it shows. It's just the right deep, rich color to display the grain. The grain on our gun wasn't perfectly filled, but it was close. The finish was vulnerable to my "universal solvent" sunscreen, though. All real oil finishes seem to be. On the plus side, it's easy to bring a proper oil finish back to life with a few drops of linseed rubbed in as you sit by the fire with a glass

The access plate on the bottom of our test gun's action was blued for contrast, but it is coin finished on today's examples.

of restorative port at hand. Oporto isn't all that far from Eibar, after all.

Wood-to-metal fit on our gun was excellent. It was absolutely correct everywhere. Well done. Even the little ears on the head of the stock that tuck into notches at the rear of the receiver to keep the stock from springing were perfect.

The engraving is what sets the Cabela's Classic apart from conventional 4/53s. The receiver has a 100-percent-coverage foliate-and-flower design on a silver coin background. It appears to be similar to AyA's No. 4 BL model. I've not seen a pattern like this from England or Italy. It is entirely hand cut and reasonably well executed. It looks good to the naked eye but suffers unfairly under a 10X loupe. It definitely livens up the gun compared to the unengraved version. Among the dozen or so shooters I asked, opinions on the engraving were divided. The standard 4/53 receiver with its unengraved case-colored receiver is extremely plain. Perhaps a lightly engraved middle alternative would be in order.

The detachable access plate on the bottom of the action is fully engraved, but on our sample gun it was blued for an interesting contrast. Again, some people liked this and some did not. Today's examples have the floorplate finished in silver coin like the rest of the receiver. The trigger guard and first two inches of the top rib are engraved also.

Cabela's AyA 4/53 Classic arrives in a plain cardboard box with the Spanish proof certificate and a five-year warranty. Originally the service work was performed by New England Custom Gun Service, Ltd. NECG is noted for good service and a quick turnaround. When I spoke to the folks there, they reported very few problems with the 4/53s. Now AyAs are imported by AyA USA and NECG is one of the main retailers.

In the end it all comes down to shooting, and, like engraving, this is a personal matter. That said, every shooter I loaned the gun to liked the balance and handling. I did too. The 29" barrels are just perfect. With a total weight just less than 6 pounds, you couldn't ask for a better-balanced 20. Because moment of inertia isn't a commonly used descriptor and all the really flowery words get used in wine reviews, I'll just say that the gun had enough weight forward to be easy to shoot consistently but not so much that it was slow to respond. I thought that the long barrels would slow the gun down, but they enabled me to make one good smooth move on the bird rather than my usual awkward lunge and desperate correction. Barrel convergence seemed good, and clay-target breaks were appro-

priate to the constrictions.

I particularly liked the feel of the slender stock wrist. It was just perfect and was a major contributor to the excellent handling. The off-the-shelf stock dimensions are fairly standard, so if you are too, you will be pleased.

AyA 4/53 prices have risen over the years but, compared to other boxlocks of similar quality available today, the price is in the right ballpark. Overall, I'd rate our test gun's mechanicals as robust and proven, its general appearance as classic, its cosmetic execution as appropriate for the price and, most important, its handling as absolutely top notch. Cabela's will be happy to supply either the engraved 4/53 Classic or the mechanically identical plain 4/53. Oh, and did I mention that the gun comes in 12, 16, 20, 28 and .410, with receivers sized to the gauge?

B. Rizzini Round Body Game Gun

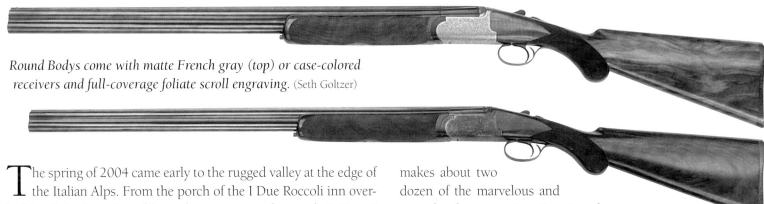

Round Bodys come with matte French gray (top) or case-colored receivers and full-coverage foliate scroll engraving. (Seth Goltzer)

The spring of 2004 came early to the rugged valley at the edge of the Italian Alps. From the porch of the I Due Roccoli inn overlooking Lake Iseo, I could see the young couples on their Ducati and Moto Guzzi motorcycles cruising along the high ridges on their way to a Sunday afternoon at Lake Garda. The flowers in the well-tended garden were just starting to explore the warm spring sunlight, and the streams were overflowing with snowmelt. Winter was past, and life was full of promise. In a moment the little Mercedes driven by my charming translator Elena Micheli-Lamboy would collect me for the half-hour ride to Marcheno and the B. Rizzini gun factory.

I had come to Italy at the invitation of Battista Rizzini. As Elena explained it, there are four Rizzini gunmaking companies in Gardone. Fratelli (the brothers) Rizzini, or Flli. Rizzini, annually makes about two dozen of the marvelous and marvelously expensive R-series shotguns. Emilio Rizzini, or E. Rizzini, now allied with Fausti Stefano, SRL, makes guns that at one time were sold in the US by Traditions and Marlin (L.C. Smith), and the firm still supplies Weatherby. Isidoro Rizzini owns FAIR (Fabbrica Armi Isidoro Rizzini), SRL, which is marketed in America by PMC's Verona. Battista Rizzini markets his guns through Rizzini USA and has trademarked the name "Rizzini." Battista, Emilio and Isidoro are brothers. The Fratelli Rizzini are their cousins. Additionally, the Caesar Guerini company is run by the Guerini brothers, Giorgio and Antonio, who are nephews of Battista Rizzini and used to work for him. It's all in the family, but you really do need a translator.

Battista Rizzini's factory is in Marcheno along the steep sides of the Trompia River valley. It's 20 minutes from Brescia and 90 from the Swiss border. The mountains, honeycombed with iron-ore mines, run right down to the river. The plant is a substantial, modern, two-story affair employing more than 35 workers, including Battista's son and two daughters. Annually, the firm makes about 6,000 shotguns plus some double rifles and paradoxes. The plant is quite modern, with plenty of CNC and EDM machinery, some of which Battista helped design. The factory is a rarity for a producer of this volume in that it's a vertical operation. The company makes just about all of its parts, including springs and pins, in-house. You'd be surprised to learn just how many well-known gun brands are merely assembled from pieces supplied by others.

A vertical operation complete with high-tech machinery gives Rizzini complete control over quality and supply. Modern CNC means precise interchangeability of parts, with very little hand-fitting needed. Battista showed me that he could take the barrels from any gun and fit them perfectly to any other with the same-size receiver. An extra barrel ordered for your Rizzini will drop on perfectly. It won't need fitting.

Two months before my visit, at the 2004 SHOT Show, in Las Vegas, Rizzini USA's national sales manager had shown me the "in the white" prototype for the new B. Rizzini over/under Round Body Game Gun. It had drawn quite a crowd and a lot of enthusiasm. At the plant Battista showed me further prototypes and said they would be available in the US in '05. True to his word, they were. I was sent a 20 and 28 Round Body for this review.

The Round Body uses the same mechanics as the other guns in the B. Rizzini line. It's a third-generation design for Rizzini. Like all Rizzinis, it has a receiver and separate triggerplate CNC'd from a billet of solid steel. The only cast parts are the inertia block and opening lever. Many modern O/U designs suspend the sears from the top tang of the receiver and have the hammers pivoting upward from the triggerplate. Any misalignment of the tang or plate will cause problems with sear engagement, resulting in inconsistent pulls. Rizzini solved the problem by building a vertical stanchion into the center of the triggerplate and suspending the sears from that. This locates the sears on the triggerplate just like the hammers and avoids any possible flexing. It also simplifies proper alignment during manufacture.

The inertia block is on a ball-bearing rider and is held in place by a simple spring so that it can be easily removed for cleaning. In fact, the entire receiver can be pulled apart by hand once you remove the vertical screw under the safety. I watched as Battista disassembled the action using a BIC ballpoint and bent paperclip. The single trigger is "gunsmith adjustable" for over-travel and engagement but not for length of pull. The manual safety/selector lever is the Beretta-type, with barrel selection a matter of simply sliding the little toggle side to side.

Lockup is by a single Browning-style tongue at the bottom of the action. Although this adds a tiny bit of depth to the action, the bottom of the monoblock wall is thinned out to compensate. The 20-gauge action is only $^{1}/_{10}$" taller than Beretta's 20. If you live long enough to need it, the action can be tightened with five different-size locking bolts. I was told that Rizzini can rebuild a 100,000-round gun in a half-hour by simply replacing a few interchangeable CNC parts. Passive locking is by two monoblock lugs that engage recesses in the floor of the action but do not protrude through the bottom. The barrels hinge on Beretta-style replaceable hinge stubs, but they are larger than those Beretta uses. The interior sides of the receiver are dead flat to mate with the flat sides of the monoblock and preclude lateral movement. The pair of large, flat cocking levers lie in the bottom of the receiver.

Both of our test guns had 29" barrels. The prototypes I saw had fixed chokes, and these are available on special request. Our test guns each came with five stainless Briley screw chokes (Skeet through Full) and the excellent Briley "fishing reel handle" choke wrench. These chokes had thin walls and did not require any swelling of the barrel at the muzzle. Unfortunately, the choke names are only on the bodies of the tubes and there are no notches indicating constrictions on the rims. You'll have to remember what you put where. Like most production Italian guns, the barrels are joined at the monoblock. Rizzini's monoblock contains the entire ejector mechanism. It's a marvel of simplicity. The monoblock sides are engine turned, but all of the edges plus those of the ejectors are left razor sharp, just as they come off of the CNC. The barrel bores are chromed, and forcing cones on our sub-gauge guns appeared to be of normal length.

The 100-percent-coverage, foliate-scroll engraving on the Round Body is laser cut and then hand-chased.
(Seth Goltzer)

The barrels are hot-blued with a lustrous, ripple-free finish. The paean to the American tort system "Warning: Read owner's manual before use" is mercifully stamped out of sight on the lower barrel. Less mercifully, the maker's name, country of origin, gauge and chamber length are applied on the top barrel with some kind of rat-a-tat-tat EDM machine that writes like an old dot-matrix printer. It's mostly hidden by the excellent bluing, but it's out of place on a classy gun like this. What isn't out of place is the sleek look of the solid side and top ribs. The solid top rib has a slight taper and a perfectly sized brass bead at the muzzle. Rizzini brazes the ribs to the barrels so they won't come loose the way some soft-soldered ones do. I suppose solid ribs have the practical value of keeping out water and debris, but I think they look great, too. They're also a little more resistant to dents than vent ribs are. A vented top rib is available if you insist. If you need vented top ribs on your field guns to minimize mirage when the barrels heat up, you hunt in better places than I do.

The wood on our sample guns was first class and at least AA. That's to be expected. Battista Rizzini has more than 10,000 personally selected stock blanks in inventory, drying out and awaiting their turn on the factory's fully automated CNC stock machine. Much of this Turkish and Azerbaijani inventory was stored in the part of the Bernardelli factory that Battista owned. The CNC must have been programmed properly, because the wood-to-metal fit on our guns was excellent. The finish was hand-rubbed oil and looked it. It had a marvelous subtle sheen. Unlike on many European guns, the grain was filled correctly. The insides of the stock heads and forends also were finished properly, to preclude possible oil soaking. (Oil soaking can be avoided by not over-oiling and by storing guns muzzle down.) The grain and color of the stocks and forends were matched. The borderless laser checkering was about 22 lpi. Checkering quality was quite good, showing that machines really are catching up.

Stock dimensions on both guns were relatively high and long at 14⁹/₁₆" x 1⁵/₁₆" x 2¹/₁₆", with 2¹/₂" of pitch and a guesstimated ¹/₈" cast at heel and ³/₈" at toe. Our Round Bodys each came with a relaxed round-knob pistol grip, the kind that seems to fit every hand well. (Guns can be ordered with English stocks if you prefer.) The trigger guard has a long tang that extends down the pistol grip for that extra touch of class, like the sainted round-knob long-tang Browning Super-poseds. The separate buttplate is made of highly figured wood. The stock is attached with a conventional drawbolt, so access is easy.

The Round Body gets an attractive, slen-der, fully checkered game forend instead of the Schnabel that Rizzini inflicts on its Au-rums. It allows your hand to get close to the sides of the barrels but seems slightly deep-er than those of some other guns because of the low placement of the Anson push button at the tip. If you want the Schnabel beak, you can request it. The metal inside the forend is minimal, as the entire ejector mechanism is in the monoblock.

It's really the cosmetics that set this gun apart from the rest of the B. Rizzini line. Like Beretta's 68X series and the Browning Superposed, Rizzini uses the same basic mechanics throughout its line, changing only the decorative exterior aspects. The Round Body Game Gun is the result of a collaboration between Ivano Tanfoglio of the Ferlib firm and Battista Rizzini. Around 2004 Rizzini bought Ferlib with an eye to producing up-market guns. Ivano was running Ferlib and had been friends with Battista for

Battista Rizzini (left) and Ivano Tanfoglio collaborated on the design of the Round Body gun.

years. The Round Body was Ivano's first project for Rizzini. The dif-ferences between the Round Body and the standard Rizzini Aurum field gun (somewhat similar to the L.L. Bean New Englander, at the time made by Rizzini) may be only cosmetic, but they are very im-pressive. The Round Body's receiver eliminates the sculpted cheeks and trunnion covers for a smooth, uncluttered look. The underside of the Round Body's action has been heavily curved. The result is a much more graceful appearance and a comfortable carry.

The engraving is a major part of the Round Body's appeal. Rizzini used Botte-gia Giovanelli for the work. The engraving is laser cut and then hand-chased to give it life. It looks absolutely first class, with 100-percent coverage in a subtle foliate scroll. Receiver finishes are a choice of case coloring or a sort of matte French gray. The latter is applied by a chemical steam pro-cess that is said to be more durable than chrome. It's certainly prettier. Many hunt-ers avoid silver receivers on game guns, but this one is nice. Personally, I'd still go for the case coloring.

Everyone who saw our test guns com-mented on how attractive they were. If looks could kill, the Rizzini Round Body certainly would save on ammo. The proportions are perfect. So many other guns have one or two features that clash and just don't look right. The Round Body is "all of a piece."

Our 28-gauge weighed just more than 6 pounds, whereas the 20 was 4 oz heavier. The extra weight of the 20 seemed to be mostly in the barrels, not in the slightly larger action. The 28 balanced right on the trunnions, whereas the 20 was 1⅛" farther forward and felt noticeably more nose heavy. The prototype guns I saw in Italy with fixed chokes seemed to have slightly lighter barrels. I preferred the feel of the fixed-choke prototype 20 to the 28, but in the production screw-choked guns I like the 28 better. For those who prefer just a little more forward bias, the 20 would be the way to go.

Both guns worked correctly. All four sears tripped at about 3½ pounds with a little take-up and a tiny amount of creep, which probably could be adjusted out if you were really fussy. The safety was crisp and large enough to be fumble-free. The inertia triggers worked well with several different brands of factory ammo. I shot a lot of clays with the guns, and barrel convergence seemed good on both. The chokes stayed in place and were easy to change. The stocks, perhaps because of the relaxed rounded grip, seemed to suit a wide variety of shooters. Both of the guns were easy to shoot well.

Rizzini expects to sell 100 or so Round Bodys per year worldwide. In the US the guns are sold by Rizzini USA. All five gauges are available on 12, 20 and 28 action sizes. Options include extra barrels complete with their own forends, fixed or screw chokes, barrel lengths from 26" to 30", and double or single triggers. A completely custom stock can be made in Italy, but more modest adjustments in length or bend can be done after importation.

The guns come housed in a good-quality ABS clamshell case suitable for air travel. There's also a limited lifetime warranty backed by a company that's been around for 30 years. The 2005 list price for the Rizzini Round Body Game Gun was $5,900. This placed it well above Rizzini's then $2,250 Aurum Classic field guns but far below the extravagantly engraved $15,000 sideplated premium models. At its price point, the Round Body has a lot of competition, but it's one of those guns that you just have to see and handle in person to appreciate. Handsome is as handsome does, and this gun is very handsome indeed.

UPDATE

Six years after this review, a few things have changed on the Rizzini Round Body, but the major attributes remain. Connecticut Shotgun is now the B. Rizzini USA distributor. CSMC also retails the gun and has added a network of more than a dozen dealers nationwide.

The name has been changed from the Round Body to the Inverness. The mechanics and option of five gauges and five barrel lengths remain unchanged, but the guarantee has been reduced to one year. Cosmetically, the guns reviewed here continue as the Deluxe model, while a new Classic engraving pattern offers 50-percent foliate scroll. The Inverness Deluxe now retails for $5,629 in the large action and $6,685 in the small-gauge actions. As mentioned, the small-action Round Bodys reviewed were $5,900 in 2005, so that's about a 13-percent increase over six years. Compared to Spanish gun price increases, that's quite restrained. The Inverness Classic, with a little less engraving and slightly lesser wood, retails for $4,985 for the larger action and $5,629 for the small gauges. These guns remain extraordinarily attractive.

Baserri Mari HR Hunter

An Italian gun with a Basque name in the American market? Now that's interesting. When Alan Thompson and Wayne Rodrigue decided to start an American shotgun company, they first thought of having guns produced in Spain. Appropriately, they selected "Baserri" as the company name. A baserri is a typical stone-and-timber farmhouse, or perhaps hunting lodge, in the Basque Pyrenees. "Mari" was selected as the model name. The foremost goddess in the Basque pantheon, Mari is the deity of thunder and wind.

But a trip to AyA and ARDESA, AyA's parts supplier, came up blank. The Spanish couldn't change their production methods to accommodate the guns Thompson and Rodrigue wanted. They suggested that Fabarm, in Italy, might be a good fit. And it was.

Fabarm, located near the gunmaking center of Brescia, was established in 1900. The firm produces a complete line of shotguns and rifles for the Continental market and recently Russia. Fabarm has never had a separate US branch, but in the past has sold here under the aegis of H&K, SIG Arms, TriStar and others. The company is also well known as a parts supplier to the industry. Caesar Guerini used Fabarm's services quite a bit when CG was just starting out and didn't yet have its own plant.

Fabarm recently came out with a new Elos model over/under for the European market, and that is the basis of the Baserri Mari. As I write this, Baserri is bringing in a steel-receiver 30" 12-gauge Mari Elite sporter as well as our test gun: the aluminum-receiver 28" 12-gauge Mari HR hunter.

The design of the alloy action of our Mari HR is about as conventional as it gets in Brescia and Val Trompia. The lock and hinge are similar to those on the Caesar Guerini Ellipse EVO, reviewed elsewhere in these pages. CG, along with B. Rizzini, Fausti, Fabarm and others, uses a Browning-style lock. The locking tongue emerges from the bottom of the standing breech and engages a slot in the bottom of the monoblock lugs. This lock type is said to make the receiver deeper compared to a gun with mid-locks like the Beretta 680 series, but when I measured, the difference was a mere $1/8"$.

Like the Browning, the monoblock has four passive underlugs. On the Baserri, only the rear two lock by engaging a recess in the receiver floor, but they do not go through it. In the Superposed all four fully engage and penetrate the receiver floor. Hinging is by the usual Italian replaceable hinge stubs, as found on Berettas and Perazzis.

Hammers pivot on the triggerplate. Sears are suspended from the top strap. Ejector cocking rods are fixed to the base of the hammers so that the auto ejectors are cocked when the hammer drops. All very standard and proven.

The single trigger is inertia operated, so the first shell must fire to set the second barrel. The barrel is selected by the usual Beretta-style safety toggle switch. The safety is automatic, whether you like it or not. If you don't, a little time at your gunsmith's shop will set things right. There's a nice additional safety feature in a lever that disconnects the trigger when the opening lever is moved to the right. The gun can't fire if the action isn't completely locked.

The Mari HR is light, well made, good looking and a lot of gun for the money.

Our test gun's trigger varied between 4^1/4 pounds and 4^3/4 pounds on both sears. That was fine, but there was also a distinct hitch in the midst of the pull. This was noticeable when measuring but not when actually shooting. Sometimes these things smooth out when a gun has more rounds through it. Trigger take-up is adjustable via an Allen key, offering a nice little extra.

The interior of the action shows a mixture of parts that are ma-chined, cast and stamped based on their usage. There were no extraneous tool marks. It was clean. Solid pins, not roll pins, are used to hold the bits in place. Well done.

The big thing about the Mari HR action is that it is aluminum. Ergal 55 aluminum alloy for you metallurgists. The triggerplate too. And not just the action. My trusty magnet showed that the forend iron wasn't iron. It was aluminum for additional weight savings.

In a relatively low-volume hunting gun, the wear on the receiver knuckle and mating forend piece, even if made of aluminum, is minimal. The high-wear area is around the hinge stubs, and those are steel on steel. My testing was too short to draw any conclusions regarding the durability of the gun's aluminum components, but Browning's aluminum O/Us hold up well.

The whole point of the aluminum bits is to lower weight, both real and advertised. It's a known fact that just about all gunmakers fudge a touch by low-balling the stated weight of their field guns. The Baserri Mari HR has a listed weight of 6 pounds 3 ounces. Don't believe everything you read—unless I write it. Our gun came in at almost 6 pounds 10 ounces. Not that it really matters. A weight of 6 pounds 10 ounces is definitely light for a field 12, and it will be a delightful gun to carry all day.

The cosmetics of the receiver include a proprietary matte-silver titanium coating and tasteful acanthus-leaf roll engraving on the receiver sides. The lower edges of the receiver are nicely rounded for a comfortable field carry.

At press time, barrels for the Mari HR come in only a 28" length. Again, perfectly nice for a field gun for most uses. What makes the Baserri's barrels different is that they are built on Fabarm's Tribore principle from thrice-bored chrome molybdenum steel that has been aged outdoors for a year. The company claims that the outdoor exposure makes the steel harder. I don't know enough about metallurgy to vouch for this, but the Baserri barrels are overproofed to 1630 BAR, as opposed to the 12-country European CIP proof standard for high-performance steel shot of 1370 BAR. The US standard SAAMI definitive proof minimum average is 1310 BAR, and the maximum average is 1413. Clearly, the Baserri has very sturdy barrels.

The Tribore-barrel concept gets a lot of hype. Baserri's Website glowingly reports that the Tribore barrel "has eliminated the forcing cone by gradually reducing the bore from .740 to .724 inch, which increases shot velocity, reduces felt recoil and provides better patterns."

Maybe yes. Maybe no. A little time with a bore mike on our test gun's barrels showed a standard 3" chamber and a very normal short forcing cone leading from the chamber to the bore. It was hardly eliminated. But then it got interesting. From in front of the forcing cone to about 15" from the breech, the bore measured a constant overbore .740". Then, over the next 10", it did indeed gradually taper down to about .724" at the back of the screw choke's skirt.

Taper-bore barrels are nothing new. In the 1890s Horatio Phillips patented the Vena Contracta, a 12-gauge shotgun barrel that reduced to 20-gauge dimensions in the first third of its length. The Tribore is not nearly that extreme and remains all 12 gauge with a modest .016" bore taper. It was nice to see that both barrels had the same interior diameter. You would be amazed at how many double shotguns have bores of slightly different sizes. The backs of the screw-choke tubes open to .733" for safety clearance, so there is a bit of a jug before the choke constriction.

The Baserri Inner Plus flush-mount screw chokes are a longish $3^{1}/_{4}$". They use a constant taper to a $^{3}/_{8}$" parallel. The four screw chokes that came with the gun were an Improved Cylinder, with .006" constriction; a .017" Modified; a .027" Improved Modified and a .035" Full. The IC is a little more open than usual for American standards, but the others are normal. They are notched for the adequate wrench and rim-grooved for identification. The IC and M are approved for steel shot.

The barrel exterior sports full-length solid side ribs and an untapered $^{1}/_{4}$"-wide vent top rib finished with a sensible single stainless front bead sight. The barrel finish is a low-glare matte black. The barrel exterior appeared smooth and properly struck, with modest swelling at the muzzle for the screw chokes.

The stock on our test Mari HR measured $14^{1}/_{2}$" x $1^{7}/_{16}$" x $2^{1}/_{4}$" with a little cast, typical on Italian guns. The dimensions are a little higher than we typically see on Browning or Remington guns. Pitch was the usual 2" of stand-off. The rubber recoil pad was $^{1}/_{2}$" thick, but there is an optional $^{7}/_{8}$" pad if you want to increase length.

The stock wrist and pistol grip were a little thicker than I like on a field gun due to a slight ambidextrous palm swell, but they were good enough. Checkering was laser cut in a simple borderless pattern. The wood-to-metal fit was a bit proud but uniform. The wood itself is listed as "Grade 2 Plus," and I'll certainly give it that. It had a good bit of figure and was said to be finished in hand-rubbed oil. As with many Italian guns, the finish showed some open grain, but it was nicely colored. The inside of the head of the stock looked as though it had a couple of protective finish coats, too. Nice. The forend had one of those Schnabel schnouts but, of the type, it was well done.

A nice plus, especially considering the aluminum mating surfaces, is an adjustable opening-tension feature. With the supplied Allen keys you can alter the pressure of the forend bracket on the barrel tenon to change resistance of the barrel rotation around the hinge pin if things begin to wear.

The Baserri Mari HR comes in a serviceable black ABS take-down case complete with the four screw chokes, functional choke wrench, 1630 BAR proof certificate, manual, warrantee registration and a useful parts diagram. You can learn a lot about the gun's design from the parts diagram.

The Baserri warranty is for three years parts and labor. Baserri recently signed on with Briley for warranty work, replacement chokes and customization. Briley's stellar reputation makes this selection an intelligent move for a new company.

Shooting the gun was interesting. You'd think that a gun with an aluminum receiver would balance like a broomstick with a brick on each end, but the Mari HR didn't. The barrels were comparatively heavy, weighing 7½ oz more than the 28" barrels on my Beretta O/U, so the gun had a definite front bias. This helped it swing smoothly but made quick starts and mid-air corrections more difficult. Pheasants beware. Ruffed grouse rejoice.

The stock dimensions seemed to suit most who tried it. Low stocks make you lift your head. That, to the utter delight of the bird in question, stops the gun. High stocks just make you hold a little under the target.

The Mari HR comes with four 3¼" flush-mount choke tubes.

The gun functioned correctly in all respects. Ejectors were properly timed. There were no misfires, even with reloads using sunken primers that balk in my Superposeds. The screw chokes stayed snug. Both barrels shot to the same point of impact. Sporting clays target breaks seemed normal for the choke.

Comments that I have read say that the gun has low recoil. To me, recoil seemed about normal for a gun of this weight. I didn't notice any magic Tribore recoil reduction, nor did I expect it. Mr. Newton laid out the rules pretty clearly. I extensively shot a Fabarm Sporting Clays Competition Extra O/U 10 years ago and didn't notice any particular Tribore recoil reduction then either. Besides, so much of perceived recoil is gunfit. But the Mari HR was comfortable to shoot. I would be quite content taking this gun afield.

And now here's the good part. The Baserri Mari HR 28" 12-gauge lists for $2,395. A little bit of the usual dealer discount would get it down to a very nice price level. It's a lot of gun for the money. It weighs less and costs less than the aluminum-receiver Browning 625 Feather. It handles decently, seems well made and looks nice. The Baserri Mari HR may be the new kid on the block, but this goddess of thunder is definitely worth a look.

Beretta A400 Xplor Unico

Consulting my copy of S.P. Fjestad's encyclopedic *Blue Book of Gun Values*, I see that Beretta started its gas-operated semi-auto production in 1956 with the Model 60. I remained blissfully unaware of the company's efforts through the ensuing Model 61, Lark series and AL-1 model of the early '70s, but I fooled around with the incrementally improved AL-2 and AL-3. The gas ports were too small to reliably run American target loads. The following 301, 302 and 303 were essentially the same gun, but Beretta finally got the ports right with the 303. I didn't have to drill those out to function with lighter loads. I also had a couple of Browning B-80s, really just Beretta 302s with slightly different cosmetics.

The Model 390 (1992 to '99) was the first big change. For the first time Beretta's standard auto was given a 3" chamber, but it functioned nicely with light loads, too. The firm did this by means of a secondary bleed valve on the front of the gas chamber to vent excess pressure from heavy loads. The remaining gas worked the action at normal speed. The 390 was popular and reliable.

The 391 (2000 to '09) was Beretta's mega-hit. It was more of the same mechanics, but it trimmed down the front end using a smaller gas piston and made other refinements. In 2002 Beretta added the completely new Xtrema $3^1/2$" gas gun, but that weighed close to 8 pounds and was best in the duck blind. For all-around use, the 391 has set today's standard for gas-operated shotguns. In sporting clays roughly one-third of the shooters use semi-autos. From what I've seen, at least 90 percent of those have been 391s. The gun has ruled the roost. It has been the one to beat.

Has been. Enter Beretta's new gas gun: the A400 Xplor Unico. "Xplor" is for the hunting model and "Unico" for the unique action. Often new guns aren't really new. They're just an excuse to raise the price for a little change in cosmetics. Not so this time. This gun really is new. New action. New look. And, of course, new price: MSRP $1,725 with the Kick Off recoil-reduction system, $1,625 without.

The big news is that the A400 is a $3^1/2$" 12-gauge gas gun. The Xtrema is also a $3^1/2$" gas auto, but again, it is hefty. Beretta's Benelli branch makes a lighter $3^1/2$" recoil-operated gun, but it doesn't love light loads. The 391 is only 3". The A400 is different. Beretta claims it weighs a field-carry-friendly 6.6 pounds, has ultra-low recoil and will handle even the lightest loads. Too good to be true? We'll see about that.

The first A400s in the US were wood-stocked field guns in 12 gauge, arriving in 2010. Our $3^1/2$" test gun's receiver is about $3/8$" longer than the 391's but close to the same height and width. At a glance, it looks pretty much the same except that the ejection port, loading port and carrier are $1/2$" longer to take the longer shell. The left-side magazine cut-off and right-side closing button are unchanged. The crossbolt safety is still at the front of the techno-polymer trigger guard, but now it is far more ergonomic and easily reversed for lefties. It really is the best trigger-guard safety I've used.

What you'll notice is the A400's matte gray/green anodized-aluminum receiver color. The last green receivers I remember seeing were on Browning Lightweight Double Autos made in the '50s.

The trigger group is redesigned and slightly lighter than the 391's. The hammer is lighter, so it should have a faster lock time. Beretta claims an extremely high cycling rate: "36 percent faster" than any other system. One thing is for sure, the trigger group is removed far more easily than the 391's, which you really had to yank on. The trigger pull on the A400 I tested was 5 pounds but, like most autos, had a fair amount of creep. I'd call it average. Rich Cole (www.cole gun.com) does a great job of crisping up Beretta triggers.

There is a new hydraulic damper at the rear of the receiver inside the stock bolt. It reduces recoil by absorbing the impact of the bolt carrier against the receiver when it's driven back during cycling. In the past this was done with a passive nylon bushing that was prone to breakage on impact.

The new bolt on the A400 uses a rotary lock-up, like the Xtrema, and engages slots just aft of the chamber. Previous 300-series models used a rising locking block engaging the barrel extension. The outer casing of the A400's bolt is welded onto the dual action rails. The front of this bolt-casing/action-rail assembly is a cylinder that fits over the magazine tube.

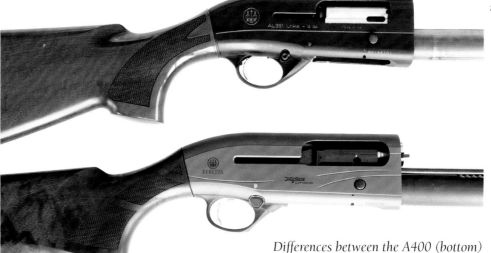

Differences between the A400 (bottom) and its predecessor, the 391 (top), include a longer receiver to accommodate $3^1/2$" shells and a high-tech gray/green coating.

Again, like the Xtrema but unlike the previous 300-series autos, the mainspring wraps around the magazine tube and is not hidden in the buttstock. I think this is a big plus, because now the mainspring is easy to inspect and clean or replace. Autos will beat themselves to death if the mainspring is worn. For protection, the mainspring is surrounded by a polymer sleeve.

A neat touch is the locked charging handle. I don't know how many times my autos have flung the charging handle into the weeds at the worst possible moment. The A400 solves this by locking the handle in the bolt until the bolt head is given a quarter-turn to release it. Foolproof and just my style.

The gas system is also new. There is the usual gas chamber under the barrel. As with the 390 and 391, the front of the chamber has a spring-loaded secondary bleed valve to vent excess gas. The manual says that this valve now requires no maintenance or cleaning. A big difference is the new piston, which rides on the magazine-tube guide rod. Instead of a piston that looks like a ridged barrel, as on the 300-series gas guns, the A400 piston looks a little like a funnel with an aggressive expanding washer around the neck. The serrated washer provides a tight gas seal and also scrapes carbon from the chamber.

A result of this change is that it takes less gas to operate the action. Less gas means less dirt and a cleaner, more reliable gun. Beretta reps told me that one of the A400 test guns had gone 10,000 rounds between cleanings! Amazing. Think about how much work that will save your wife.

The barrel also has other changes. As befits a $3^{1}/_{2}$" gun, the barrel extension that guides and locks the bolt is longer. It's also bright-chromed for easy cleaning. There is now a fitting ring to seal the joint where the barrel slips into the front of the receiver. This damps barrel wobble and vibration.

Beyond the $3^{1}/_{2}$" chamber, the forcing cone is most unusual. It is the same length as the chamber. That is *loooong*. I have my doubts if cones much longer than $1^{1}/_{2}$" do any good, but if more is better, then this is best. The bore on our gun miked .732", a relatively modest overbore.

Three of the new nickel-plated Optima-Choke HP chokes come

with the gun. There is a Cylinder Bore miking .000", a Modified of .020" and a Full of .037". The Cylinder and Modified are OK for steel. The Full isn't. I'm surprised Beretta didn't include a .010" Improved Cylinder with the gun, though it is available as an extra. The chokes are $2^{3}/_{4}$" long with $^{1}/_{2}$" parallel after a $2^{1}/_{4}$" taper. The rears of the chokes were .010" larger than the bore, a normal drop for mass production.

The outside of the barrel on the gun I tested was nicely matte-blued with no ripples or machining marks. Beretta makes good barrels. The narrow, $^{7}/_{32}$"-wide, untapered, vented field rib has a simple single steel bead at the muzzle. Or it did until it unscrewed and fell off. More Loctite next time.

The first thing I noticed about the wood was that it was nicely figured. Well, I got taken in. It's called Xtra Grain, and it's a cosmetic treatment that paints a fancy grain pattern over relatively plain walnut. It's nicely done, fools most people, and soaks into the wood, so you might be able to refinish lightly. This sort of thing has been done for years by many makers, and Beretta does it well. It is much nicer than the company's earlier Xtra Wood enhancement with fragile layered film.

Our stock had the extra-cost Kick Off recoil system, which I discuss in the review of the Beretta Perennia over/under. This system also has been offered on synthetic stocks for the Xtrema and 391 Urika. Like the GraCoil and others, it cushions recoil with dual hydraulic cylinders between the recoil pad and the stock. Beretta claims 60-percent recoil reduction with the device.

The recoil pad on all A400s is Beretta's new Micro Core model, complete with the usual claimed miracle damping properties. It seemed fine, and I'll give it one thing: It wasn't sticky, so it didn't hinder mounting the gun in the field. Micro Cores of different thicknesses are available to alter the length of the stock.

The stock dimensions feel similar to those on other Beretta autoloading field guns. The pistol grip is thankfully more open than the target 391's. This first run of A400 Xplor Unico field guns came with sling studs in the stocks and forend caps. Slings are popular in Europe and with some duck hunters here, but they are uncommon in the American uplands.

The forend looks high-tech because of a subtle swoosh line, and it feels very comfortable. The front has a plastic molding incorporating a gas vent and a tight barrel seal. Checkering is laser-applied at 24 lpi and quite nice. It goes all the way around the bottom of the forend for a good grip and even manages to tastefully incorporate Beretta's Three Arrows logo. As on the 391s before it, the forend mates tightly with the front of the receiver for a smooth transition.

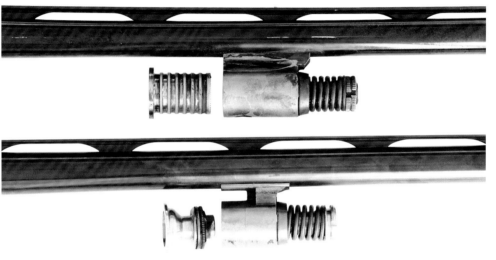

Another difference between the A400 and the 391 (pictured at top) is a new gas system with a funnel-like piston shape and an expanding gas-sealing washer.

Beretta invited some writers to South Dakota to test the gun and learn of its wonders. We shot pheasants and clays for a couple of days. The gun I drew had 28" barrels, and I felt it was just a touch muzzle-heavy in the field. I would pick the 26" for upland hunting, but most of the people I showed my 28" review gun to preferred that length. A 30" tube is also available. It's nice to have the choice.

We shot 2¾" 1¼-oz loads on the pheasants, but we also tested 3½" 1¼-oz high-velocity steel and 3" 1⅝-oz lead interchangeably. The gun handled everything without a hiccup. I was really impressed when my review gun arrived home and I ran a bunch of ⅞-oz, 1,150-fps powder puffs through it just to see. It worked perfectly. I never had a jam or malfunction of any kind with any ammunition. Well done. Very well done, indeed. I was given to understand that the upcoming 12-gauge target model will have a 3" chamber, but my 3½" field gun functioned so well with such absurdly light loads that I don't see the need.

The A400 Xplor Unico comes in a nice plastic compartmented case suitable for air travel. Inside are the three chokes, a good choke wrench, a bottle of oil, an extra stock-adjustment-shim set, sling swivels, an informative manual and a one-year warranty extendable to three years on submission of the registration. Before disassembling the gun, make sure to read the manual to learn the trick to removing the charging handle. After that, disassembly is a snap.

Recoil was another matter. My test gun weighed exactly 7 pounds, not the 6.6 pounds advertised. Still, it's pretty light for something meant to shoot 2¼-oz chiropractor specials. For me, in spite of the

Kick Off device and new recoil pad, the gun was still uncomfortable with heavy loads. Some friends who own 391s felt the A400 shot softer, but I felt the other way. The A400 certainly didn't seem as soft as the heavier Xtrema. Perhaps it's a matter of fit. For me, the Kick Off A400 was a little short at 14^1/$_4$", and short guns always kick more than those of proper length. Let's just say that the Kick Off is probably worthwhile, but it's not a miracle.

As to looks, the general opinion, including mine, was that the gun was very attractive. It is appropriately modern but not at all overboard. It's really nicely done.

And finally, will it run 10K before cleaning? My sample looked normally dirty after a couple of flats of ammo, but it never once failed to cycle properly with a wide variety of loads. Maybe it *could* go 10K. My test was too short to know long-term reliability, but the design and construction sure look good.

The Beretta A400 Xplor Unico is a heck of a gun. The 391 has become a legend, but this really is a step up. The 3^1/$_2$" chamber offers great possibilities for steel waterfowl loads, and the modest weight, good handling and excellent ergonomics will work for those who prefer an auto for the uplands or pre-season target work. The gun will handily shoot any 12-gauge shell. Ease of maintenance and good looks put the cap on it. If you cook with gas, make sure to Xplor this gun.

UPDATE

The 3" A400 Xcel Sporter came to market early in 2011 along with a 3"-chambered Xplor Light field model that saves 5 oz of weight. At this writing, the A400 20-gauge is still in the offing. In 2011 Beretta told me that the 391 would remain available alongside the A400 for a limited time, probably to work through inventories while production of the new gun ramps up.

Beretta Silver Pigeon V 28-Gauge

I was looking over things in the Beretta display at the 2007 SHOT Show when the 28-gauge Silver Pigeon V over/under field gun simply jumped into my hands. Like a puppy at the dog shelter, it picked me—I didn't pick it. It handled perfectly as I waved it at various klieg lights and logo banners hanging from the ceiling. I could shoot this gun! And it was good-looking too. What could a gun reviewer possibly do but try one out? It was my duty.

Beretta makes a ton of 28s. Currently you can get Beretta boxlock 28s in nine field grades and three sporting clays grades. The interior mechanics are all the same, but the exterior embellishments change as the list prices go from the $2,075 White Onyx to the $7,275 687 EELL Diamond Pigeon Sporter, plus a good bit more for the Giubileo model. There is something for everybody. In the middle of the pack is the Silver Pigeon V at $3,775. I was drawn to its particular combination of scaled receiver, perfectly shaped forend and optional English or pistol-grip stock.

The Silver Pigeon V's 28-gauge receiver truly is 28-gauge-sized. In today's Silver Pigeon lineup, the S, IV and V come with true 28-gauge receivers. The others currently are built on 20-gauge frames.

Does the difference in frame size really matter? Both the 20- and 28-gauge receivers are $3\frac{1}{8}$" front to back. Interior widths are the same, and the 28-gauge barrels seem like they could interchange if fitted. On the outside the scaled frame is a minuscule .08" narrower and a slightly more noticeable .11" shorter. You can just notice the difference when the guns are placed together if you look for it. This may be a princess-and-the-pea-type deal but, when carrying the guns by the receivers, you can feel the difference.

The basic 680 action design has been around forever and doesn't need any further praise from me. It works. It's reliable. It's clean and tidy. It is proven beyond the slightest doubt. I've had a half-dozen 680 Series Berettas over the years and cannot remember a single serious mechanical problem. One of the biggest pluses is that it is a sealed action with no locking lugs running through the floorplate like the Brownings. This keeps it clean. The stub hinge pins are easily replaced if they ever should wear. The split locking lug engages halfway up each side of the monobloc and comes in different sizes for easy replacement as it ages.

The gold-plated single trigger on our test gun released the under sear at 4³/₄ pounds. It was consistent and crisp but with noticeable over-travel. The over sear let off at a reliable 4 pounds but with some creep. This is perfectly adequate for a mass-produced gun, and only the most digitally sensitive soul would require further tuning.

The safety on our field gun was automatic. You easily can have a gunsmith return it to manual operation if you prefer. The size and let-off of the safety were fine, but once or twice a shooter inadvertently switched the barrel selector when opening the gun. The barrel selector is a little left-right toggle on top of the safety. When pushing the opening lever to the right, a shooter might brush his thumb over the selector, accidentally selecting the over barrel. It happened, but only rarely and shouldn't be a problem once you are familiar with the gun.

On the outside, the receiver, forend iron and trigger guard have a case-colored look. The colors are applied by a new chemical process, not in the traditional bone, charcoal and oven procedure. The advantage to Beretta's approach is that there is no possibility of the metal warpage that can occur during the oven process. It involves less labor, too. On the downside, not everyone liked the application. The color was very nice indeed, noticeably more vibrant than some oven coloring I've seen. The problem is that the chemical process left some uncovered areas. To some shooters it looked as though it had been dipped and hadn't taken at several of the edges. Opinions differed, as others felt it looked fine. The "holidays" were more extensive in some samples than others. I have no way of telling how durable the finish is, but just about anything holds up better than real case coloring. The receiver has two gold-washed birds on each side and a gold logo on the bottom. The gold looks pretty against the colors. The underlying engraving is mechanically applied and perfectly nice.

The SPV 28-gauge is available with 28" or 26" barrels. Ours were the former. The barrels themselves are typical Beretta: very nice indeed, thanks to the most modern cold-hammer-forging machinery. There were no ripples or flaws. This is noteworthy, because the barrels are joined by brazing, a more durable but higher heat process than soldering. Brazing requires more care to avoid rippling due to overheating. The untapered and narrow .235"-wide vented field rib was on straight and level. There is an appropriate simple steel bead at the muzzle.

The side ribs are solid, but they run only from the muzzle to 8" from the breech. The area under the forend has no side ribs. My wife's faithful 15-year-old Beretta 686 Special 28-gauge has full-length side ribs that go from muzzle to monobloc. The SPV's shorter side ribs are lighter but are positioned to move the barrel balance forward. The big issue with little guns is almost always whippiness because they are so light. Moving all the weight possible forward helps, and Beretta has made that effort with the SPV.

The barrel interiors are chromed, as they are on all the Beretta 680 Series guns I'm familiar with. Chroming makes the bores easier to clean. For the slothful among us, chrome is rust resistant if you fail to clean as often as you should, and it also rustproofs the choke threads if you forget to lube them. On the downside, it makes further forcing-cone alterations more problematic, though certainly not impossible.

Chambers on the Beretta 28s I've measured have been 2³/₄", unlike some of the German 3" 28-gauge chambers. The chamber forcing cones on our gun were 1" long—plenty of length to gradually introduce the shot into the barrel and keep shot deformation to a minimum. I've seen shorter cones on many 12-gauge guns.

The barrel tubes are joined by the usual Beretta monobloc. Beretta has used this jointure for more than a century. The seam is disguised by a small engraved line. The monobloc carries Beretta's simple ejectors powered by spring-loaded plungers.

Both barrel bores are .551". Nominal bore for 28 gauge is .550", so these are about dead on. It's nice that both barrels have the same I.D., which is not always the case with other shotguns. Barrels with different I.D.s play havoc with changing screw-in chokes. The Silver Pigeon V comes with five screw-in Mobilchokes mounted flush with the muzzle. They are Cylinder Bore (measuring .004" constriction), Improved Cylinder (.010"), Modified (.015"), Improved Modified (.023") and Full (.028"). These constrictions are certainly in the ballpark for their designations. The .004" and .015" would make ideal 20- and 30-yard upland chokes.

The choke tubes are only about $1^1/2$" long, but each has a surprising $^3/4$" to 1" of parallel after an abrupt constriction. The shot is quickly squeezed down and then allowed to stabilize in the parallel. Perazzi takes the opposite approach in its 28-gauge barrels, using 4" fixed chokes with 3" of gradual constriction and then 1" of parallel. The Perazzis produce exceptional patterns. It is interesting that Beretta, within the confines of a short screw-in, chose to maintain the long parallel at the expense of a short constriction section.

One area where Beretta didn't get it right was with the supplied choke "wrench." It is a wretched flat stamping, awkward and inconvenient to use. But it was cheap to make, I'm sure. Beretta's 12-gauge

The SPV 28's frame is scaled appropriately, and the receiver, forend iron and trigger guard have chemically applied colors.

screw-choke wrench with the plastic collet is ever so much nicer. Briley makes a very nice fishing-reel-handle wrench for all gauges.

The standard Beretta sub-gauge field stock has been unchanged for many years. My wife's old gun has the same stock and pistol grip as our test SPV. Unlike the oversized vertical pistol grips of many Italian competition guns, the Beretta field pistol grip is nicely relaxed and seemed to suit a broad variety of those who tried the gun. And if you prefer an English stock on your over/under field gun, the SPV is available in that configuration also. It looks gorgeous. I believe that the SPV 20, 28 and .410 are the only versions of the 680 series currently available with an English stock. All the English-stocked guns come with 28" barrels. There's a gold-colored metal oval on the underside of the stock for initials or a family crest.

According to my faithful Combo Gauge, the stock dimensions of our gun were $14^7/16$" x $1^7/16$" x $2^5/16$", with 3" of stand-off and a modest amount of cast-off for a right-handed shooter. This is pretty standard stuff, but the gun seemed to me to mount just a touch higher than others. Perhaps it is the relaxed pistol grip changing the angle of the right wrist and thus raising the shoulder.

The forend is slender and very nicely shaped and was one of the things that attracted me to the gun. It eschews the finger grooves and passé Schnabels of the other models. It reminds me of the marvelous minimalist forends of the early Browning Superlights. Again, this delightful forend comes only on the SPV and Silver Pigeon C grade. The latter is made for the discerning English market.

The forend is attached with a properly fitted Deeley pull-down latch. I think this is much nicer than the Anson buttons I see on some other over/under field guns, because it allows a smoother forend-tip transition. Boss over/under fans may disagree.

Checkering on our SPV was done by laser, with a narrow double-line border and a moderate lpi. The amoeba-like shape of the checkered panels might put off the purists and does make the checkering look machine-cut, but it is well executed. Unlike some recent samples of laser checkering I've seen, Beretta's work did not look burnt.

Wood-to-metal fit on our gun was pretty good. There was certainly nothing egregious, but the wood around the receiver was about $^1/_{32}$" proud. There were no gaps. It was just a little high to allow for shrinkage and the like. There was considerably more of an issue where the stock met the top rear of the receiver and the wood overlapped by $^3/_{32}$". That's too much, and Beretta ought to tweak the pantograph.

The stock ends in a $^1/_2$" solid-black-polymer recoil pad. Our gun case also contained a fitted green $^1/_2$" Beretta Gel-Tek pad in case you prefer its slicker surface and higher recoil absorbency. Thicker pre-fit pads are available if you need more length. Nice touch.

The finish on the SPV is listed as oil. It successfully resisted my universal-solvent sunscreen, so there is obviously more to the oil than just linseed. Our gun had a dark-stain, non-reflective matte finish with considerable open grain. The figure of the walnut was fair on one side, so-so on the other. It wasn't great wood, especially considering the price for this model.

And therein lies a lesson. Shotguns aren't identical. If you are paying extra for an upgraded model, make sure your gun meets your cosmetic requirements. Most of the SPVs I've seen have had very nice wood. This particular one didn't. It happens. There are good photos of available wood and guns at two of the larger US Beretta dealers: www.joeletchenguns.com and www.colegun.com.

The Silver Pigeon V comes in a decent plastic takedown case. It's fine protection for the boot of the shooting brake but no match for a testy

In an effort to lighten the barrels and move weight forward, Beretta has removed the side ribs beneath the forend on the SPV (top). Note how the author's wife's 15-year-old 686 Special 28 (bottom) has side ribs extending to the monobloc.

baggage handler. The case contains the aforementioned wretched wrench, five chokes, a TruGlo luminous light tube front sight for those shooters with a psychedelic bent, sling swivels for the Europeans and the extra Gel-Tek pad. There's also a generic tri-lingual manual. The factory warrantee is for three years.

This gun was a hoot to shoot. It was everything I'd hoped it would be when I saw it at SHOT. Of course, I'm biased. I'm an unabashed fan of the 28 gauge. If you miss with a 28, everyone sympathizes with your handicap. When you finally do make a shot, you're a hero. That's my kind of deal. A killjoy might note that the 20 gauge is more versatile and, in the case of the Beretta, weighs about the same as the 28. I don't care. The fact is that out to 30 yards or so, the 28's ³/₄ ounce of shot is just fine for appropriately sized birds. It's the ideal quail gauge. With enough choke, a 28 can take doves at silly distances.

Of course, not all 28s are equal. This Beretta is simply more equal. It feels so absolutely right. The balance and handling are prefect. Because of the excellent, very slightly weight-forward bias, the gun was a delight to shoot. The light 6¹/₄-pound weight made very fast shots possible, and the balance made more measured swings easy. As expected, mechanical reliability was 100 percent. The ejectors were properly timed and tossed empties about four feet. That's not hard enough to discipline your loader for a snide comment, but it's enough to clear the chambers.

My only real complaints were about the cosmetics of this particular test gun. It had spotty case coloring and wood that wasn't up to the price point. I've seen other examples of the same model that were better in both respects, so just pick one that meets your preferences and you'll be happy. The balance, handling and reliability are built in. Don't worry about that.

There's a very good reason why Beretta has been in business for almost 500 years. The company makes good stuff. When you buy a Beretta over/under—any Beretta over/under —you can expect reliable performance honed by years of experience. The firm makes enough different models that there's a good chance you'll find one that pleases you. I certainly found one that pleases me.

Beretta SV10 Perennia III

When I first saw the SV10 Perennia III at the SHOT Show, I thought that the folks at Beretta had lost their minds. It looked like a totally new gun in direct competition with the Silver Pigeon/680 series over/unders. Why on earth would the world's oldest company compete with its own tremendously successful 680 series? Over the years I've owned a half-dozen guns from the 680 series and shot many more. Generally well balanced and always reliable, they are never a bad choice and often an excellent one. Why mess with success?

When my test gun arrived, the first thing I did was pull it apart. In true master gunsmithing tradition, I Googled videos on Perennia features and disassembly on YouTube. Then I disassembled my own 1998 Beretta Essential. The Essential was the company's bottom-of-the-line over/under 10 years ago, but it had the same mechanics as all of the other stout-hearted 680s. Lo and behold, the interior actions of the Perennia and Essential are basically identical. I immediately felt better. The Perennia isn't about the basics. The 680 already has those. The Perennia is about extra features.

Introduced in 2008, the Perennia's first three years of production included only 12-gauge models. The field model comes in two versions: the Perennia III, which we tested, and a limited run of 300 Perennia Is. The only difference was the receiver engraving. The price was unchanged. Options were limited to 26" or 28" barrels without the Kick-Off hydraulic recoil-reducing buttpad and only 28" barrels with it. Originally, suggested retail for the Perennia III was $3,250 ($3,650 with the Kick-Off), but the price had dropped to $2,600 ($2,900 with the Kick-Off) by 2011 to boost sales. Sporting clays versions—the SV10 Prevail and SV10 Prevail Game Scene—were introduced in 2010 and were based on the same action.

The first thing everyone notices about the Perennia is the bright nickel-coated receiver. It has a new action shoulder creating a raised outline (Beretta calls it an "arrow") on each side, which is echoed by the deeply convex stock inletting at the head. It is all very modern but not over the top like the Browning Cynergy. The design house of Giugiaro has cosmetically influenced some of Beretta's other guns, and perhaps it had some input here. The mechanical engraving's 100-percent coverage breaks up some of the receiver shine. The engraving is marked "Perennia III."

Inside the action it's old home week with some major additions. The 680 series was always a triggerplate boxlock, but now the triggerplate is detachable. Remove the stock, apply a half-turn to the little Torx bolt under the safety, give a yank and out it comes. Removing the trigger group will give you better access to cleaning things and the very occasional parts replacement. It's one of those things that isn't necessary but is nice to have and fun to show your friends. The Beretta 680 was never the simplest action, so easy access to all of the bits and pieces is probably a good idea.

By the way, the trigger blade itself may look like it's stainless, but it is made from titanium. I'm sure there was a perfectly good reason for that. Most of the interior of the action is nickel-plated to prevent rust and make cleaning easy. The trigger is inertial.

The modern look and feel of the SV10 Perennia belies its heart: the well-proven guts of a 680- series gun. Other changes include a delightful array of extra features.

The first pulls on our gun varied from 4 to 4½ pounds with above-average creep; the second pulls were a consistent 4¾ pounds and crisp, with no creep. Like it or not, the safety is automatic, and as in past Berettas, it incorporates the barrel selector via a lateral toggle.

Basic lockup and ejection remain unchanged from the reliable 680 standard, but there is an addition. At the very front of the monobloc, just above the ejectors on both sides, are slot heads. Turning them a quarter-turn with a screwdriver changes the ejectors to extractors. This will be convenient for those who never have learned to catch their ejecting hulls by hand. Those who have this skill can simply ignore the feature.

Another change in the monobloc is a slight reshaping of the side lumps, which engage recesses in the top of the receiver sides. This is mostly a cosmetic bit to give the monobloc a different look. A real difference is that the replaceable hinge stubs on the Perennia are considerably larger and stronger than those on the 680. There are also new internal reinforcement shoulders just to the front of the stubs to further strengthen the action. Because of these changes, 680 barrels will not fit the Perennia.

Advertising hype has it that overbored barrels improve patterns and reduce recoil. In this spirit the barrels of the new Perennia I tested measured an overbored .737" compared to the .723" of my older Beretta barrels. Beretta was one of the last major makers to go to the 12-gauge overbore, but these barrels are there now in several models. Overboring has a price, and that is weight. The 28" barrels on our Perennia weighed 3 pounds 2 ounces, whereas those on my 28" Essential are 2 pounds 13 ounces. True, some of that huge 5-oz difference is because the Essential has no side ribs. But some of it is due to the overboring. That's because overboring may put bigger holes in the tubes, but engineers insist on maintaining barrel-wall thickness. You end up with larger, heavier tubes.

If some is good, more is better. The forcing cones on the SV10 are a whopping $3^1/2"$ long. The cones on my Essential are only $1^1/4"$. The jury is definitely still out on whether cones longer than about $1^1/2"$ improve patterns, even with large shot. On the negative side, the longer the cones, the more possibility of gas blow-by with fiber wads or some plastic wads in very cold temperatures. Some feel that long cones combined with overbored barrels reduce subjective, or felt, recoil, though the recoil formula numbers cannot show this.

As usual, the interiors of the Beretta barrels are chromed for ease of maintenance and cleaning. As a Superposed owner who has watched his bores rust, I love chrome bores. The Perennia barrel exteriors are a nice ripple-free subdued blue-black. This is most appropriate for a field gun.

The Perennia sports the new Optima Choke HP (High Performance) screw chokes. They are nickel-coated steel, not stainless, and are OK for hard nontoxic shot from Cylinder up to Modified. The chokes are of the taper/parallel design. The $2^3/4"$ length of these flush-fit chokes gives enough room for at least a $1/2"$ or more stabilizing parallel section. The drop from the bore to the choke's rear skirt is only .006". This offers the shot charge a less bumpy bore/choke transition than the usual .010"-plus and shows good machining tolerances. The screw chokes cause a tiny .043" swelling at the muzzles, but you can't see it, so fuggetaboutit. These are nice chokes. No one has proven to me that they actually perform better than the old Beretta 2" Mobilchokes, but the tech specs read better.

The bottom line is that the Perennia's barrels are very much up to date with their overbores, extended cones and long screw chokes. They have hit all the buttons.

Our Perennia had the .235"-wide untapered lightweight field vent rib. It is the same one that's on my Essential. There is a simple steel bead at the front and mercifully no center bead to clutter things. The skinny rib is very nice, but it is also very fragile; I've dented the one on my gun several times. Fortunately, Brownells (www.brownells.com) sells the perfect fix. It's the Murray's Vent Rib Tool ($40). It makes straightening rib dents a snap. Still, a solid top rib would be so much stronger and classier.

Normally I wouldn't mention Beretta's forend iron. All the ejector and cocking stuff is in the receiver. The forend of the 680 series just has a couple of forend-iron levers and no real mechanism. Until now. According to the Perennia Website (www.sv10perennia.com): "The new fore-end iron boasts a new patented internal mechanism that maintains a constant barrel-receiver-iron fit." It goes on to say that this improves "the strength of the locking system and the service life of the gun."

The new forend contains a Belleville washer spring (a stack of slightly conical washers) that keeps just enough pressure on the iron to maintain a snug fit on the main joint between the forend and the receiver. Frankly, the snugness of the forend hasn't been a major problem with the 680 series, but I'm all for improvements. In theory this addition will make new guns easy to open without letting old guns get sloppy. Our test gun certainly opened and closed smoothly.

But there is no free lunch. The new forend "iron" isn't; it is aluminum. Why change from steel to aluminum on a part that sees a good bit of wear? Your guess is as good as mine, but here's my try: Overboring the barrels while maintaining wall thickness increased weight. To counteract the increased weight, the forend iron was made from aluminum. To make up for aluminum's greater wear tendency, a spring was added to maintain constant tension. Everything certainly worked fine on our gun, so all's well that ends well. On the outside, the steel forend latch is now longer for better leverage and the new metal escutcheon around the lever is now aluminum.

The shape of the field forend is absolutely perfect. Petite and purposeful and spared the dreaded Schnabel schnout, it is right up there with the field forend paradigm of the '67 Browning Super-lights. Well done, Beretta.

The field stock on our Perennia seems to have been made on the same relaxed pistol-grip pattern as that of my Essential. It feels just right. Measurements are about the same and so are the pistol-grip dimensions and profile. The Perennia Website lists two available stock dimensions—the low one is 14.7" x 1.5" x 2.36", and the higher one is 14.7" x 1.38" x 2.17"—but a Beretta rep told me that probably only the lower stock would be imported. Our test gun was stocked higher than either, so perhaps it was a European spec. Beretta offers pre-fit recoil pads and buttplates of varying thicknesses to easily alter length.

Our gun's stock had Beretta's new Kick-Off recoil-reduction device, a $300 option. It has been offered previously on the Xtrema and Urika synthetic-stocked autos, but I haven't seen it applied to a wood-stocked field gun before. The device fits into the butt of the stock and looks like a thick recoil pad. It consists of two metal, oil-filled hydraulic cylinders about $5/16$" in diameter and a couple of inches long to absorb recoil and three coil springs to return the device to battery. This is all capped

The Kick-Off recoil-reduction device operates on two oil-damped cylinders.

by a standard Beretta recoil pad. The Kick-Off can compress about $3/8$" on recoil. Beretta claims a reduction of 69 percent of recoil. The body of the device is made from some sort of black techno-polymer plastic. It works on the same principle as the CounterCoil, R.A.D., Isis and some others. Most of the other reducers are made of metal and are a good bit heavier, so their market is the target gun.

The Kick-Off has a nicely designed black polymer sleeve covering the awkward gap where the device compresses. In all it is easily the best-looking example of the type that I have seen. It comes with a price, though. The device adds about 5 oz to the butt compared to a standard pad on a wood stock.

With the Kick-Off in place, the standard drawbolt attachment of the stock was out of the question, as too much disassembly would have been required to reach the stock bolt. Thus, Beretta came up with the patented Q-Stock. This involves a small metal trap door in the grip cap that allows Torx-driver access to unscrew an angled bolt that engages a stub drawbolt in the rear of the receiver. It is a little Rube Goldberg but seems to work and draws in the stock snugly. It certainly is quick and easy.

The wood on our gun was nicely figured, clearly a step up. Unfortunately, the dark oil used to finish the wood hid most of the figure. The oil finish also failed to completely seal the grain. This is surprisingly common in oil-finished European guns. The checkering is mechanically done but nicely so. The pattern is traditional. Wood-to-metal fit was fairly good on this early gun, but it was too proud at the top tang and where the stock heads up.

Our test gun did not ship with the extras that you'll get when you buy your own. According to the Website, Perennias come with a plastic takedown case, five chokes (Cylinder, Improved Cylinder, Modified, Improved Modified and Full), a choke wrench, sling swivels in case you really must, an extra-thin plastic buttplate and some oil. There also is a Torx wrench for the stock and trigger, but you'll need to get two more to disassemble the forend and Kick-Off. The guarantee is for one year, but Beretta will add two more years to that if you send in the registration.

I shot the gun at clays and loaned it around. General opinion was quite favorable. Most people liked the looks of the new receiver and didn't worry about the flashy reflection as much as I did. It was an easy gun to shoot well. Balance was just at the rear of the hinge pin. This made the gun feel livelier than its weight would indicate.

The Kick-Off looks great, although the option adds 5 oz and $400.

Without the Kick-Off, it would have balanced more to the front.

Some people liked the Kick-Off stock and some didn't. It really depended on shooting style. The Kick-Off reduces recoil by collapsing slightly on firing. This spaces out the recoil similar to the way it is done with an autoloader. In exchange for this time delay, the stock moves an extra half-inch along the face during recoil. So if face slap is an issue, it might be worse with the Kick-Off. If it isn't, the recoil reduction will be more apparent. Personally, I've found that familiarization with the gun let me adjust my hold to avoid face slap and better appreciate the recoil reduction.

The only real downside I found was the gun's weight. At 7 pounds 9 ounces, it is at the upper end of what I want to lug around all day. But you may feel differently. For ducks, doves or driven, the weight won't matter.

In the end you have to compare the SV10 Perennia to the existing line of 680/Silver Pigeons. The lower revised price point puts it about midway between the 686 White Onyx and the 687 Silver Pigeon II. The Perennia offers a slew of new features, and you are the best judge as to whether they are important. Beretta clearly put a lot of effort into this gun. The company always has made a point of offering choices, and here is another good one. We can never have too many of those.

Blaser F3 Competition Sporting

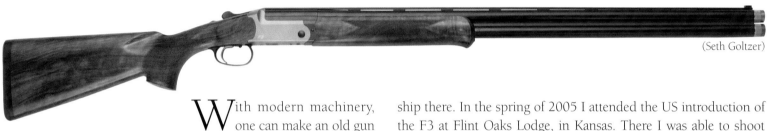

(Seth Goltzer)

With modern machinery, one can make an old gun in a new way. Add imaginative modern design into the mix and you can produce something truly new. The Blaser F3 over/under started with a clean slate. It turned out to be more revolutionary than evolutionary. This review will be a little more detailed than usual, because the gun has so many innovations.

Blaser (Blah-zer), from Isny, Germany, has long produced excellent modular rifles. The F3 is Blaser's first shotgun. Although the company is new to shotgunning, its management isn't. The personable Bernard Knobel, Blaser's president, worked for Krieghoff for 10 years, and the design personnel on this project clearly were top-notch.

Though I previously had heard rumors of the Blaser F3 Competition O/Us, my first specific reports were from friends who had seen the guns at the 2004 FITASC World Sporting Championship, in Signes, France. British sporting great John Bidwell was a consultant on the F3 design, and he used one to win the Veteran's championship there. In the spring of 2005 I attended the US introduction of the F3 at Flint Oaks Lodge, in Kansas. There I was able to shoot some examples and talk to the gun's designers, management and marketers.

The F3's action is smallish, squarish and elegant at the same time. The interior is more complex than the monastic simplicity of a Perazzi's but nowhere near as Byzantine as a Krieghoff's. I have been to the Blaser factory in Germany, and it is absolutely modern. The receiver starts as an MIM (metal injection molding) piece that is cut to shape with CNC machines and EDM. The action hinges on Beretta-style replaceable hinge stubs and uses a single underbolt like Brownings. In spite of the underlug, the action is only 2.39" high and 1.59" wide—a bit higher than a Cynergy's and lower than a Perazzi's. The monoblock has one large lug that not only receives the underbolt but also locks through the floor of the receiver for additional strength. The front of this lug is replaceable for initial fitting or later wear. The total lockup seems very secure but not nearly as fussy as some other exuberantly multi-latched German guns.

This is a triggerplate action, where all the bits and pieces inside ride on a separate bottom plate. The plate is easily removed with one screw and a drift pin. With a nod to Blaser's rifle heritage, the F3 uses innovative massive linear strikers instead of conventional hammers. Blaser claims a very short lock time because of this. Although rare in shotguns, a striker system is not unique. The Swedish Flodman, nee Caprinus, and Browning Cynergy use the same striker theory but have different executions. The F3's coil mainsprings are trapped inside the strikers, so that they will function even when broken.

The Blaser trigger is mechanical with an inertial-block delay to prevent doubling. The trigger blade is nicely curved and rides on a rail adjustable for trigger-pull length. The rail slopes upward to the rear, so that when the trigger pull is shortened it also is raised to accommodate a smaller hand. Nice touch, and one that I've not seen before. The barrel selector is a small switch immediately in front of the trigger blade. It worked well enough, but you definitely won't be selecting a barrel with a bird in the air. The safety is a conventional fore-and-aft top-tang toggle. It's backed up by a secondary striker interceptor that operates independently of the safety in the event of breakage or a jarring blow. The opening lever appears conventional but hides a neat feature. It can be converted to left-handed opening! Just push out two pins, drop in a left-handed lever and move two parts. Lefties of the world rejoice!

The face of the standing breech holds a large inset plate with six holes. Two holes are for the firing pins. Two are for the Allen keys used to remove the plate and access the pins. The final two holes are for the innovative Blaser EBS (Ejection Ball System). When the gun is fired, the strikers push these pins through the breech face against receptors in the face of the ejectors. This cocks the ejectors. Most guns cock the hammers on opening and the ejectors on closing. Because Blaser hammers are cocked on

opening and the ejectors on firing, closing the gun is effortless.

The receiver is hardened and nitrated to a durable dull matte gray. I was told that the front shoulders of the receiver are wire-EDM'd to exact radius after hardening. This allows correction of any minute hardening warpage, but the EDM is accurate enough not to cut through the hardened layer. The only decoration on the receiver—indeed, on the entire gun—is an unobtrusive "F3" in yellow paint, not gold, on the lower rear sides of the receiver and "Blaser" in black on the bottom. It looks restrained, elegant and tasteful, especially compared to the disco-madness motifs inflicted on some Italian and Japanese guns.

The triggers on all of the F3s I shot were, without exception, superb. I don't mean merely good. I mean *superb*. A good trigger has less to do with pull weight than it does with crispness plus absence of creep, over-travel, side-wobble and play. The best triggers I've used through the years have been on Krieghoff K-80s. The Blaser's is very, very close. Blaser claims to set the pulls to $3\frac{1}{2}$ pounds, but those on my gun were about a pound heavier. No matter. Combined with a comfortably formed trigger blade and a sensible length adjustment, this trigger was a pleasure to use.

Barrels are built on the two-tubes-and-monoblock approach that we see on most modern guns. Right now Blaser goes outside for cold-hammer-forged barrels, but the company intends to make its own in the future. Three-inch chambers with "particularly flat" forcing cones are forged integrally with the barrels to ensure perfect alignment. After extensive testing, Blaser (like Beretta, but unlike Browning) concluded that there was no pattern disadvantage when using $2\frac{3}{4}"$ shells in 3" chambers. Bores are slightly overbore at .735", just like Krieghoff's. The interior is hard-chromed and proofed for use with steel shot.

Competition barrels are available in 28", 30" and 32" lengths. They all balance in the same place regardless of length. This is achieved by varying barrel-wall thicknesses. It requires special steel, extra effort and cost. I have not seen this done previously in a mass-production gun. Even though the balance point remains the same, moment of inertia (the effort required to swing the gun) does increase slightly with barrel length. The 32s do not feel exactly like the 28s, but it's much closer than with other guns. Game barrels are available in 27", 28" and 29" lengths. For these, wall thickness does not change with length, so longer barrels are heavier.

The top rib is absolutely, blessedly flat. There is no step at the rear to hide a dropping bird or make the gun shoot artificially high with a level sight picture. The top surface is nicely scribed to a dull glare and provides a visual center channel. The tops of the receivers on the guns I saw were slightly above the ribs. When I commented on

The F3 features Blaser's EBS (Ejection Ball System), in which, upon firing, the ejectors are cocked via pins being pushed against receptors in the ejectors.
(Seth Goltzer)

this, I was told that the company was aware of this and that it was being addressed. Again, counting our blessings: There is no center bead to clutter things up and collect gun-case lint. The gun comes with an interchangeable front bead. The top rib on our test gun was tapered from $10^1/2$mm to $8^1/2$mm, but $10^1/2$mm and $8^1/2$mm parallel ribs will be available. The rib posts are precision CNC-aligned and welded to the barrel. The rib floats on cushioned inserts, so there

should be no heat distortion or looseness. Side ribs joining the front two-thirds of the barrels are soft-soldered using a higher-temperature soft solder. This process is strong but won't warp the barrels. The exterior barrel finish is innovative. It's plasma-nitrated and then conventionally blued to hide the nitrating's silver color. The result is a black non-glare matte finish with superior rust resistance.

Our F3 Competition came with five extended Briley Spectrum chokes. The constrictions were Skeet, Improved Cylinder, Modified, Improved Modified and Full, but others are available. Threading is proprietary to Blaser, and barrel muzzles are jugged ever so slightly to accept the chokes. Although the choke extensions are knurled for slothful hand-tightening, they also are notched for proper snugging with the supplied Briley "fishing reel handle" wrench. You'll want the wrench, as the chokes took 17 full turns to seat. The choke tips are color coded, but unfortunately the choke name is etched only on the body of the choke where it is hidden when installed. Briley flush chokes are standard on game barrels.

Proper barrel convergence (both barrels shooting to the same point of impact) is a big issue with any double. Unlike less-expensive guns, F3s are shot for convergence in the white after soldering, and then final-finished and shot a second time. Blaser's experience in regulating its double rifles pays off here, and our test gun's convergence was dead on.

Handsome is as handsome does, but a little glitz never hurts either. The first thing that everyone notices about the Blaser F3 is that it comes with highly figured walnut, even in the base models. Every Blaser I saw had snappy lumber. The company definitely understands the US shooter in this respect.

The stock is nicely finished in oil with technical dryers. Typically German, the grain is not entirely filled. The forend and head of the stock were finished properly inside to forestall oil seepage. The wood was generally very slightly proud, but not too much so. It could take one refinishing without fallin below the metal. Checkering is laser-cut in tiny circles on the base and Luxus grades, hand-cut on the fancier grades. The laser work is nicer looking than the Beretta 682's little oval islands, but neither works as well as real checkering.

Our test gun came with the standard 14.6" x 1.5" x 2" stock. It had a moderate $1/8$" at heel and $1/3$" at toe right cast, a medium right-handed palm swell and a normal pitch of about 2". The pistol grip was more relaxed than those on current Italian competition guns but a little more vertical than those on older Browning target guns. Stocks also are available in 15.4" lengths and with 1.6" x 2.2" drops at no extra charge, as is a Monte Carlo stock. Left-handed stocks and adjustable stocks are available for an extra charge. A completely custom-dimensioned stock, included free on Perazzis, is a whopping $1,200. The buttpad on the sporter stock has a plastic horseshoe inset into the top for smoother mounting. The stock is instantly removable with the provided hex wrench.

Inside the stock there is another bit of innovation called the Blaser Balancer. It's a threaded rod that screws into the standard stock bolt. On the rod were two 2.4-oz weights located with grub screws. It looks as though there is enough room for two more if you wish. Gun balance can be fine-tuned with any combination of weights and placement. Nice touch.

The forend, like so much else on the F3, is novel. It uses a sort of Anson pushbutton, except that the entire latch is at the front of the forend. The forend is inflicted with a clumsy Schnabel tip—the inescapable stigma of sporters these days. It looks like a Hapsburg lip on an otherwise very attractive gun. The semi-beavertail from the F3 trap model might look better, but the marvelously slender forend on the English-market Perazzi sporters would be ideal.

The individual parts of the F3 are innovative, as is the underlying concept. Blaser has followed the example it set with its R93 rifles and has made the F3 completely modular. At the factory, all barrels are fitted to a master receiver and all receivers to master barrels. All barrels, receivers, stocks and forends are interchangeable. This means that with one receiver and enough barrels and stocks, you can set up any type of field, skeet, sporting or trap gun you wish. I was told that the action will even handle double-rifle barrels, though it is not yet marketed as being able to. The gun is equally modular inside and requires no fitting when changing parts. Just order whatever has broken and stuff it in.

The Blaser F3 Competition comes in a decent takedown Negrini ABS case with five Briley Spectrum chokes, a nice choke wrench, a stock wrench, a manual and a 10-year guarantee to the original owner covering the metal but not the wood. Currently, the gun is made in 12 gauge only in a choice of field or target models.

At Flint Oaks we shot sporting under John Bidwell's patient tutelage. At first I preferred the 30" tubes, but as I got to know the gun better, I felt more comfortable with the 32s. That's the length I ordered in our test gun and the length Blaser feels will be most popular for sporting. The 32" tubes gave the gun just a touch more "gravitas" on the longer birds but were light enough to move quickly on the short stuff.

The first thing one notices about any gun is presence or absence of recoil. In Kansas we shot light 1-oz loads, and the gun felt comfortable. In my later tests I used 3-dram $1^1/8$-oz shells, and things changed. I got more face slap than a frat boy at the drive-in. Normally, I wouldn't mention face slap, because I think it's mostly a function of stock fit and can be eliminated with a proper fitting. Blaser does offer numerous stock options. Still, more than half the experienced shooters I loaned the gun to also complained of face slap. This is more than usual. It's got me stumped. The standard stock looks normal and sets up well. I can't think of any dimension I'd really change. It is relatively flat nose to heel and has a nicely rounded comb and not too much pitch. There was little muzzle rise, thanks to the low placement of the barrels in the receiver and the interior bore work. Still, if I were to get the gun, I'd need the adjustable or custom stock. To be fair, some who shot the gun had no problem and felt the gun was soft-shooting. Go figure. It's all in the fit, and no one set of dimensions is right for everyone.

With light loads, the gun was comfortable and the magnificence of the trigger became apparent.

The F3's trigger-plate action is easily removed and uses massive linear strikers, which are said to improve lock time. (Seth Goltzer)

A good trigger is like caviar: You can live happily without it, but once sampled, you're hooked. Everyone commented on how good the trigger was and how easy it made the timing of the shot. A minor minus was that the laser checkering, even with gloves, felt a little slippery. Naturally, the Schnabel lip interfered with those who hold their forehand index finger well forward.

You can pretty much tell the balance and swing rate of a gun when you first pick it up. The F3 felt wonderful. Balance was just ahead of the hinge pin, and the long barrels gave the gun a controlled swing. It never got whippy—sure death in a sporter. When you needed more speed, you just pushed a little harder. Yet, thanks to its appropriate target-gun weight of 8 pounds 2 ounces, it was stately enough to provide the precision required on long targets. The gun really felt right. So many less-expensive 32" guns feel like railroad ties because the money wasn't spent to make the long barrels thin. Blaser gets an "A" for handling.

Naturally, I can't tell how durable a completely new gun will be. The components of the F3 look strong. It was designed with Teutonic thoroughness and innovation. Blaser has a marvelous reputation for good rifles. Everything worked flawlessly for the time I had the gun. It all augers well, but only time will tell.

What we don't need time to tell is that the F3's SRP of $4,895 puts the gun into its own category. Assuming that it will sell for close to list, it's twice the street price of the Citori 525, more than $1,500 above the Beretta 682 Gold, a little less than Beretta's DT-10 and several thousand less than a Perazzi or Krieghoff. Blaser also offers a number of engraved models ranging from the $6,395 Luxus to the $25,895 Royal. Extra barrels are $2,495.

The Blaser F3 Competition O/U is innovative, well made, attractive and fairly priced. It has a fantastic trigger and, best of all, the right feel and balance. For those who find the gun comfortable to shoot, it would be an excellent choice.

UPDATE

This review was written in 2006. In the five years since then the Blaser shotgun line has matured. Due to demand for the guns, Blaser opened its own US distributor, Blaser USA. It is headed up by Norbert Haussmann, who is, like Blaser CEO Knobel, a past Krieghoff employee.

The price of our review F3 Sporting Standard has risen from $4,985 to $6,895, an increase of 40 percent, yet sales have increased as the F3 has gained in reputation. The line has been broadened to include seven levels of engraving and wood. The F3 Sporting Imperial tops out at $29,995.

While the flat-rib F3 Sporting Standard remains popular, the latest sporter from Blaser is the F3 Super Sport: $7,881 with Standard engraving. This model features an adjustable raised rib and adjustable-comb stock. In combination with the original stock balancer and the new Barrel Balancer weight system (a series of removable 1.5-oz weights attached between the barrels under the forend), I found the new model far more comfortable to shoot. By raising the rib, the point of recoil at the shoulder was lowered, and the adjustable stock assured less face slap. So much of perceived recoil is gunfit.

Browning Citori Superlight Feather

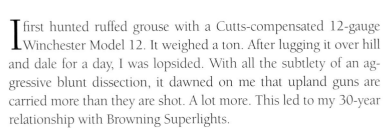

I first hunted ruffed grouse with a Cutts-compensated 12-gauge Winchester Model 12. It weighed a ton. After lugging it over hill and dale for a day, I was lopsided. With all the subtlety of an aggressive blunt dissection, it dawned on me that upland guns are carried more than they are shot. A lot more. This led to my 30-year relationship with Browning Superlights.

The year 1967 was a bad one for Browning. The salt-wood-curing process that Morton had sold the Belgians in 1965 now afflicted 90 percent of their wood stocks. Almost unnoticed amidst this maelstrom of misery, the Browning Superlight was born. A little rooting around in Ned Schwing's marvelous book *The Browning Superposed—John M. Browning's Last Legacy* (Krause Publications, 1996) shows that Browning tested the American market with 237 Superlights, a tiny percentage of the almost 17,000 12-gauge Superposeds the company sold that year.

One of those 1967 American-market Superlights later came my way. My gun was pretty typical of the first guns, with its English stock, dainty field forend, rounded receiver, solid rib and blond wood. I shot at a lot of grouse with it. At less than 6 pounds 10 ounces, the gun

was lively and a pleasure to carry. At the time, the Belgian Superposed 12-gauge came in three weights: Standard, Lightning and Superlight. The Superlight saved a half-pound compared to the Lightning by using less wood, a thin rib and, for the most part, 26½" barrels. After shooting the gun for a few years, something drove me to test it for barrel convergence. The top barrel was shooting way high. We parted company.

Between 1967 and 1977 in the US, Browning sold about 4,600 12-gauge Superlights and about 1,000 in 20 gauge. Most were Grade I 26½"-barreled guns. Then Browning was purchased by Fabrique Nationale, which always had manufactured the gun anyway, and changes began to occur. From 1977 to 1984, the Superposed, including the Superlight, was available mainly as a semi-custom Presentation Series gun with extra-cost features and new engraving patterns. Prices skyrocketed. Sales sank. In 1983 and '84 there were some small custom orders by a couple of major American dealers for some Grade I Superposeds with nice wood.

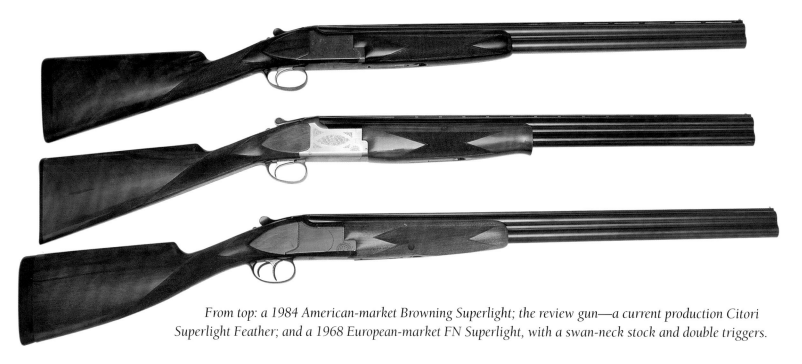

From top: a 1984 American-market Browning Superlight; the review gun—a current production Citori Superlight Feather; and a 1968 European-market FN Superlight, with a swan-neck stock and double triggers.

I bought one of those '84 guns: a 26½" 12-gauge Superlight with conventional Grade I Superposed hand engraving that actually was signed by the engraver. (Browning engravers had refused to sign the acid-etched engraving on certain Presentation models.) My Superlight has stunning wood and a light (and fragile) vent rib. When I bought it, it had an unfortunate Schnabel forend in place of the attractive minimalist forend of the originals. I had the Schnabel lip exorcised. The gun weighs 6 pounds 12 ounces, as the stock and forend both seem a tad thicker than those on the '67 gun. I happily tote it around to this day.

FN also made Superlights for the European market. Rooting around on www.GunsAmerica.com a few years ago, I found and quickly bought a 12-gauge FN Superlight with longer, 27½" barrels, a solid rib, double triggers and a swan-neck stock. The diminutive forend, receiver rounding and engraving are identical to that on my '67 Superlight. This gun weighs 7 pounds and is about as good a Western Plains pheasant gun as you can get.

None of the Belgian Superlight 12s I've handled have been truly lightweight. Still, at 7 pounds or less, they are handy guns suitable for carrying long distances and reliably delivering 1¼-oz loads of lead or soft nontoxic shot. Like all Belgian Brownings, the chambers will rust while you watch, the thin vent ribs will shoot loose after many thousands of rounds, and the ejector extensions sometimes will crack. None of these problems will stop you from hunting, and they are not too difficult to repair. Other than that, the Belgian Superlight is beautifully balanced and about as bulletproof as a gun can be.

Careful perusal of used-gun lists occasionally will turn up a Belgian Superlight. Expect to pay a premium for it compared to the $2,000 a good used Standard or Lightning Superposed brings. If you want a new Belgian Superlight, Browning's custom shop will be more than happy to oblige—with most starting around $20,000. (No, that's not a misprint.)

But to today's newer shooters, "Browning shotgun" does not mean Made in Belgium. It means Made in Japan. In the 1970s rising costs compelled Browning to look elsewhere for reasonably priced shotgun production. For a number of years Miroku had been making an over/under very similar to the Superposed. In the US it was sold under the Charles Daly aegis. After long negotiations, Browning assumed the sole US distribution of the Miroku gun. The company named it the Citori, and it first came to market in 1973. It is now the best-selling O/U in the US.

The basics of the Citori have changed little since the gun's introduction. Although clearly a close copy of the Superposed, it has a number of improvements and also some changes that are less clearly improvements. The main difference is price. The 12-gauge Citori Superlight Feather that we tested from Browning has a suggested retail price of $2,390. That's about $1,000 less than a good used Belgian Superlight 12 (if you can

find one) and a whole bunch less than the custom shop's version. The Citori Superlight Feather is a popular model and has been in the Browning lineup for a dozen years. Since the 12 was reviewed, it also has been joined by a 20-gauge Superlight Feather at the same price.

The main difference between the Japanese and Belgian actions is not the design so much as the more modern methods of manufacture. The interiors of the actions are mechanically very similar. The Belgian receiver uses a separate riser to connect the top and bottom tangs, whereas the Japanese action is one piece. The machining of the receiver interior on our Citori was devoid of the many tool marks present in the Superposed. Other than that, the design of John and Val Browning's action is so well known that a description isn't necessary. It was reliable then; it is reliable now. And, yes, the action is a tiny bit taller than a Beretta's, but the widths are the same.

The silver-nitrided receiver of the Japanese Citori Feather (top) and the blued receiver of an '84 American-market Superlight.

Though mechanically identical to the steel Citori actions, the "Feather" part of the Citori Superlight Feather means that the receiver is made of aluminum. The Japanese Feather's receiver weighs 17.2 oz, whereas the Belgian Superlight's steel receiver weighs 30.4 oz. The Feather's internal parts are made of steel, as is the hinge pin. Also, there is a steel plate inserted in the face of the standing breech to provide a secure firing-pin guide as well as a stop for the metal shotshell rims.

Part of the floorplate that buttresses the rear monoblock lugs is also steel. The aluminum Feather receiver is also used in several Citori target models, indicating Browning's confidence in its durability and longevity.

The Citori's gold-plated trigger is inertial. It is not adjustable for length of pull, as are the triggers on target models. The pull on the lower barrel's sear on our test gun was 5.5 pounds; the upper barrel's was 5.8 pounds. This is perfectly fine on a field gun where overly light triggers can cause serious trouble during a stumble. Unfortunately, the triggers also had a fair amount of scratchy creep. The machine-cut triggers on recent Beretta O/Us are nicer. The Citori's safety is manual, and the barrel selector is built into the safety.

Our Feather's receiver and all other metal parts except the barrels were silver-nitrided to a low-gloss, almost brushed, argent glow. The receiver engraving is light, machine-applied scroll. There's a gold-washed feather on the bottom of the action as well as a gold Browning "Buck Mark" logo on the trigger guard. The guard itself has an attractive long tang that fits perfectly with the English stock. In general, the cosmetics are restrained and traditional, avoiding the disco dementia decor that has cropped up elsewhere.

Currently, the Superlight Feather is the only English-stocked gun in the Citori line. The steel-receiver Citori Superlight was discontinued a dozen years ago. An English stock, even on an over/under, has a certain look that many find appealing. The practical advantages of the English stock on a field gun are that it saves a little weight and permits an easier port arms carry. On the downside, the lack of a pistol grip slightly limits right-hand control. Unlike the original 1967 Belgian Superlight but like the 1984 Belgian edition, the Citori Superlight Feather has been subjected to a Schnabel forend. Unlike the original's, the Citori's forend is blessedly detachable.

Our test gun's stock measured 14¼" x 1⅝" x 2½" with zero cast and about 2½" of pitch. This is fairly standard stuff and is the same

as the original. The butt is finished with a ¼" plastic buttplate cut on a curve. You'll have to cut wood if you want to add a pad. The wrist of the stock has a deep oval cross-section that allows good right-hand control.

The Feather's stock finish was a glossy techno-polymer that will show every ding and fence-wire blemish. The medium-colored walnut had nice figure on the stock's left side but was plainer on the right. The forend wood was featureless. Checkering was cut in a conventional pattern. It appeared machine-cut at a relatively coarse 15 lpi, but it was neatly executed.

Although the action gets the attention, especially on this gun, it's the barrels that define any gun. This Citori has the current Invector Plus screw chokes. The installation causes noticeable muzzle bulging, making the front end look like a 10-gauge. The barrels are overbore at .742". Nominal 12 gauge is .729", and most of the Belgian Superposeds I've measured had bores around .725". The Japanese Superlight Feather's 26" barrels, the only length available, weigh a full 6 oz more than the half-inch-longer fixed-choke barrels of the Belgian Superlight. Part of this is attributable to the 1.1-oz average weight of each Invector Plus choke. The rest is due to the larger diameter and thicker walls of the mass-produced Citori barrels, which always have been a little chunky.

Improved Cylinder, Modified and Full flush chokes are included, but any constriction you can think of is available in the aftermarket. Browning Invector Plus chokes tend to be more open than the nominal .010" for IC and .020" for M, but make sure to pattern them before drawing any conclusions. The chokes and barrels are "steel proof," so you can use any nontoxic shot you can afford. Choke designations are written on the barrel of the choke and also are indicated by rim cuts visible when the choke is in place. I wish every maker would do that. On the downside, this Browning originally came with absolutely the worst choke wrench I've ever used. It was a wretched, flat, stamped Star Chamber implement guaranteed to cause scraped knuckles, torn nails and general disgruntlement. To Browning's credit, the current choke wrenches are much nicer.

Interior barrel dimensions are interesting. In contrast to the .742" overbore, until very recently Browning chose to cut standard-length short forcing cones in its Citoris. For years Beretta went the opposite way, with tight bores and relatively long cones. The Belgian Superposed came with short cones and tight bores. Krieghoff's are overbore with long cones. All four are capable of excellent patterns with the right shells, so that ought to give you some idea of where the science of barrel design is today. Also, unlike guns from Beretta and many other Italian and German makers, the Citori Superlight Feather 12-gauge comes with only 2³/4" chambers. The Blaser folks told me that they found no pattern degradation when using 2³/4" shells in 3" chambers, but Browning's designers must feel differently. Besides, you really don't want to shoot a 3" Roman candle in a light gun. With a nod to the "rust while you watch" chambers on the Superposed, the Citori's chambers are nicely chromed.

Cosmetically, the barrels are topped with an untapered ¹/4"-wide flat rib that is appropriate for the gun. There is a tasteful single brass bead up front. The barrels are finished in a high-gloss, ripple-free, blue-black hot bluing. Before 1995 Miroku used chopper-lump barrels. Now the barrels are joined with a monoblock. The upper-barrel-joint seam on our Feather was invisible. The factory must be doing it right, because our test gun had no convergence problems.

The aluminum receiver from the test gun. (Note the steel-strip reinforcement on the standing breech.)

On paper I had my doubts about the Superlight Feather. Compared to a Belgian Superlight, the Japanese gun weighed 6 pounds 6 ounces and was a full 6 oz lighter, thanks to the aluminum receiver. That's welcome in a field gun. But if the entire gun was 6 oz lighter yet the barrels were 6 oz heavier, wouldn't it steer like an oil tanker? The balance point of the Belgian gun was under the hinge pin, whereas the Japanese gun balanced an inch farther forward.

Well, balance point isn't everything. With the 26" barrels, the moment of inertia wasn't all that high, and the Superlight Feather handled well in its own way. It is lighter than most 12s and benefits from having a little weight forward. A light gun with neutral balance can be too fast. I found the Feather to be quick enough for short shots, though not lightning fast, and stable enough for slightly longer shots where the forward bias seemed to compensate for the shorter barrels. Although it lacked the traditional neutral game-gun balance, it proved surprisingly effective. Of course, if it had the light fixed-choke barrels that Miroku sells in the UK, it would be a marvel. Obviously, a light gun has a little more recoil than a heavy one, but you'll never notice it in a hunting situation. In all, the Superlight Feather is a workable compromise between handling and weight, especially compared to the massive 8-pound *avoirdupois* of the 26" steel 12-gauge Citori Lightning field guns.

The coarse checkering did a good job of providing a secure grip on the normally slippery English stock. The Schnabel forend is a finger biter for those who extend their forehands. The fragile Schnabel lip is also vulnerable to damage in the field. The safety button is perfectly formed, with a nice bump for the thumb and a crisp let-off. It combines with Browning's traditional U-shaped barrel selector. I'm sure that there are those who can select a barrel when a bird is in the air, but I never could. I simply select the top barrel by firing the lower one first. As is often the case, the trigger creep wasn't as noticeable when actually shooting the gun as it was when measuring things. The plastic buttplate, although almost guaranteeing that the gun eventually will swan dive off of a gun rack, made mounting the gun smooth and easy.

The test gun came in a cardboard box with the usual minimalist manual, three Invector Plus flush chokes, the aforesaid wretched wrench and unique safety chamber locks. Joining what is becoming a trend in the gun industry, Browning offers no written warranty. According to the company, the gun should be sent to factory service to determine if a problem will be covered at no charge. In my experience, Browning always has been more than fair.

The 12-gauge Citori Superlight Feather is a perfectly nice upland gun with its own personality. It's generally attractive, as light as most 20s, positively reliable and priced fairly. As a lightweight 12-gauge over/under with an English stock, it has little competition today. In exchange for the light weight, you get more forward bias than is customary, but many hunters will prefer this. It comes down, as it always does, to personal inclination.

Browning Superposed

(Richard Procopio)

Everyone loves a bargain. You're about to read about what may be the best bargain available in a used gun today. It's John Browning's classic Superposed, the gun that did the most to popularize the over/under with American shotgunners.

I won't take up your time by relating the history of the Superposed. Ned Schwing tells you everything you need to know in his definitive *The Browning Superposed* (Krause Publications, 1996). Instead I want to talk about what the guns are like to shoot, how they hold up over time and where they stand in value in today's used-gun market compared to the current crop of new guns.

I'd like to be able to say I started this gun review some 35 years ago, when I bought my first Superposed, but that would be a fib. Through the years, though, I've owned a couple of dozen of them, and currently I have five. All were and are shooters. I'm not a collector, and I never really went out of my way to get the fancy models, though I did have a couple. I kept buying the guns because I simply shot them better than anything else available.

The guns we shoot best are those that are the most transparent to us. Pointing a shotgun should be as effortless as pointing a finger. Like carrying an overfull cup of tea, the more you concentrate on the act of shooting, the more difficult it becomes. Gun fit, balance and weight all must be in harmony. I would be the last to claim that all Superposeds are magic wands, but the guns are invariably well balanced for their weight. Browning stock designs, particularly in the grip area, seem to suit a wider variety of owners than many contemporary Italian efforts.

Through the years the Browning Superposed has come in nearly every possible variant. I've seen Standard model 12-gauge field guns of around $7^3/4$ pounds, Lightning 12-gauge field guns close to $7^1/4$ pounds and 12-gauge Superlights around $6^3/4$ pounds. I had a field 20-gauge Fabrique Nationale Superposed (made for the European market) that came in at $6^1/4$ pounds. Obviously, these guns handle differently, but they all have handled well for their type. Browning made a real effort to alter weight throughout the gun, not just in one place. Compared to the Standard-weight, the Superlight has thinner barrels, a hollowed stock and a slightly shaved receiver. It plain costs more to make thin barrels, because machining tolerances must be kept tighter. It would have been easier to reduce weight with an alloy receiver, but the balance would have shifted forward and the moment of inertia would have increased dramatically.

You won't find screw chokes in an unaltered Superposed. Although newer shooters who have known nothing else may question this, if you have been shooting for a while, you likely know that fixed chokes generally mean more responsive barrels and better patterns. Most factory-installed screw chokes are heavy, because they are made thick to be steel-shot proof. Unfortunately, this often adds noticeable weight right at the tip of the gun. If you have a screw-choke gun and want to know what it would have felt like if it had been built with fixed chokes, remove the screw chokes and then test for balance and swing. Draw your own conclusions. To me, the feel and balance of a gun is its most important attribute. I'll sacrifice everything else for the sake of handling.

The Citoris made for Browning by Miroku have screw chokes on the US models, but they aren't simply Superposed clones made in Japan. It's a different gun based on Miroku's interpretation of the original Browning design. Citoris are excellent assembly-line guns, but due to heavy screw chokes and different barrel contours, they don't feel like Superposeds. If you insist on a screw-choked Superposed, there's nothing to stop you from retrofitting the excellent Briley Thinwalls or Teagues. They don't change the balance. The Superposed isn't meant to shoot steel, but barrel-friendly Bismuth and Kent Impact Tungsten Matrix are better anyway. Unfortunately, the Superposed can't handle the awesome but ultra-hard HEVI-Shot—that's a loss.

The oft-copied Superposed action should be familiar to experienced shooters. It's all machined steel, with the full-width replaceable hinge pin and replaceable wedge-shaped locking tongue engaging the bottom rear of the monoblock. It also has two large and two smaller locking lugs that drop into cuts in the bottom of the action. Detractors have complained that the full-width hinge pin causes the action to be unnecessarily deep in comparison to Italian guns with hinge stubs on the sides. That's pure twaddle. Lay a 682 Beretta receiver on a Superposed's and you'll find less than $^2/_{10}"$ difference in height and none in width.

The same critics point out that the Superposed forend is attached to the barrels and can't be removed easily for cleaning. They are 100-percent right. It is a royal pain. John Browning is said to have designed it that way because he once misplaced a forend and never wanted that to happen again.

The Superposed always has had a decent trigger. Most have a dependable inertia design, but some of the guns made in the past 25 years have the excellent Mark V mechanical trigger. Although not as crisp as Krieghoff's, both Browning designs are very good and extremely reliable if kept clean. They hold their settings for a long time before recutting sears is necessary.

One of the questions I'm most often asked is how long a particular gun will last. It's usually accompanied by the statement that "this next gun will be the last one I ever buy." Sure it will. And I'm only going to eat one peanut. The fact is that very few hunters will use any gun enough to shoot it out. Field guns get worn out from the outside, not the inside. Target guns are the reverse.

If longevity is a concern, the Superposed is as tough as anything ever made, maybe tougher. In another life I tried to make the US Olympic International Skeet team. It took me more than a dozen years and a quarter-million rounds before I realized that I wasn't quite good enough. Talk about slow learners. For five of those years I shot a Browning Standard Superposed that I had bought second-hand. I put 106,000 carefully logged rounds through it without major maintenance. It was finally starting to get a little loose when I sold it, but it was nothing that a quick trip to the gunsmith couldn't have fixed. One of my Fabrique Nationale Special Trap No. 6 Superposeds—a model made for the European market—came to me well used and lasted only another 50,000 rounds before needing a refurbished locking tongue. I have no argument if you say that other guns last just as long. Maybe, but my vote goes to the Superposed. Parts are still readily available from Browning and Brownells. Rebuilds are reasonably priced. In addition to Browning factory service, Midwest Gunworks, in Festus, Missouri, and Art's Gun Shop, in Hillsboro, Missouri, do excellent work on Superposeds.

The Superposed is good but not perfect. The chambers, unless chromed as some of the European Fabrique Nationale Superposeds were, will rust while you watch unless kept clean and oiled. If you shoot a ton of shells at one time and really let your barrels heat up, the thin top ribs on the Superlight and Lightning models can loosen, as they will on any soft-soldered gun. That said, I've not had that trouble often—and never with one of the 10mm FN target ribs or the even wider Broadway ribs.

John Browning's classic over/under.
(Richard Procopio)

The "new style" ejectors on Superposeds made since the late '60s sometimes crack the lower barrels' ejector extensions. The older ejector extensions with the little square blocks never did this. I usually just cut a couple of coils off of the ejector hammer springs to lower the impact of the ejector hammers. This keeps cracks from recurring and ejection remains fine. If for some reason you want an extractor gun, just pull out the ejector cocking rods. You can always reinstall them if you change your mind. As an added plus, if you fully depress the ejector extension stop pins, you'll be able to instantly remove the ejectors for complete cleaning when the barrels are off, but they'll stay in place when the gun is assembled.

The Superposed is easy to work on once you figure out how to remove the stock. As a ham-fisted tinkerer who occasionally enlists the aid of a shop assistant named Forza Bruta, I learned early on to grind a special screwdriver to fit the screws in the "long tang." Then, using a monster screwdriver for the stock bolt, stock removal was a piece of cake. Make sure to pull the stock off once a year to lightly oil things after cleaning out the inside. Occasionally I've neglected this and had dirt build up just under the trigger lever. It was enough to cause a few misfires until I cleaned it properly. Sloth hath its price.

The only real problems I've run into with Superposeds have been salt wood and barrel convergence. Two of my Supers mis-converged, shooting the top barrel very much higher than the bottom. One was a 12-gauge solid-rib Superlight that I'd successfully hunted with for years. I adored that gun and thought I was sudden death with it. One day the devil, in the form of a well-meaning friend, asked if I'd ever tested the gun for barrel convergence. I told him there was no need to because I'd been shooting it very nicely, thank you. You know the rest. I couldn't let well enough alone; I tested the gun, found the top barrel shooting 24" higher than the lower barrel at 40 yards. I sold it but have never shot another Superlight as well, which must prove something. However, any O/U can be afflicted with convergence issues, not just the Superposed. If you are buying a used gun, use your trial period to test convergence. Barrels shooting apart by four or five inches at 40 yards might be acceptable, but a lot more isn't. With fixed chokes, moderate divergence can be rectified by a little eccentric choke grinding. If there is enough metal at the muzzle, Briley actually can install screw chokes at an angle. I should have kept that cross-eyed Browning, but I swapped it for a salt-wood Superposed .410.

The "salt wood" issue, well covered in Schwing's book, affected only some Superposed guns made from about 1966 to '72. If the used Super you're examining is from that time period, Schwing advises scraping a bit of wood under the buttplate/pad and applying the 1-percent solution of silver nitrate that you keep handy for emergencies. (It's available where photography chemicals are sold.) If the solution remains light purple, you're good to go. If it turns white, there's salt in the wood. The only fix is to refinish any salt-eaten metal and replace the wood.

Some have said that the Superposed is the hardest-kicking O/U. Well, it isn't. The original Winchester 101 is. So much of recoil is related to gunfit that I hesitate to state that one brand of gun kicks more than another. Except the 101. If a gun hits you in the cheek, it's gunfit or shooting technique. If the punishment comes through your shoulder and up the back of your neck, then blame recoil.

Though I've referred to the Browning Superposed as a used gun, it is still very much in production. The Fabrique Nationale plant, in Herstal, Belgium, still produces Superposeds at a rate of about 150 per year. About two-thirds of these go to the British and Continental markets. In the US new ones are available through the Browning Custom Shop at prices ranging from $20,000 to $70,000. Browning keeps a small inventory on hand for instant gratification. At one time Griffin & Howe also sold its own version of the Superposed called the Madison.

And therein lies a problem. The factory has produced almost 400,000 Superposeds. A majority of these have found their way to the American market. Now consider the fact that the Superposed is almost impossible to wear out, and you can appreciate the situation. A quick glance at gun ads in magazines or online will show plenty of good used Grade I 12-gauge Superposeds for sale at $1,500 to $2,000, with 20-gauge guns running $1,000 or so more. And now consider the price of a new Superposed from the Custom Shop. Can you spell "arbitrage"? It's such a good deal that an active reverse gray market has arisen. Used US Grade I Brownings are going to Europe and the UK for upgrading and resale. The guns are highly prized there, and the market for upgraded Superposeds is lively.

Considering what a new gun costs and that the old ones are just as good, a used Browning Superposed is an incredible bargain. Just one thing, though: The secret password is "Belgian" Browning, not the "Belgium" Browning you see in some gun ads. It isn't a "Spain Arrieta" or "Italy Fabbri." A classic gun deserves classic English.

Caesar Guerini Apex Field

Caesar Guerini certainly has come a long way in a short time. It was about 11 years ago when brothers Giorgio and Antonio Guerini left Rizzini SRL, where they worked for their uncle, Battista Rizzini, and struck out on their own. They leased a building, set up with a dozen employees and began making guns. I remember seeing their little plant, located just under Ivano Tanfoglio's Ferlib shop, when I visited the Val Trompia area of Italy. Like many small gun companies, the Guerinis outsourced most of their parts while they stuck to the design, assembly and finishing of the guns.

Soon after starting and aiming at the US market, they partnered with Wes Lang to form Caesar Guerini USA. They had gotten to know Lang when they were selling Rizzinis to Sigarms for import as their Aurora line. Lang's background included work at Seminole Gunworks, Beretta USA's and Sigarms' marketing departments, and Emap Petersen magazine publishing. In addition to his marketing skills, Lang is a Master-class sporting clays competitor and an avid hunter. He had an immediate positive influence on configuring the guns.

Recently the Guerinis moved their Italian operation to a considerably larger modern factory, and now they make a high percentage of their parts in-house on the latest machinery. They have gone upscale and currently offer 13 models of over/under field guns ranging from the Woodlander, at $2,995, to the Forum, at $9,375. They also offer six sporting clays and four trap models. In 2009 the American side of Guerini, in Maryland, opened a custom shop with services that include custom wood, extra barrels, refinishing and special engraving.

Elsewhere I review the Caesar Guerini Magnus Light alloy 12-gauge and also the 28-gauge Woodlander. Here, for those who want a more elaborate gun with a bit of a British feel, I'll cover the Apex. The field model costs $7,295 in 12, 20 and 28 gauge; $9,205 as a two-barrel 20/28 combo; and $11,275 as a 20, 28 and .410 three-barrel set. The Apex also comes as a $7,850 sporter and in four trap single-barrel models starting at $9,395. Our test gun was the 20-gauge field version.

The basic Caesar Guerini action is a blend of the Belgian Browning Superposed's full-width underbolt and the Woodward's hinge stubs. The action might have been made a touch lower by using a

Beretta/Perazzi mid-breech lockup, but all the Rizzini-related gunmakers (Caesar Guerini, B. Rizzini, Fausti and FAIR) seem to do it the same way. For extra strength, the receiver bottom is recessed at the rear to receive two monoblock lugs. The action bottom is clean, because the recesses do not protrude through the receiver the way they do on the Superposed. The bottom of the receiver is cut out to accept the triggerplate, which fit perfectly. In fact, all the metal seams were almost invisible, with one exception. There was a slight gap between the tops of both receiver sides and the barrels' monoblock shoulder ridges. The breech fences are nicely sculpted and contribute to the gun's upper-class look.

The forged-steel action has coil-spring-driven hammers hinged on the bottom and sears suspended from the top strap. Firing pins and the opening lever are standard configurations. With only one unimportant exception that I could see, the action pins were satisfyingly solid, not roll pins. Internal parts appear substantial, with the possible exception of the thin, stamped spring-steel butterfly brackets that activate the wire ejector trip rods. However, this is by design, as the rods only trip and don't cock the ejectors. The interior of this Apex action bore no machine marks.

The manual safety is the Beretta-style, with the little side-to-side barrel selector built in. The inertia trigger was quite good, with little creep, slop or overtravel. Pulls were the right weight but a touch inconsistent on our gun. The bottom barrel varied from $4^1/8$

Ornate scroll engraving with gold accenting covers the coin-finished receiver and sideplates.

pounds to $4^5/8$ pounds, whereas the top went from $3^7/8$ pounds to $4^1/2$ pounds. Lang told me that since this gun was made, the trigger has been slightly redesigned for improved performance.

Overall, the action is nicely made but a touch heavy for a 20, at 1 pound 15 ounces. The sideplates and long trigger tang account for about 4 oz of that. It's the price of beauty.

The hand-polished and specially coated coin-finished receiver and sideplates have 100-percent-coverage engraving in an ornate scroll with a little gold accenting. The work is done by Bottega Incisioni C. Giovanelli. Lang told me that Giovanelli was secretive about the exact process used, but it involves EDM, laser, hand engraving and a separate gold application. The background is darkened for a deeper look. The receiver's total lack of screw heads makes for an unbroken canvas, and the decorative sideplates provide more area for artistry.

The Apex has a clever screwless long tang extending from the trigger guard down the front of the pistol grip. It is held in place by the skeleton grip cap. The tang and cap really look classy. The grip cap and brass front bead were the only metal parts of the gun I could find that were not steel.

The barrels on all of the Guerinis I've seen use a standard monoblock that houses the ejectors, ejector springs and plungers. Guerini recently acquired a new CNC machine capable of machining the monoblocks to tolerances of .0001". Like Perazzi, Guerini has included a simple method of removing the ejectors for cleaning. Just push them in, remove a small retaining button and out they come. The company outsources its tubes and ribs but does the final machining in-house.

Apex field barrels come standard at 28" long, with 26" and 30" optional. Our 28" 20-gauge had 3" chambers. It was not proofed for steel shot, as Guerini usually does that only for 12-gauge field guns, but steel proofing for the 20 is available if you request it. Bores are chrome lined, and the barrels are screw-choked.

The bottom barrel was stamped with a 15.8mm inside diameter and measured .622" just behind the choke. The top was marked 15.9mm and did have a slightly larger ID than the bottom but not enough to make any real difference. Nominal bores for a 20 are .615", so the Apex has a trendy slight overbore. Forcing cones appeared normal. Both barrels had bore-taper constrictions of a few thou for 6" before the screw chokes.

The Apex came with five screw chokes. The chokes are just over 2" long, with about .015" relief at the skirt tapering forward to a $^{1}/_{2}$" parallel at the front. Constrictions of the chokes were: Cylinder, .001"; Improved Cylinder, .007"; Modified, .015"; Improved Modified, .020"; and Full, .027". That's about right for the 20 and really all you need. I would have preferred to see a little less relief at the skirt for a smoother shot transition. The 12-gauge Guerinis are much better in this area. The chokes are flush mounted, which is appropriate on a field gun, and rim-notched to designate the constrictions. The chokes were a pain to change, with 36 full turns required to extract and replace using the inconvenient wrench supplied. Get one of Briley's fishing-reel-handle wrenches.

Outside, the barrels showed a high-gloss blue and were free of ripples. Rib-solder seams were correct and without blemishes. Side ribs were solid all the way back to the monoblock. The top rib was a very attractive 8mm-down-to-6mm tapered solid rib with a cross-hatched non-glare top surface. A solid rib is perfect for a hunting gun, because it's durable and doesn't collect brush. There was an appropriate simple brass bead at the muzzle.

The front 6" of the barrels are slightly jugged out about .10" to accommodate the choke threads, but it was hard to notice unless you really looked.

For seven large you ought to get pretty walnut. If our sample is any indication, you certainly do. Both the stock and forend were heavily figured with blessedly equal grain on both sides. The finish is listed as high-gloss oil—probably Tru-Oil or similar—and it has a much more subtle and smoother look than high-gloss synthetic. Wood pores were 98-percent filled. Just one more coat would have done it. It was nice to see that the inside of the forend and stock head also received some protective coats of oil. Checkering is borderless. Without going blind trying to measure it, I'll trust the catalog statement that it's 26 lpi. If it were any finer, it wouldn't fulfill its purpose of providing a good grip. My guess is that the checkering is machine-cut, because it's almost too perfect.

The forend has a delicious shape. Long and slender, yet nicely

The Apex comes with fancy engraved sideplates, a subtly curved pistol grip, an ergonomic forend, killer wood and more.

rounded, it is just perfect in placing the hand as close to the barrel as practical. Guerini's over/unders, like Rizzini's and many of Boss's and Woodward's, have Anson push-button forend releases. I've never been a fan of these, because I feel they make the forends deeper than necessary, but I have to admit that this forend is nice. The Anson button has the advantage of being self-adjusting for wear, too. I'm not going to say anything about the lack of a passé Schnabel forend. I'll just do a little dance of joy.

After a gun's balance, the stock is the most important contributor to ease of shooting. Our test Apex measured 14³⁄₄" x 1³⁄₈" x 2¹⁄₈" with normal right-hand cast. That's a touch longer and higher than the generic 14¹⁄₄" x 1¹⁄₂" x 2¹⁄₂". Experienced shooters often use longer and higher stocks, because they have more-practiced mounts and a bit more cheek pressure. You exceptions know who you are.

One stock can't fit everyone any more than a 42 Regular suit can, but this Apex has an edge. It has a relaxed English-style Prince of Wales grip that allows more flexible placement of the hand. It offers a far more comfortable bend at the wrist, and it does not force a low elbow and high handhold the way a vertical grip does. The Italians have always seemed to struggle with the PoW grip, but this one is spot-on perfect.

Pitch is given as the standard 4°. I measured 2¹⁄₂" stand-off. I would have liked just a touch more, because the buttplate, although made of a gorgeous piece of walnut, lacks the frictive grip of rubber to hold it in the shoulder pocket for the second shot. The wood butt is also easily dinged and may cause the gun to fall when stood in a rack or corner. On the plus side, it's easier to mount, and it sure is pretty.

The Apex comes in a Negrini ABS takedown case with odd decorative leather-like patches on the outside. Inside are the aforementioned five chokes and wrench in a plastic box, cloth sleeves for the barrels and stock, and the usual generic multi-lingual instruction manual. Nothing too special there. But the gun does come with two extras that matter. The owner is entitled to send his gun back three times for a free annual "pit stop" factory tune-up and cleaning. And now the best part: The original owner receives a lifetime guarantee from Caesar Guerini USA.

Any guarantee, even a lifetime one, is no better than the factory service. From speaking to many Guerini owners over the past eight years, I have heard nothing but praise for the quality and speed of the company's service. It is also interesting to note that both Orvis and L.L. Bean have adopted Caesar Guerini as a house brand, so Wes and his team must be doing something right.

I spent a little more time than usual shooting this gun, for the simple reason that I liked it and shot it well. Everyone I loaned it to felt the same way. One comment was, "If looks have anything to do with it, it will shoot for itself." And it just about does.

Our gun balanced about ¹⁄₂" in front of the hinge, and the weight seemed to be distributed throughout the gun, not just at the ends or in the middle. One of the reasons that the gun feels so good and shoots so well is that, at 6³⁄₄ pounds, it has some gravitas to it. Up to a point, heavier guns are easier to shoot. However, this is a heavy carry for a field 20, where I would hope for about 6¹⁄₄ pounds. I'm sure the Apex *avoirdupois* is due to the sideplates, solid top with long tang and heavily figured wood. You are the best judge as to how much the extra weight matters to the way you hunt. Personally,

I'd rather carry a slightly heavy gun that I shoot well than a light, whippy one that I don't.

To sum up, the Caesar Guerini Apex is fairly expensive, very attractive, a little heavy, and it shoots like a dream. The basic-model Woodlander costs half as much and is mechanically identical, but you won't get the fancy engraved sideplates, clever screwless long tang, skeleton grip cap, subtly curved pistol grip, sexy solid rib, smooth ergonomic forend, fancy wood buttplate or killer walnut. Your call.

The Apex has two other downsides that I have to mention. Some hunters may consider it simply too pretty to risk afield. An even greater problem is that the gun shoots so well that you might limit out early and have to cut your hunt short.

Caesar Guerini Ellipse EVO

I review four Caesar Guerini guns in this book. That's a lot, but I have my reasons. Since its inception 11 years ago, Guerini has earned a prominent place in the shotgun world. The company's lifetime warranty and factory service are first-rate. The guns are well made and have proven durable. Certain of the Guerini guns are absolutely gorgeous. The prices are not egregious. And, most important, every Guerini I've spent time with has been an easy gun to shoot well. Every one.

The subject of this review is the Caesar Guerini Ellipse EVO over/under, the company's first gun with a truly rounded action. This field gun costs $5,605 and at this writing is built on a 20-gauge action with 28" barrels in either 20 or 28 gauge. As a 20/28-gauge two-barrel set, it runs $7,365. If it were just the usual Guerini with the annual cosmetic upgrade, I wouldn't spend much time on it. But it's not. It is an excellent example of how a good basic gun can be transformed into something far greater.

The interior of the Ellipse action is standard Guerini issue. In my review of the Guerini Apex, I described it as sort of Brescia generic.

The replaceable Woodward hinge stubs and Browning underbolt are typical of B. Rizzini, Fabarm, FAIR, E. Rizzini, Fausti and others. Beretta is the notable exception with its mid-breech locking cones. The bottom of the Guerini action is solid, so the two locking lugs on the monoblock engage it but do not penetrate through as they do on a Superposed. There's a large cocking rod up the middle of the floor, and ejector tripwires run inside the lower edges of the action out to the knuckle. Sears are suspended from the top strap, and hammers pivot on the triggerplate. Interior machining is crisp, though machining lines can be seen on the inside of the top and bottom tangs. In all, the action is a good one and well proven.

The receiver is machined from forged steel. By varying the time and temperature of the heating process, only the exterior is hardened to avoid brittleness inside. The rounding of the Ellipse begins at the receiver. Just how do you significantly round the underside of an over/under action? You can't just grind away metal, because the ejector tripwires run through the receiver's lower edges. Guerini first widened part of the action. The other Guerinis have sort of a cheek on the side of the receiver, much like some Berettas. The usual

Guerini receivers are cut away some .035" in front of the cheek up to the knuckle. In designing the Ellipse, this cutaway was restored so that the front of the receiver had the same width as the rear. This wider receiver enabled a greater rounding of the lower edges.

But when the front of the receiver is widened, the forend iron must be widened also. Then Guerini had to widen the monoblock shoulders of the barrels. None of these changes were much over $^1/_{32}$", but they meant new machining for each part. The result was a modestly rounded receiver and a most comfortable one-hand field carry.

The changes didn't stop there. The Ellipse receiver has a beautiful semi-circular cut at the rear. It results in a much more attractive line than the usual vertical junction of the stock head at the back of the receiver. The curve flows smoothly into the tapered top tang. It's really classy, but it took some work.

The rest of the Guerini line—and most other modern Italian boxlock O/Us—usually use a tab on the top of each side of the head of the stock to engage a cutout in the receiver. This tab keeps the stock head from spreading apart as it is snugged down. The Ellipse's sensual curve eliminates this cutout, but the stock still has to be kept from being split apart by the wedge of the upper tang. On the Ellipse the stock head was given two very substantial interior side tabs, which engage cutouts on the inside of the receiver's rear sides. It is all invisible until you remove the stock. It's much more difficult to machine but much smoother and more pleasing to the eye.

The single trigger is inertia operated and has a couple of nice touches. Just aft of the blade are two small screws; one adjusts take-up and one over-travel. Getting to those screws may require an engineering degree, but at least the option is there. These are the only exposed screw heads on the outside of the gun. Trigger pulls on our sample were a consistent $4^1/_4$ pounds lower and $4^3/_4$ upper. Just about perfect.

What I didn't find perfect was the manual safety. It worked cor-

rectly, but the Beretta-style safety/barrel-selector toggle has been eliminated. Our Ellipse's trigger was non-selective. I asked Caesar Guerini USA president Wes Lang about this change. He said that it was done because the non-selective safety was slimmer and more in keeping with the attractive lines of the gun. True enough, it is slick-looking and many upland hunters always shoot the bottom barrel first. But, Lang added, if a buyer prefers the traditional toggle-selector safety, Guerini will install it for free at any time. Personally, I'd get the selector.

As mentioned, barrels for the first run of Ellipses are 20 and 28 gauge, and they are all 28" long. Perhaps

From the rounded, curved receiver to the relaxed-knob grip to the multi-depth engraving, the EVO is one beautifully designed gun.

other choices will be added later. Our 20-gauge test barrels were similar to those of the Guerini Apex in that they were properly hot-blued, ripple-free, chrome-lined, 3"-chambered and screw-choked. There is a bit of barrel bulge at the chokes, but it's not too bad.

Five flush-mounted nickel-plated chokes come with the gun: Cylinder, Improved Cylinder, Modified, Improved Modified and Full. They appear to be of average quality. At 2⅛" long, they have about ½" parallel after the constriction and about .010" jump from bore to the relieved rear of the choke. The chokes use a very fine thread that required 72 turns of the supplied wrench to remove and insert just one.

The side ribs of the barrels are solid and extend back to the monoblock. The top rib is a glorious, upper-class solid rib so appropriate on a field gun. As on the Apex, this 8mm-to-6mm tapered rib gives the gun a more attractive line. It is more resistant to the inevitable field knocks and dings. There is a proper brass bead at the muzzle and no silly mid-bead to clutter things.

The wood on our Ellipse EVO—and the wood on the other EVO samples I've seen in photographs—is really snappy walnut. Obviously samples will vary, but an effort has clearly been made to put the good stuff on these guns. Wood samples I've seen have ranged from blondish to dark. All have been heavily figured.

Standard stock measurements for the Ellipse are the same as they are on the Apex 20-gauge field: 14¾" x 1⁷/₁₆" x 2¼", with a touch of cast-off and 4° of pitch. Our sample was true to the standard. The Ellipse comes with a very relaxed round-knob grip. Few Italian guns get the round-knob genre right, but this one is good. I really

Guerini designers skipped the usual thinning taper of the front of the receiver in favor of rounding the bottom edges.

liked the relaxed, capped Prince of Wales grip on the Apex, but the one on the Ellipse is also very nice. On special order, left-handed and English stocks are available.

The forend appears to be identical to that of the Apex, and that's a good thing. Eschewing the trite Schnabel beak, the Ellipse's forend is slender and smooth with a nicely rounded front. Your hand will be comfortable anywhere along it. Guerini uses an Anson push-rod for the forend release, necessitating a slightly deeper forend than with the usual Deeley latch, but Guerini does the Anson well and the forend retains its grace. An interesting note is that the only non-steel metal I found on the gun, other than the brass front bead, was the aluminum pushrod. Good place for it, as it saved some weight at no expense in strength.

The borderless laser checkering of 26 lpi was mechanically perfect and in a conservative pattern. As befits a field gun, the Ellipse uses a wooden buttplate. It looks classy, but if you find it slippery, it is easy to substitute a rubber pad. The medium-gloss stock finish is listed as hand-rubbed oil, and it was first class. The grain was properly filled, and everything was smooth. Even the inside of the stock head and forend got a coat or two for protection. Wood-to-metal fit was about .020" proud everywhere to provide a bit of leeway for eventual refinishing.

I've saved the engraving for last because it is so outstanding. Like the work on Guerini's other engraved guns, it is done outside the factory by Bottega C. Giovanelli, the largest of Italy's mechanized engraving houses. Giovanelli is not always forthcoming about the engraving processes used, but Lang felt it probably involves laser, hand chasing and perhaps some EDM. It is far, far more advanced than the engraving on the company's Summit that I compared it to. I think it's also nicer than that on the more expensive Apex, but that's just personal taste. It is multi-depth engraving, not all on a single plane like most other laser efforts. The varied depths in the foliate pattern also show up better because of the new receiver finish. Instead of the protective nickel plating used previously, Guerini simply polishes the metal and coats it with a proprietary clear-coat process. It is said to be extremely durable and rustproof, and it certainly shows the engraving to advantage.

Another big thing about this engraving is that it goes around the curves. Often you see machine engraving that stops at a rounded edge and then starts up again after a space because it can't turn the corner. On the EVO you really notice the unbroken engraving as it runs from the side of the action down around the curved receiver edge to the bottom of the action. It's not unique, but it is an important next step. French gunmaker Chapuis uses a five-axis laser engraver that also can turn corners on a rounded action. And the Fausti Dea Round Body has light engraving that runs around the action's curved underside as well. But the Ellipse EVO's engraving is deeper than either and in a different class entirely.

The Ellipse is also sold in the Limited model. Mechanically identical, the Ellipse Limited has a chemically case-colored receiver, modest border engraving, and wood that is just a notch less magnificent than that on the EVO. But you get the same sensuous lines and marvelous handling for $1,500 less.

The EVO's engraving is outstanding, and it runs unbroken from the side of the receiver to the bottom of the rounded action.

The Ellipse EVO comes in a standard ABS takedown case with odd-looking pseudo-suede patches on the outside. Included are a plastic box of five chokes and a wrench. It also comes with Guerini's lifetime guarantee, backed by an enviable service reputation. The guarantee and service have earned a loyal following for the brand.

I shot the Ellipse at skeet, 5 Stand and sporting clays, all low gun. It was mechanically correct, with no flaws or failures of any kind. Chokes stayed put, ejectors ejected, triggers stayed crisp and nothing fell off. Like the Apex before it, it moved well. The relaxed grip allowed shooters of different statures to adjust fit a bit. It was an easy gun to shoot.

One of the reasons it shot so well was that the balance was slightly forward, and at 6 pounds 11.3 ounces, the gun had a bit of heft. Great for shooting, less-good for carrying. Most of the Beretta 680-series 20-gauge guns are around 6 pounds 4 ounces, so the Ellipse is a bit buxom. Of course, if you ever take advantage of the 3" chambers, you'll welcome the extra weight.

At the range, I showed the gun around. Without exception, everyone felt the Ellipse EVO was absolutely gorgeous. The Ellipse's rounded lower edges and curved receiver smoothly transitioning into the tapered top tang give it a design artistry unequalled in its price range. The engraving pattern and its quality really are a step up. The solid rib, tastefully smooth forend and graceful grip seal the deal. And, good looks aside, it's a shooter. It has the feel. That's the highest compliment I can pay any gun.

Caesar Guerini Magnus Light and Woodlander

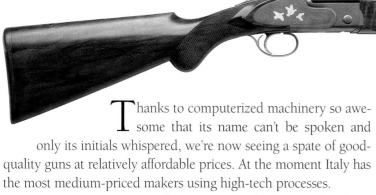

The Magnus Light has an aluminum-alloy receiver.
(Lee Thomas Kjos/Courtesy of Caesar Guerini USA)

Thanks to computerized machinery so awe-some that its name can't be spoken and only its initials whispered, we're now seeing a spate of good-quality guns at relatively affordable prices. At the moment Italy has the most medium-priced makers using high-tech processes.

Caesar Guerini is just such a company. The Guerini brothers, Giorgio and Antonio, worked with Battista Rizzini in Gardone, Italy, making B. Rizzinis. Those very nice over/unders were sold in the US by Sigarms, L.L. Bean, Rizzini USA and now Connecticut Shotgun Manufacturing Company. In 2000 the Guerinis decided to build their own. They moved up the valley to Marcheno, leased a building and set up a dozen employees with modern machinery.

If you sell shotguns, the American market is the big enchilada. Guerini began looking for an American distributor at about the same time Wes Lang was considering his next step in the gun business. Lang had started with Seminole Gunworks in choke development and gun customization, then moved to the marketing department of

Beretta USA. Later he'd gone to SIG's shotgun section and had been responsible for the overall configuration of the company's excellent B. Rizzini TT25 sporter. After SIG he'd headed west to work with Emap publishing, overseeing shooting magazines, but he'd always wanted to market his own guns. With a résumé like that, he was entitled to. Lang formed Caesar Guerini USA as sole importer and has used his experience to tailor Guerinis to the American market.

At the time of this original review, in 2004, the Guerini USA O/U line had seven models built around modern Italian 12- and 20-gauge boxlock frames. Seven years later the line has expanded to 11 field models, six sporting models, four trap models, plus two Ellipse and two raised-rib Impact models. Within the field versions, the prices vary from $9,375 for the Forum to $2,995 for the Wood-lander. The difference is mostly in the cosmetics. The upland guns we received for review were the Magnus Light 12-gauge ($4,075) and the Woodlander 28-gauge.

The Magnus models have engraved sideplates and come in 12,

20 and 28 gauge as well as .410. The Magnus Light is the same, but with a lightweight alloy receiver. The racy Woodlander is the English-stocked version with a steel boxlock receiver, again in all four gauges. Across the model lines, the three sub-gauges are built on 20-gauge actions. All the upland guns come in 26" and 28" lengths.

The Guerini action is typical of what I'm seeing from modern Italian mid-range producers. It's a standard boxlock with replaceable stub hinges, like those from Beretta, and an underlocking tongue, like that from Browning. The jeweled sides of the monoblock are dead flat. Two massive lugs on the bottom of the monoblock engage recesses in the bottom of the receiver but do not protrude through the way Browning's do. This is about the same setup that the B. Rizzini, Kimber and Fabarm actions use. Receiver walls in the 12-gauge Guerinis are a hefty ¼" thick. All the Guerinis I've shot have been initially stiff to open and shut because of close-fitting parts.

The major internal action parts are steel and appear robust. The only possible exceptions are the thin stamped brackets holding the ejector trip rods. Because these rods only trip and don't cock, they are low-stress, so a lightly made part may be appropriate. The inertia trigger has an adjustable blade on the sporters and a fixed blade on the field guns. Pulls on our test guns averaged five pounds and were fairly crisp after a bit of takeup. The safety/barrel-selector combo switch is like Beretta's. Workmanship inside the guns was clean, but there were a few machining marks inside the receivers. This was in contrast to flawless exteriors.

The barrels are laser-aligned during manufacture. They use a normal monoblock that houses the ejectors, ejector springs and plungers. Like Perazzi's, Guerini's ejectors are easily removed for cleaning. Just push the ejectors in, remove a small retaining button and out everything comes. I do wish the field guns included a Perazzi-style stock-removal wrench for easy disassembly after wet days. Early on the 12-gauge bores were "pre-overbore Italian standard," or about .723". More recent production employs the .735" Maxis overbore. All the bores are chrome-plated, so they won't rust if camp cocktails and dinner take precedence over gun cleaning. Originally, all the field guns had flat, untapered 7mm or 6mm top ribs with single brass beads and solid side ribs. Later production has offered some of the upland guns with most-attractive solid top ribs.

Field Guerinis come with five flush screw chokes in Cylinder, Improved Cylinder, Modified, Improved Modified and Full. Lang's experience with Seminole was useful in perfecting the choke ta-

The Woodlander, with its racy English stock, is clean, subdued and attractive.
(Lee Thomas Kjos/Courtesy of Caesar Guerini USA)

pers. My only complaint about the chokes is that they use odd notch spacing on the rims. I often misplace my choke wrench and couldn't snug up these chokes with the brass rim of an empty shell the way I usually do. The chokes never shot loose, so it wasn't really an issue.

If there's one thing that Guerini understands, it's glitz. Because the market for $3,000 guns is crowded, Guerinis are built as good basic guns with enough extra gingerbread to make them stand out. The Magnus and Magnus Light models have nicely engraved pinless sideplates from Bottega Incisioni C. Giovanelli. The engraving is a combination of machine and hand cutting of good quality and design. It's far more attractive than the rolled neo-disco efforts I've seen from another major Italian maker. The gold-washed birds lend a nice touch and will help identify what you're supposed to be shooting. The Woodlander has polyurethane-protected case colors, whereas the Magnus Light has a durable matte-gray nickel/Teflon finish called Tinaloy. The Woodlander has a conventional steel boxlock receiver without sideplates that is unengraved except for a gold flushing grouse on the bottom of the receiver. The look is clean, subdued and very attractive.

One other thing that has stood out on all of the Guerinis I've seen has been the wood. The

Gold-washed birds add a nice touch to the Magnus Light and Magnus.

American market is known for its penchant for fancy wood, and I'm wholeheartedly in that demographic. Every Guerini I've looked at has had nicely figured Turkish walnut. It's oil-finished, and the company recommends an occasional rub with boiled linseed. The finish shows the dark lines and blonde accents to advantage. The field guns have 14½" stocks to figured walnut buttplates. (Guerini realizes that it's easier to shorten a long stock than lengthen a short one.) Wood-to-metal fit on the guns I've seen has been good, though a little proud, and the machine-cut checkering has been aggressive enough to actually provide a grip. The Magnus Light stocks have comfortable, relaxed, round-knob pistol grips like the sainted Browning Superposed, whereas the little Woodlander has the racy English stock it deserves but can be special ordered with a round-knob pistol grip if you wish.

When they first came out, all of the field-grade Guerinis except the now-discontinued Flyway waterfowler had Schnabel forends. This is not my favorite field configuration, because Schnabels can be fragile and that darn Hapsburg lip keeps dinging my forefinger. I said that I'd love to see a minimalist forend like those on the Merkels, Perazzi field guns or early Superposeds. And that's just what Guerini eventually did. The Woodlander and Magnus remain stuck with the Schnabel, but the fancier Forum, Apex and Ellipse field models get a most-attractive proper rounded field forearm.

While we're up front, I should also mention that the Guerinis use the self-adjusting Anson pushbutton forend iron rather than the more common Deeley latch.

Both of our test guns weighed just 6 pounds 1 ounce, but they were very different otherwise. The 12-gauge Magnus Light is a good example of the deluxe upland ultralight concept. In a gun that's meant to be carried more than shot, the Magnus Light's aluminum-alloy receiver saves about a pound. If you hunt hard, you'll really appreciate this at the end of the day. Recoil changes at about the same ratio as weight, so the Magnus Light picks up about 15 percent more recoil than the steel Magnus. In the heart-stopping flush of a grouse, you'll never notice it. For preseason clays practice, the gun will be most comfortable with the lightest available loads.

Durability is a concern with alloy receivers, but the Magnus Light hinge stubs are steel, as is the locking tongue. Both engage the steel monoblock. Guerini did not choose to use a steel or titanium insert on the standing breech like Beretta's, Franchi's and Browning's alloy guns, but it will take many more rounds than I can shoot in this test to see if that's an issue. Guerini USA guarantees all its guns for life, so it's the company's problem, not yours.

Guns with alloy receivers can be nose-heavy, so Guerini made its forend iron out of the same alloy as the receiver, to reduce foreweight. With its 28" screw-choke barrels, the Magnus Light balanced about 1½" in front of the hinge. Although it's weight-forward, the weight was located along the barrel, not at the tip, so the gun moved smoothly and handled well. You may notice the balance at first, but you won't after a day.

The 28" 28-gauge Woodlander had a delicious feel right out of the box. It was more center-balanced at ½" in front of the hinge. The gun was alive but not whippy. It was extremely easy to shoot. The Woodlander's English stock was higher than the Magnus Light's, as sub-gauge guns are often stocked higher than 12s, but everyone I loaned it to shot it well. Very well. Two wanted to buy it on the spot. A pretty 28-gauge will do that to you. This gun really had *the* feel.

Lang personally inspects each gun before sending it to his dealers. It's nice to see a personal touch in guns with such a personality. I was impressed with these new guns, and dealers have been too. Guerinis have been selling well in a competitive market because they are well made and good looking. For that you can thank the CNC and EDM gods. To give thanks for the beautiful wood, you have to go a little higher.

CSMC A-10 American

It was in early 2009 that we first began to hear rumors of a new over/under from Connecticut Shotgun Manufacturing Company. The firm's RBL boxlock side-by-side had been in production for four years and was nearing the end of its limited-production run. It had been a success, and everyone was waiting to see what would be next. A boxlock O/U was assumed. Still, we were surprised by the September 1, 2009, announcement of a sidelock O/U: the A-10 American. We were stunned by the introductory price of $3,995.

Most of CSMC's production is side-by-sides. The Model 21s, Foxes, Remington Parkers, RBLs and exquisite A. Galazan Round Body side-by-side guns are well known. But since 1990 the company also has made the five-figure A. Galazan Boss-style rounded-action sidelock O/U. Clearly CSMC knew how to make a sidelock O/U, but for less than $4,000? A Beretta SO or Merkel 303 sidelock starts well over $25,000. British "best" O/U sidelocks are several times that. The only O/U sidelock I can think of that was roughly in the $5K range is the discontinued Kimber Marias. It was gorgeous,

but the non-selective single trigger and non-intercepting sears were drawbacks. Normally, Connecticut Shotgun copies existing designs and innovates with new production methods. What does the A-10 emulate?

The answer is Beretta and Beretta again. The sidelocks are just about dead ringers for those of the Beretta SO5. Both bridles are machined integrally with the lockplate, not as a separate piece. That's why there are only four pins showing instead of the seven pins used on some other Beretta SOs. Both the A-10 and the SO5 use a flat V-leaf mainspring located under the bridle.

In fact, the only real difference in the mechanics of the locks that I could see was that the SO5 has a locking screw securing the hammer pin while the A-10 has a lone Torx pivot pin. The A-10 has a hard coat of gold titanium nitride on the sears, hammer and pins. It's tough stuff, as no wear showed on the faces of the hammers when I disassembled the gun after my tests.

Outside, the A-10 locks are hand detachable via two hidden flip tabs on the right sidelock. With the little nylon tool provided, you simply push the tail of a tab and it pops up. Then you twist and remove it. The tabs fit the sidelock surface so well that you have to look twice to see them. It's really classy.

That's not all that's detachable. The A-10's inertia trigger is mounted on a plate that is held in the rear by a Torx bolt passing through the short, stubby trigger tang. To detach the trigger, just loosen the stock via its drawbolt (a rarity in sidelocks) and unscrew the Torx. In literally minutes you can break down the action into the main receiver, triggerplate and two sidelocks. This is great for cleaning and general admiration. A little less admirable was the slightly imperfect fit of the triggerplate to the receiver on our test gun. This was noticeable because all of the other metal fit was so good.

The action's lockup was an interesting choice on CSMC's part. Instead of copying the SO action's Kersten crossbolt, the A-10's stays with a Beretta design, but it's the lock of the 680 boxlock series.

A mid-breech U-shaped locking lug has two sturdy $1/4''$ flat-bottomed studs that engage sockets midway up the barrel's monoblock. This is a simpler, cleaner system than the Kersten crossbolt and has proven durable in the 680s.

Like the SO and 680, the A-10 has no Perazzi-style side lumps, so the inside of the receiver is clean. Hinging is by replaceable hinge stubs as on the SO and just about every other modern O/U except those by Browning. The smooth floor of the receiver, with its huge rounded cocking rods, is pure SO.

The heavily tapered monoblock contains the usual Beretta-style selective ejectors, again tried and true. It also has the usual little half-moon cutouts

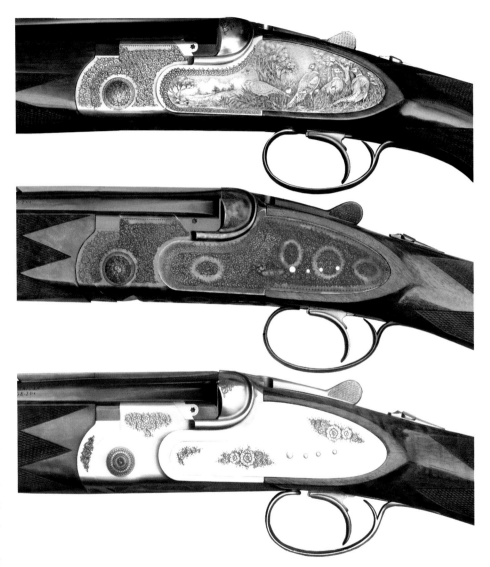

Three of the A-10's four levels of engraving include (from top): Platinum, Rose & Scroll (shown with optional case coloring) and Standard.

for the hinge stubs on each side. Standard stuff, but worth copying because it works. No great effort was made to disguise our review gun's monoblock seam, but on a couple of 20-gauge A-10s I saw at the SHOT Show the seam was well polished and almost invisible.

Here is a good spot to mention that the A-10 was built with the most modern machinery. Connecticut Shotgun extensively retooled specifically for this gun, installing a new machining line. The gun was computer designed in-house and made in a totally vertical operation. The company even makes the barrels— something most gun-makers don't do. CSMC says that 1,300 different steps go into the manufacture. CNC and EDM are used extensively. Finished parts are inspected by computer-coordinate measuring machines, and then they are hand fitted for the best of both worlds. The guns are extensively tested too. I've seen CSMC's indoor test range knee deep in hulls.

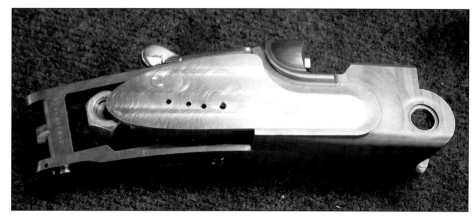
Because the bridles are machined integrally with the lockplate, only four pins show on the outside of the action.

The A-10's barrels offer a little extra. The tubes themselves are drilled in-house, not hammer forged. Then they are vertically honed. Length options are 26", 28", 30" and 32". On the 12-gauge frame you can have 12-, 20- or 28-gauge barrels. On the 20-gauge frame it is 20 or 28. Our test gun's 30" 12-gauge barrels had 3" chambers. Chamber forcing cones were of conventional length. The barrel bores were fashionably overbore. On this particular set of barrels, the lower barrel was .735" while the upper was .003" larger at .738".

The barrel interiors are coated with CSMC's Tuff Bore plating for steel-shot compatibility. It is durable, rustproof and makes barrel cleaning a bit easier. The barrels are also cryogenically frozen for stress relief. CSMC claims that this "allows for more accurate and consistent shot patterning." I'm sure it can't hurt.

Each barrel set comes with five Trulock stainless-steel screw chokes. They are short little things, only 1½" long, having about an inch of taper and a half-inch of parallel. They have rim notches for proper wrench seating, but there are no identification notches on the rims to identify inserted chokes if you forget.

The rears of the chokes are about .007" overbore for safety. The chokes are marked as to designation and nominal constriction, but you'll have to remember that your barrel IDs are about .735" for the latter to make sense. The Modified, Improved Modified and Full were about the usual .020", .030" and .035" constrictions, but the Skeet and Improved Cylinder were .005" tighter than normal at .010" and .015". The IM and F are not recommended for steel shot, but the others are. The five choke tubes and a decent wrench come in a classy faux-leather box, but you will want something more practical for field use.

The outsides of the barrels are rust blued to a nice matte finish. I could see some faint lengthwise carding lines on our sample but nothing egregious, and the exterior was ripple free. There was the slightest swelling at the muzzle due to the chokes. The side and top ribs are laser welded to the barrels. This should be tremendously strong and avoid the problem that soft-soldered ribs have of popping off after a while. The top rib is machine-scribed for low glare and has a small red bead at the muzzle.

There are no side ribs under the forend, but there is an attachment plate for the special weight system. CSMC says that six weights are included—two of 2.25 oz each and four of .5 oz each—but our review gun came with two of 1.5 oz and two of 2.25 oz for a total of 7.5 oz. The weights were easily and cleanly attached singly, in pairs or all at once. It was a slick way to shift balance forward and totally invisible with the forend in place. This weight system is not available in the 20-gauge action.

The A-10 comes with another weight set to fit

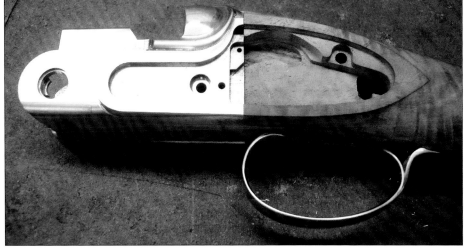

The A-10 is built with the most modern machinery, and there are 1,300 steps in its manufacture.

in the stock's drawbolt hole. It is a 6³/₄" threaded rod with four screw-on weights locked in place with a supplied Allen key. Weight added to the stock can vary from 3.8 oz to 11.4 oz. The screw-on weights have O-rings for a snug fit in the stock hole, but the weight set is not anchored fore and aft. It should be.

You have the choice of the English field stock that came on our gun or a pistol-grip sporter stock. Factory dimensions for the Eng-

lish stock are given as 14⁵/₈" x 1¹/₂" x 2²/₅", neutral cast and 4.25° pitch. The factory pistol grip dimensions are 14¹/₂" x 1¹/₂" x 2³/₈", neutral cast and 4° pitch. The neutral cast should please you lefties. Length can be altered by recoil-pad selection. The trigger blade is adjustable fore and aft in three positions over ¹/₂", but that realistically affects grip comfort more than practical stock length. On the 12-gauge the pistol grip is flat, while on recent 20s I have seen it has either been a round knob or an attractive capped flat-knob Prince of Wales. Two forends are available. Our test gun had the svelte field forend, with a slightly fuller sporting forend being the other choice.

The checkering is borderless and not overly fancy, and it appears to be laser cut. It is properly aggressive for a good grip and did not have the slightly burned look that the checkering on some RBLs have. The checkering on the rear of one of our stock panels was not sharp, but the rest was correct. The wood finish is oil and nicely done to a low gloss. The grain was properly filled, and it looked really good. The finish is said to be in the wood, not on it. Factory literature says that "the wood is coated on every possible surface inside and out," but the inside of our gun's stock head appeared untreated. The wood-to-metal fit on our gun was generally good.

CSMC uses mostly American black walnut. Standard wood is 2X, but you can order 3X for $350, 4X for $600 and Exhibition for $900. Regardless of grade, every A-10 owner I've spoken to has said that the wood exceeded their expectations.

Whereas nature gets credit for the wood, man is in charge of the engraving. One of the main reasons that sidelocks are considered upper crusty is that they offer a larger canvas for the engraver. The A-10 comes in four levels of engraving: Standard, Deluxe, Rose & Scroll and Platinum. All of the receivers are French-grayed and plasma hardened except that the Rose & Scroll has the option of case coloring.

Engraving on the Standard and Deluxe is the very light bulino style cut by a new laser process and hand chased by a half-dozen in-house engravers. The Standard pattern is a light rose & scroll of about 25-percent coverage, while the Deluxe has dog and bird scenes on the locks with a tight rose & scroll elsewhere. I didn't feel that the engraving on these models was a strong point, and others I spoke to felt the same way. It seemed more *chiaroscuro*, relying just on light and shadow. It needed a bit more depth. The deeper 100%-coverage engraving on our test Rose & Scroll gun was adequate, but that was mostly because it was so nicely disguised by CSMC's real bone-and-charcoal case coloring. The overall combined effect was attrac-

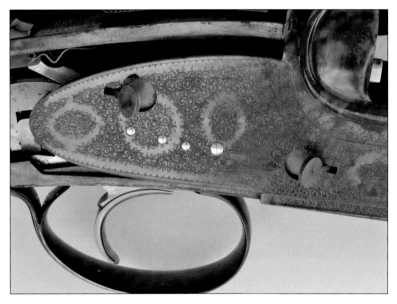

The A-10's locks are hand detachable via two flip tabs on the right sidelock.

tive though. I had only a glance at the Platinum model's engraving, but it looked like the real deal—with a price to match.

The A-10 comes in a sturdy aluminum takedown case fit to withstand the most disgruntled baggage handler. It has a removable black nylon cover Velcroed on, but that makes it inconvenient to open, so you'll use it only when you travel. In addition to the gun, the case contains the afore-mentioned five chokes and wrench, fore and aft weight sets if a 12-gauge, Allen keys for the weights and trigger (but no Torx), a nylon push tool for the sideplate tabs, a surprisingly literate and informative manual that you really should read carefully, plus the warranty. CSMC guarantees the Standard version for five years, and the others are guaranteed for the life of the original owner.

Our 12-gauge A-10 weighed 7 pounds 7.3 ounces with its 30" barrels, English stock, field forend and no added weights. This is a bit heavy for convenient upland carry but just about ideal for driven shooting or doves. The gun was beautifully balanced, and I don't say that casually. To me, balance is the most important aspect of any gun. For targets I might go with 32" barrels and sporter wood plus a little tinkering with the weights, but for driven or perhaps open-field shooting our test gun was perfect.

Stock fit is always an individual thing. Some feel that the RBLs and A-10s don't have enough pitch and that the stock toe digs into their pecs when shooting on the level. But that's easy to fix, and on high birds pitch doesn't really matter.

I first tried the gun on our local 5 Stand layout. I like to shoot singles and shoot the pieces with the second barrel. It's a great test to see how well you stay into the gun and to get ready for double-tapping those iron-clad South Dakota roosters. Unfortunately, the A-10 wouldn't fire twice. My grotty 1,125-fps $^7/_8$-oz 12-gauge reloads weren't strong enough to reliably cycle the trigger's inertia block, even though my other guns, including the autoloaders, run those shells. To be fair, every 1-, $1^1/_8$- and $1^1/_4$-oz factory load I tried functioned perfectly. Just be careful of the absurdly light stuff.

Trigger pulls were pretty good. The bottom was $4^1/_2$ pounds with a touch of slop and creep. The top, at $5^1/_4$ pounds, was crisp. The Beretta-style automatic safety/barrel selector worked correctly. If you prefer a manual safety, ask for it when you order the gun. On our particular gun the choke in the lower barrel kept coming loose, while the one in the upper barrel was sticky and hard to remove. A couple of SSM readers wrote me about sticking firing pins in their early A-10s, but both reported

The sears, hammers and pins are coated with gold titanium nitride to prevent wear.

prompt factory repair. The test gun had no such problems.

The gun shot well for me. Really, really well. As well as anything I own. Perfect balance will do that. I loaned the gun around, and those who tried it, though varying in stature and build, also had good luck. The SSM readers I corresponded with who owned 12-gauge A-10s also mostly reported that they shot the guns well. I took the gun dove hunting, and it proved ideal for high crossers. I think that it may just be one of those blessed guns. It would really shine at driven shooting in Spain, England or Scotland.

The pricing on the A-10 is interesting. When the gun was first announced in September 2009, the price of the Standard model was $7,995, but a total of $4,000 in various discounts was offered for a limited time. The Deluxe was $1,000 more. The 20-gauge added another $500.

This was a marvelous bargain: $3,995 for a well-made, beautifully balanced sidelock O/U. Unheard of. Amazing. The orders poured in. Deliveries started in April 2010 but very, very slowly. CSMC didn't want to release guns unless they were right and that meant a slow ramp up, just like the RBL before. One offshoot of this was that it was difficult to get a review gun. The customers actually came before us media flaks.

Imagine that. CSMC really does deserve its excellent reputation for customer care. We are deeply indebted to Steve Barnett of Steve Barnett Fine Guns, one of the new Galazan Premium Dealers, for the loan of our test gun.

As advertised, when orders reached a certain undisclosed point, all discounts ceased. By

called the Grand Master, comes as a 12-, 20- and 28-gauge barrel set, and has a new engraving pattern. Limited to a run of 100 sets, it will sell on pre-order for $25,000.

CSMC also has a complete custom shop capable of any alteration, such as a solid rib, double triggers, custom wood, special

Embellishment on the Standard model is light rose & scroll—cut by a new laser process and hand chased by CSMC's in-house engravers.

engraving and the like. It costs $1,000 to "enter" the custom shop, and to

October 2010 the prices were fixed for the Standard at $7,995, the Deluxe at $8,995, the Rose & Scroll at $10,000 and the Platinum at $15,000. At the 2011 SCI Convention, in Reno, CSMC introduced a new A-10 model. The receiver, forend metal and lockplates are machined from titanium to reduce gun weight by a pound. It's

that is added the cost of the work requested.

At $4,000 the A-10 American Standard was an insanely good buy. Even at today's $8,000, if you wish a sidelock O/U there is nothing like it at the price. Classic yet innovative. Proudly American made. Attractive and, above all, a real shooter.

CSMC RBL Launch Edition

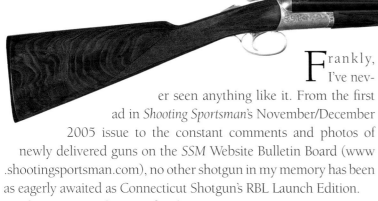

(Courtesy of Rock Island Auctions)

Frankly, I've never seen anything like it. From the first ad in *Shooting Sportsman*'s November/December 2005 issue to the constant comments and photos of newly delivered guns on the *SSM* Website Bulletin Board (www .shootingsportsman.com), no other shotgun in my memory has been as eagerly awaited as Connecticut Shotgun's RBL Launch Edition.

There was good reason for the anticipation too. Since its inception in 1975, Connecticut Shotgun Manufacturing Company has earned a reputation for producing high-quality guns. The firm makes modern versions of the all-American Fox, Winchester Model 21 and high-grade Remington Parker as well as a Boss-style over/under and an exquisite round-body sidelock side-by-side. Prices start around $15,000 and go up rapidly to more than six figures.

The RBL (which, I was told, stands for "Round Box Lock") was introduced as a 28" 20-gauge side-by-side at $2,499 if you paid up front—$300 more if you didn't. There was no middleman; you dealt directly with the factory. The glossy photos in the ads were stunning. They showed the gun with a fully accessorized takedown case. Free options included single or double triggers, a choice of two stock lengths, and an English or pistol-grip hand. Extra-cost options included wood upgrades, assisted opening, beavertail forend and case coloring. The looks, specifications and price of the gun from a company with a stellar reputation created a flood of orders. And the wait began.

Meanwhile back at the factory, Tony Galazan, the owner and operator of Connecticut Shotgun, had his hands full. He had just moved from a large plant into an even larger one in New Britain, Connecticut. It was one of the old Stanley Tool Works buildings and covered three acres under one roof. (That's about 2 1/2 football fields, including end zones.) The plant had to be completely refurbished even as it was being set up for RBL production, and the company still had to maintain production of all of its other guns. It was a massive undertaking, especially considering that Galazan was determined to run a completely vertical operation, with every process to be performed in-house eventually.

Galazan always has relied on the latest high-tech machinery combined with handwork where necessary. Obviously, his high-end guns demand more of the latter, whereas the RBL was to rely as much as possible on the former. It was designed from scratch as a manufactured gun.

When I toured the new plant in 2006, I was impressed by the shear number of high-tech machines. I'm used to seeing CNC (computer numerical control) machines in gun plants, but Galazan has an army of the latest ones. He also uses a number of very expensive and precise EDMs (electronic discharge machines). Then there are state-of-the-art machines for barrelmaking, stock duplication, laser engraving and laser checkering. There's even a vacuum wood-drying vault. As I discuss the RBL Launch Edition, I'll tie in how the machinery has enabled high production standards for a modest cost. The story here is partly about the RBL and partly about the processes that made this gun possible.

The action of the RBL is A&D via SKB. No, these are not teeny-bopper BlackBerry thumb-typing acronyms. It's a quick way of stating the RBL's provenance. The RBL sports a tried-and-true Anson & Deeley boxlock action. Arguably, the A&D action is the most reliable one for a side-by-side. It is certainly the most copied. In this case, the RBL's interior looks very much like that of the now-discontinued Japanese SKB boxlock. And I mean *very* much like. I can't say that all of the interior mechanicals are absolutely identical, but from the comparison photographs I've seen, it is hard to see any mechanical difference.

This isn't a bad thing. The SKB side-by-side boxlock actions were excellent. The single triggers really worked, and the guns were durable. With Galazan's history of copying good designs and improving them through more modern manufacturing methods, this move makes perfect sense.

While in Galazan's plant, I chatted with Englishman David Wilkes. He had apprenticed and then worked as a gunmaker for British side-by-side maker Webley & Scott before coming to Connecticut Shotgun. It turns out that Wilkes' considerable expertise in making boxlock side-by-sides heavily influenced the project. Galazan referred to him as the spearhead in setting up the RBL's production.

I was told that when SKB was designing its boxlock side-by-side, employees had visited Webley & Scott to learn how Webley built guns. The SKB and W&S actions are certainly not identical, although they do operate on the same principles.

It would be fairest to say that the SKB and RBL actions share much of the same design, but there is a major difference in the manufacturing techniques. This certainly reflects the approach Galazan has taken previously with the Fox, Winchester 21 and Parker, where he blended classic designs with modern manufacturing and materials. I also should add that the interior of the action may be similar to the SKB's, but it stops there. Elsewhere the RBL is an entirely different gun.

The RBL has a "rounded" boxlock action, not a true "round action" like Scotland's Dickson. The underside edges of the action are rounded for aesthetics and a comfortable carry. This involves more work than it seems but doesn't require a major redesign of the interior. When you get inside the RBL's A&D action, the first thing you notice is the golden titanium nitrate coating on most of the interior parts. Connecticut Shotgun has trademarked it as "Hard Gold." This is similar to the coating used on high-speed drill bits and has high lubricity, is rustproof and is very durable. It also looks good.

But it's the things you don't notice about the production of the receiver that are really interesting. The receiver is machined from a solid forging of American steel. The upper tang is a separate piece attached by an electron-beam welding process. EDMs capable of incredibly fine tolerances cut the hammer and sear notches so precisely that the trigger pulls are set by computer control of the EDMs, not by any later handwork. The machines are capable of cutting to within a couple of 10,000ths of an inch. EDMs also make the complicated cut on the floor of the receiver where the barrel hooks are received. These are cut at an angle to bear fully on the hooks' surfaces. Cheaper guns are cut square and only bear on the edges.

The bulk of the receiver work is done on CNC machines. Parts are placed in a "tombstone," or multiple-piece rack, before the workers go home at the end of the day. The machines run unattended at night. The machinery monitors the sharpness of its own tool heads and changes them as required. It also selects different tools for different operations. In the morning the completed parts are waiting for the workers to take them to the next step.

These machines certainly aren't unique among gunmakers, but the extent of their use by Connecticut Shotgun may be. As Galazan told me, part of his business is making guns and part is making the machines that make guns.

Our RBL test gun is my personal gun. I ordered it in October 2005 and received it 13 months later. The serial number is just under 100, so it is one of the earlier ones. The gun has an English stock, splinter forend, longer 14³/4" length of pull, standard-grade wood, case coloring and a single trigger.

I picked the single trigger because I just felt like giving one a try. I'd never had one on a side-by-side before. Although single triggers on side-by-sides have been a challenge for some makers, SKB had a

reliable single trigger and so did Winchester on its Model 21. Galazan has experience in this area.

The RBL's single trigger is inertial, meaning that recoil from the first shell being fired is required to set the second sear. It's also a selective trigger that uses the same little transverse button at the top of the trigger blade as the SKB and the 21. Trigger pulls on the test gun were 3¹/2 pounds for the right barrel and 2³/4 pounds for the left. Pulls were extremely crisp with no noticeable creep or over-travel.

The trigger guard is actually an off-the-shelf part taken from Galazan's extensive accessories catalog. It is rolled on both edges for left- or right-handed comfort. In a unique touch, the long trigger tang is fitted to the stock without any visible screws. A small hook at the inside rear

The RBL comes in a fitted luggage case complete with a treasure trove of first-class accessories. (Courtesy of Rock Island Auctions)

of the trigger-guard tang engages a bracket in the tang channel of the stock to hold it securely.

Lock-up of the action is by the tried-and-true Purdey double-underbolt system. Unlike the Webley & Scott's, the RBL's hinge pin is replaceable in the very unlikely event that this becomes necessary. Firing-pin holes in the breech face are not bushed, so access to the pins can be accomplished only by removing the stock. Traditional leaf springs, not coils, are used to power the hammers. Many feel that leaf springs have quicker lock times and crisper trigger pulls than coils. The floor and triggerplates of the action are each held in place by a carefully hand-indexed screw. Even the interior screws under the floorplate that hold the leaf springs are indexed.

The floorplate seam on our gun was so perfect that it was difficult to see. The safety is automatic, engaging each time you open the gun.

The ejector mechanism is the Southgate system, again tried and true. Ejectors are probably the most common failure area on a side-by-side and an area where experimentation is fraught with risk. The ejector sears, actuating rods and hammers all are treated with the titanium-nitrate process used on the interior of the action.

The forend iron uses the traditional Anson pushbutton at the front of the forend. It lacks the usual escutcheon bushing to support the rod. The mechanism is simple, reliable and self-adjusting because of the spring return. Ours worked smoothly, without the undue pressure so often required of new Anson button installations. This indicates very careful machining. Exceptional care also was taken to mate the forend iron to the receiver. During production the forend iron and receiver are jigged together and polished as a unit for a perfect hinge seam.

Like virtually everything else on the gun, the barrels are made in-house. They start as 4140 steel-alloy bar stock and go through the big Miroku-brand drill machine that runs perfect bore holes down two blanks at a time. The outsides are machined to proper contours by a separate machine.

The barrels are joined at the rear, not by a monoblock but by a brazed-on dovetail plate that incorporates the hooks. Top and bottom ribs are silver soldered but at a low-enough temperature to avoid barrel warpage. The barrels are trued in a four-step process. The barrel qualification is within an incredibly precise tolerance. The breech face is said to be machined to a precision that will allow interchange-ability of barrels without further fitting. That said, once any barrel "settles in" to an action with use, the addition of an extra barrel, no matter how carefully machined, should be checked for proper fit.

The seam between the ejectors is almost invisible. The two ejector pieces are soldered together, machined as a pair and then separated for a perfect fit.

The interiors of the barrels are chrome plated. Galazan sent a man to Europe to learn the process so that it could be done in-house. The 20-gauge chambers on all the RBLs are 2^3/4" long, not the customary 3". When I asked Galazan why he'd avoided the longer and virtually standard chambers, he said he was dissatisfied with the patterning performance of 3" 20-gauge shells and didn't want new owners blaming his gun for poor patterns. The 2^3/4" chambers have conventional forcing cones.

In addition to the chromed bores, the entire barrel set is stress-relieved by cryogenic deep freezing that can go to minus 300° Fahrenheit. Galazan calls the process "Cryo Pattern" and feels that it stabilizes the movement of hot barrels, thus producing better patterns. This process has proven effective in many areas, including rifle barrels and certain musical instruments. It is not commonly applied to production shotguns, and Galazan is a leader in the use of this technique.

RBLs come with five flush-mount 2^1/2"-long screw chokes: Skeet (.004" constriction), Improved Cylinder (.010"), Modified (.016"), Improved Modified (.026") and Full (a very tight .040") measured on 20-gauge bores of a nearly nominal .618". The factory has tested them as safe with steel shot and other hard nontoxics. Each barrel is tested with proof loads in the plant's underground test-fire range. While at the range, I saw huge piles of yellow Remington 20-gauge hulls. Galazan said that once every week or so a gun is pulled from production and every person on the RBL project is encouraged to fire it a couple of hundred times to test for parts wear. Because there are more than a dozen workers on the RBL team, that's a pretty good test.

The chokes are plated inside and centerless ground on the outside. Centerless grinding is a high-tech method of ensuring a surface finish and dimensional tolerance of the highest degree. The threads at the front are proprietary to Galazan. A stainless steel Teague-style friction-fit wrench is used to fit the notchless chokes. Choke designations are written on the barrels of the chokes but are hidden when the chokes are in place. It pays to remember what you have where.

The top rib on the barrels is a swamped English game rib. I'd thought that an all-American side-by-side more likely would have the slightly raised rib so popular on our classic guns. I asked Galazan why he'd chosen that rib, and he said that the RBL was his gun and

The engraving is a scrolled acanthus-leaf design that was created by Richard Roy.

(Courtesy of Rock Island Auctions)

that's the way he felt like doing it. Personally, I'm grateful for the low game rib. It lends a cleaner and less-bulky line to the gun. It caters to the style of the instinctive field shooter who shoots with peripheral reference to the muzzle of his barrel rather than sighting down a rib. I think it was a good choice for this little gun. The muzzle sports a tasteful brass bead.

As is traditional on game guns, the swamped rib has the same blue finish as the barrels. Lou Frutuoso, Connecticut Shotgun's director of sales and marketing, told me that our test gun's barrels were done with a military-spec thermal-set coating, not bluing as

such. It is supposed to be impervious to everything non-nuclear, and it certainly looks nice enough. However, this was changed later. As production increased, the company decided to use more cost-effective traditional rust bluing instead.

All the RBL barrels I've seen have been smoothly struck without any ripples or exterior flaws. Early prototypes had slight muzzle swelling at the chokes, but production barrels show none of this. They give no exterior evidence of being screw-choked.

The Launch Editon's barrels were available with a most interesting option. For an extra $450 you could have a Holland & Holland-style assisted opener added. It's a small spring device that fits invisibly on the barrels under the forend. It makes the gun a little harder to close but vastly easier and faster to open. It could be handy in driven situations or when defending some water tank from an onslaught of doves. It's removable too, in case you want to revert to a conventional action. An assisted opener is an expensive option usually reserved for high-grade sidelocks. It is extremely rare to see it offered on a moderately priced boxlock.

As mentioned, the RBL Launch Edition was available with an English stock, pistol-grip stock, splinter forend or, for an extra $175, a beavertail forend. Our test gun was English/splinter. Dimensions were listed as $14^{1}/4"$ (or optionally $14^{3}/4"$) x $1^{1}/2"$ x $2^{3}/8"$, with zero cast. The stock measured exactly to these dimensions but exhibited just 1" of pitch. My only complaint about the aesthetics of the wood is that the splinter forend is a little blunter at the front than I would have liked. It's a touch more German or

Japanese than English. The steel-capped pistol grips I've seen are most attractive, as are the modest beavertails.

Checkering on the wood is burned by laser, and the machine is fascinating to watch. A CAD/CAM setup next to the laser tirelessly supervises it. Each side of each V cut takes a single pass. The points are actually not quite pointed up, as that would be too sharp. A thin ribbon of smoke rises off the laser beam, and the outcome is fine, borderless 22-lpi checkering. I thought it might look burnt, but it doesn't. It's not hand-cut, but it looks pretty good.

The stock finish is a high-gloss oil/shellac combination. It is a flawless, fully filled surface that far exceeds the price level of this gun. The finish is durable but not indestructible. After I had been shooting the gun a few weeks, the sunscreen I use started to erode the finish on the comb. Frutuoso advised me that buffing would make things right, but I have not yet taken that step.

Wood was uniformly ever-so-slightly proud but not objectionably so. It's just about right to accommodate a refinishing or a little wood shrinkage. The only place you notice it is where the triggerguard tang is slightly below the surface of the stock wrist. There were no wood-to-metal gaps of any kind on the test gun or on several other RBLs I've seen.

The stock is finished with a plain, black, hard-rubber (not plastic) buttplate. I expected to see some clever logo here, but there are only modest grooves to hold the gun to the shoulder. The screws holding on the buttplate were correctly indexed.

The RBL stock is attached with a standard through-bolt, as seen on most O/Us, instead of the vertical fasteners through the tangs that most English side-by-sides use. I think that this is more secure and allows better heading up of the stock, but it makes any future stock bending for fit a bit more problematic.

As an insight into production, while on the shop tour I asked Galazan what a certain pile of foot-long steel billets was going to be.

He replied that they would be machined into the stock drawbolts. This is a part that could have been outsourced from almost any machine shop at a very low price; it was kept in-house to assure quality and maintain a completely vertical operation.

And then there is wood quality. The RBL came standard with "2X grade" walnut and upgrades of $350, $500 and $750. The upgrades offered were a choice of American, black, Claro, Turkish and California English. The test gun had standard wood, and I've seen several others with it also. All are highly figured and very nice indeed. Many of the upgrade stocks I saw drying in the plant were spectacular.

Galazan buys his wood in bulk, often by the entire tree trunk. Once cut into blanks, the wood spends months in a temperature-controlled drying kiln. From there it goes into a vacuum room, where moisture content is regulated and stabilized. The dried blanks then go onto a 10-spindle CNC stock pantograph, where they are formed. Forends use a three-dimensional milling machine. When completed, the final heading up of the stocks is by hand to account for any slight warpage.

After the fancy wood, the next thing that stands out on the RBL is the engraving. The original pattern was done by Richard Roy and is a very attractive scrolled acanthus-leaf design. Cut by laser in-house, the engraving process entailed a steep learning curve. On some early guns I saw the engraving was attractive but somewhat shallow. Later the engraving gained depth and dignity. The engraving on our test gun's receiver, top tang and trigger guard was excellent. The depth was correct and, with the naked eye, it was very hard to tell from hand-cut work. The give-away was the perfection of it. The engraving on the barrel chambers and rear of the rib was a little less successful, because the mil-spec finish process had filled it in a bit. The rust-blued barrels may be sharper.

Two receiver finishes were offered—French gray being standard and case coloring being a $250 option. The laser process leaves the background of the French-grayed finish dark enough to really show off the engraving. Early samples of the French gray were brighter and less to my taste, but this was changed during production. The graying process is proprietary to Connecticut Shotgun and exact details were not forthcoming.

The case coloring is done in-house. Galazan uses the traditional bone-and-charcoal oven process with which he colors his high-end guns. Because of the heat involved, the receivers have to be blocked to prevent warpage, but the result is worth the extra labor. The combination of the engraving and case coloring is absolutely stunning. It is well worth the money and the annual re-lacquering required to protect it.

Normally I gloss over the extras that come with test guns.

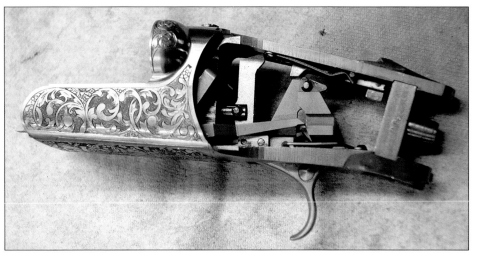

A completed French-gray RBL action ready for installation.

They usually include a cardboard box, a choke wrench and a legalese manual. Not with the RBL. You get an absolute treasure trove of first-class goodies. First there's the fitted luggage case with an elm frame covered with attractive gold-hued linen cloth, a solid-brass lock, and leather corners and straps. This is a good-quality case. The leather is sewn through the frame, not just glued on. The inside is lined with wine-colored felt. Accoutrements include a rosewood cleaning rod, a brass brush and swab, two chromed "RBL"-marked snap caps, a chromed oil bottle, a leather choke-tube pouch to hold the five chokes, protective safety glasses, and earplugs. It's a couple of hundred dollars worth of stuff and of excellent quality. The factory warranty is for six months—and Connecticut Shotgun has an excellent reputation for service.

As usual, I shot the gun a good bit at clay targets and loaned it around. I was fortunate to be able to take it to the *Shooting Sportsman* Readers & Writers shoot at Santa Fe Trail Hunts to test it on wild blue quail and hardened bobwhites. At one evening's "show and tell" everyone had a chance to comment on the gun, and many readers were able to shoot it later in the trip. Comments from this knowledgeable group were generally very positive, and the overall opinion was that the gun was worth a good bit more than the asking price.

The rounded action and light weight make the RBL a pleasure to carry in the field. I wish that I could say I shot the gun so well that the quail simply surrendered instead of rocketing away, but that wasn't the case. I shot like a pig. For my physique and style of shooting, the RBL stock was a little low and I couldn't compensate. The surprising lack of pitch made my gun mount inconsistent, as the toe of the stock caught on my chest.

But that was my problem. The dimensions really are mostly standard. Several of the people I loaned the gun to shot it very well indeed. They sagely ascribed my poor performance to lack of talent rather than lack of fit. Frutuoso told me that of the hundreds of RBLs sold, there were very few complaints about stock dimensions, so perhaps I'm the odd man out.

Stocks can be adjusted. Balance and handling are more critical. With a weight of 6 pounds 2.4 ounces, the RBL is absolutely perfect for a 20. Guns that are too light can be as hard to shoot as guns that are too heavy. A 20 in the 6- to 6½-pound range is excellent. The balance point is about ½" in front of the hinge pin, to give the gun just enough weight forward to be forgiving but not logy. Unlike two of the prototypes with heavier jugged barrels, the production guns have the weight properly distributed along the tubes. I had a Webley & Scott 20 that was the same weight but carried most of it in the center. It was a little too fast for me. With the weight just a little farther forward, the RBL is more forgiving.

Galazan's barrel-indexing machinery must be doing something right, because barrel convergence was spot-on perfect at 30 yards. Can't ask for more than that. The gun does shoot flat, so you'll want a stock high enough to see a bit of rib. The ejectors ejected briskly, and timing was correct. The single trigger worked perfectly, as did the barrel selector and safety.

Obviously, any new production-line gun is going to have some glitches. A friend of mine had an RBL with trigger and rib issues. Connecticut Shotgun fixed it in about a week. The company is obviously very anxious to get the RBL off to a good start.

Is there anything I didn't like about the gun? Other than the stock fit, which is my particular cross to bear, and the overly blunt forend, I would have preferred a slightly smaller trigger guard, as the one supplied seemed a touch oversized. The screw chokes on my gun needed constant retightening. The gun was tested with Remington ammunition and worked perfectly with that brand, but it occasionally pierced a primer when using shells with Rio primers. I'm not a big fan of automatic safeties. I thought that the light 2¾-pound pull of the left trigger sear would create a problem, but it never did, and after a while I didn't notice it. I do wish that the stock finish were lighter, to better show off the nice grain of the walnut. These are relatively minor complaints. The major things are right. It is quite a gun for the price.

CSMC RBL 28-Gauge

The RBL-28 is the second in the RBL side-by-side boxlock series from Connecticut Shotgun Manufacturing Company. The first was the RBL-20 Launch Edition, announced in late 2005. The Launch Edition was eagerly anticipated and caused more Internet comment—replete with photo postings of each lucky new owner's gun—than any other shotgun in recent years.

The 28-gauge was announced two years later, in the fall of 2007. The base price had been raised from $2,799 for the 20 to $3,650, but then the 28 always has been an upper-crust gauge. It's not that 28s actually cost more to make. The volume isn't there, so margin becomes more important. It's the same in the cost difference of 28- versus 20-gauge shells. Options had changed slightly on the RBL-28. Case coloring, which had been extra at $250, was now standard. A single trigger, which had been a free option on the 20, was now $175 extra. Wood options included 2X standard, 3X ($350), 4X ($600) and Exhibition ($900). The H&H-type assisted opener was still available at $450. Chokes were now fixed, not screw-in as on the 20. The gorgeous canvas-and-leather, fully accessorized case was included as before.

There was no question that I needed one of these guns. Quail attacks had been reportedly increasing in the Southeast, and I knew my duty. The only question was how to set up the gun to best deal with the threat.

Many feel that the 28 is the ideal plantation-quail gauge, and I'm in that camp. Its $3/4$-oz payload is large enough to be very effective but small enough to offer an excuse when you muff a shot and need sympathy. It's a win/win deal.

Half the fun of ordering a gun is determining how to spec it out. The RBL isn't exactly a custom gun, but the advertisements showed enough options to provide some entertainment.

I went for the English stock and splinter forend, because I prefer that look on a small side-by-side. Admittedly, the very nice pistol grip and beavertail forend would allow for a touch more control, but sex sells. The 30" barrels were appealing, because a little extra weight up front might be advantageous in a light gun. Besides, I'd never owned a 30" 28 side-by-side, so it was time. The single trigger got the nod, because my double-trigger technique isn't the best on a light gun and I get a little gun movement shifting triggers. Those traditionalists with more digital dexterity would pick DTs. And finally, I splurged by ordering exhibition walnut, because I asked my dog and she sort of nodded.

A few months after ordering, I was at the 2008 Safari Club International Convention, in Reno, and spent an inordinate amount of time at the CSMC booth handling all of the different iterations of the RBL-28. Seeing the guns in person caused me to make one change. When shouldering the 30" gun, I felt that the long barrels drew my eyes away from the target too much, although the extra weight up front was nice. I called to switch my order from 30" to 28" and asked if the gun could be made with Skeet and Improved Cylinder quail chokes instead of the listed Modified/Full.

The gun arrived 13 months from the date of ordering—the same time it took for my RBL-20 to gestate. Frankly, I sort of like having a gun "on order." It is something to look forward to; something to make plans for.

As I go through the gun, I'll concentrate on the differences between it and the RBL-20. The manufacturing process and basic makeup of the RBL series are described in the review of the 20-gauge.

The RBL-28 is light, mechanically correct and properly proportioned. It also comes in a fully accessorized case and is available with first-rate exhibition-grade walnut.

The RBL-28's action is mechanically unchanged from the 20's. It's a proven Anson & Deeley design with Purdey-style double under-bolts, Southgate ejectors, flat V mainsprings and a reliable inertial selective single trigger or double triggers as you wish. The major interior wearing parts are coated in durable gold-colored titanium nitrite just like a high-speed drill bit. The coating is tough, rustproof and looks nice.

Is the gun built on a true 28-gauge action? Maybe yes, maybe no. I put the 28-gauge barrels onto the 20-gauge receiver and the 20's barrels onto the 28's receiver just to see if I could. Everything fit. The opening levers came over the correct amount, and the guns locked up nicely. Kudos to the magic of CNC and EDM. The only real differences were the larger fences on the 20 and a few thou of width at the sides near the forend iron. I did not measure the difference in receiver weights, but it couldn't amount to much. Frankly, this sized receiver stuff doesn't really matter. The 28's receiver *looks* in correct proportion, and that's what counts.

All the RBL-28s have case-colored receivers. The optional French gray of the RBL-20s has been discontinued. Coloring is oven baked in a traditional bone-and-charcoal pack. As before, the engraving is done by machine, but the RBL-28's scroll with setter and pointer on the sides and a grouse on the bottom seems shallower, or at least less distinct, than the engraving on the 20. The 28's engraving gets lost in the case coloring.

The barrels on the 28 carry a good-quality, medium-gloss rust blue. CSMC tried a military-spec, thermal-set barrel coating on the early RBL-20s but went back to doing it the old-fashioned way. Chambers are 2³/₄", as befits the 28 gauge, and forcing cones are standard length. As before, the barrel bores are chromed, but this time screw chokes are out and fixed chokes are in. My guess is that this was done to keep the barrel weight down and the gun's balance neutral. Barrel lengths of 26", 28" and 30" were offered instead of only 28" on the 20-gauge. If you request it, CSMC will give you whatever fixed chokes you wish. If you don't stipulate,

Thanks to modern machining, an RBL-28's barrels will actually fit on an RBL-20's frame. (Note the larger fences on the 20.)

the 26" barrels get Skeet and IC, whereas the longer tubes come Modified and Full. The top rib is a beautiful English-style swamped game rib, which lends a graceful look to the gun's profile.

Due to a hiccup in communication, my 28" barrels came through with the M/F chokes, but I was promised one-day factory turnaround to open them up. This is a good place to mention that CSMC has earned an excellent reputation for quick and courteous service. The company was quick to make good on any initial flaws

in the early production RBL-20s. I measured both bores at .551", almost a perfectly nominal .550" for the 28. The barrels on my gun are quite light, and no wonder: Barrel-wall thickness just behind the chokes is .065". This is certainly safe, but it is a good bit svelter than so many of the clunky mass-produced barrels made by some other makers today. Give credit to first-rate machinery, first-rate machinists and those fixed chokes.

The wood options on the RBL-28 are the same as they were on the 20: English or pistol grip and splinter or beavertail forend. As it should be, the wrist on my 28 is slimmer than the wrist on the 20, and it feels much better. The 28 retains the "no screws" long trigger-guard tang that slips into a hidden fastener in the stock.

In all, the 28 is a gorgeous and properly proportioned package. My only little touches of aesthetic whining are that the trigger guard seems a bit oversized, the curve of the single trigger isn't particularly graceful (but it is comfortable) and the bright silver of the Anson forend push button seems out of place against the bluing and case coloring of the rest of the gun. But these are small things, and you may very well prefer them the way they are.

Then there is the wood. My gun was ordered with exhibition walnut for an extra $900. All of the RBL exhibition walnut I've seen has been absolutely first rate, but my piece hit the lumber lotto. Lascivious walnut won't improve my shooting, but it sure takes the pain out of the misses.

I took the gun through a combination of barrel testing, considerable clay shooting and three days of plantation quail. The barrel tests showed that the chokes shot tight as expected for M/F. If I were to use the gun for distant doves, these might work, but for quail, grouse, woodcock or snipe you would be well to consider the .006" and .012" Skeet and Light Modified for best coverage in the 15- to 30-yard range.

Barrel convergence—the ability of both barrels to shoot to the same point—is spot-on perfect. This is a critical but often overlooked aspect of a gun. Surprisingly few doubles have perfect convergence, so this is a tribute to CSMC's barrel regulation. One major maker feels that 8" separation is acceptable at 40 yards, but I don't. That would cost you a third of your effective pattern.

The gun is set up to shoot flat. For most people, the standard stock drop of 1¹/₂" at comb and 2³/₈" at heel will show a fair amount of rib, but the gun does not shoot as high as it looks. It worked out perfectly for the majority of the shooters I loaned it to. Initially, many complained that the stock was too high, but they were pleasantly surprised when the gun shot dead on for them. Others who are used to high combs felt that the gun shot a little lower than the sight picture indicated, and they had to cover their targets to get a hit. Light-barreled sub-gauge side-by-side guns, like this 28, are reputed to have more barrel down flip than other guns. This might be why the gun shoots so flat while showing an elevated sight picture. The choice of 14¹/₄"

or 14³/₄" lengths of pull makes the gun suitable for a broad range of shooters. I felt that the stock could have used a bit more pitch, but no one else commented on this, so I must be the odd man out.

The most noticeable shooting characteristic of the gun was its swing speed. At a featherweight 5 pounds 10 ounces—versus 6 pounds 2.4 ounces for a similarly set up RBL-20—and balanced on the hinge pin, this RBL-28 is Ferrari fast. It reminded me very much of the 28-gauge Parker Reproduction: Both move like lightning. In exchange for the reflexive speed and the ability to make instant corrections, you will be required to concentrate more on your swing so as not to stop the gun. The inertia of the gun won't keep it moving for you the way it will on a gun with more weight forward. For comparison, I tried a 30" RBL-28 with a beavertail forend and pistol grip. It was a little more sedate, but not much.

Compared to the RBL-20 Launch Edition, the RBL-28 is a more specialized gun. It is featherweight, lightning fast, mechanically correct and absolutely gorgeous. It's a classy gun in a classy gauge. And it won't stop there. CSMC is now also producing RBLs in 12 and 16 gauge. The hefty 3" magnum RBL-12s I've handled have been built with a weight-forward bias meant for waterfowl and sporting clays. The scaled-frame RBL-16s are a good bit lighter and more neutrally balanced for upland work. CSMC has even added a 20-gauge rifled version of the RBL-20 for saboted slugs complete with iron sights and scope mounts. All continue the RBL tradition of an American-made shotgun of good quality at a reasonable cost. Well done, indeed.

FAMARS Dove Gun

This gun review must be a little different. Usually I have a test gun for a couple of months. During that time it is shot a ton. The gun is also subjected to tinkering and rumination. T&R time includes general parts dislocation and fussing. By the time it's done, there may be a few interior bits left over, but I can give you a pretty good idea as to how, why and whether things work.

Not so this time. Blame it on something called a *carnet*. That's sort of a passport for merchandise. The significant import duties levied on an expensive gun brought into this country for resale are waived if that gun is imported temporarily to display at a show and then promptly sent home.

Awash in blissful ignorance of the *carnet*, I journeyed to North Carolina in April 2009 for the Southern Side by Side Championship & Exhibition. This is a first-class shoot and very much worth attending. (Naturally, *Shooting Sportsman* is one of the sponsors.) The Italian gunmaker FAMARS (also a sponsor) exhibited among the half-dozen tents full of vendors and by prior arrangement of-

fered its new Dove Gun for me to try. I was hoping to take the gun home for a few weeks of testing, but Cristina Abbiatico, president of FAMARS and daughter of co-founder Mario Abbiatico, told me about the *carnet* restriction. I was welcome to examine the gun at the show, but it had to return to Italy immediately afterward.

On the plus side, both Senior Editor Vic Venters and Editor at Large Silvio Calabi were there and were kind enough to give me their takes on the Dove Gun as we looked it over. Vic knows more than most about fine guns. He is especially familiar with FAMARS, having written an excellent article on the company in 2001 for *Shooting Sportsman*. Silvio has been with *SSM* for years in several editorial capacities and continues to write for the magazine. He flat-out knows his guns, too. Don Amos, the engineer and fine-gun aficionado who popularized measuring and comparing the moment of inertia (MOI) of shotguns, also kindly offered to have a look. With that kind of expertise on tap, three days was enough to get a good handle on the gun.

FAMARS was founded in 1967. The name is an acronym including the founders' names: Fabbrica Armi Mario Abbiatico e Remo Salvinelli. Salvinelli was one of Italy's best gun-designing minds, whereas Abbiatico was able to nurture the great engravers. I was told that Fracassi, Pedersoli, both Galeazzis, and Pedretti all worked for FAMARS at one time. Today FAMARS has a modern CAD/CAM, CNC and EDM shop plus the skilled artisans on the second floor whose expert handwork is needed to turn out about 100 guns a year in the $20,000-and-up (way up) price range. The firm currently makes about a dozen models under its own name and also does work for other high-end makers. In addition to over/ unders and side-by-sides, FAMARS makes two double-rifle models and an amazing four-barrel, single-trigger sub-gauge shotgun.

The Dove Gun I looked at was a sleek 32" over/under 28-gauge on a petite, proportioned frame with detachable trigger. The 2009 price was $19,600, but as I write this in 2011 the price has increased to $20,900. The 20-gauge version is about $1,000 less. A two-barrel 20/28-gauge set is also available. The Dove Gun is similar to the FAMARS Excalibur Round Body, though slightly less elaborate and a good bit less expensive. Total production of the Dove Gun will be limited to 100 guns.

Like the guns of Perazzi, the Dove Gun action uses Boss/Woodward bifurcated side lumps on the inside of the receiver and hinge-stub barrel pivots. Similarly, lockup is by protruding mid-breech lugs.

The 20- and 28-gauge Dove Guns have detachable triggers. It is a real trick to fit a detachable trigger into a tiny, fully rounded action. Perazzi does not offer this in its 28-gauge-sized action. When removed, the Dove Gun's trigger is definitely a showpiece, from the serpentine walls of the triggerplate to the smoothly sculpted inertia block. A selective detachable trigger is a $900 option for the Dove Gun, and an automatic safety is an additional $500. A double trigger, also detachable, is a no-charge option. The Dove Gun's trigger is removed by sliding the safety rearward past the safe detent and pulling down on the trigger guard. On the gun I examined it came out very smoothly—a tribute to fine machining and finishing. A detachable trigger really isn't necessary on a gun with an easily removable stock, but

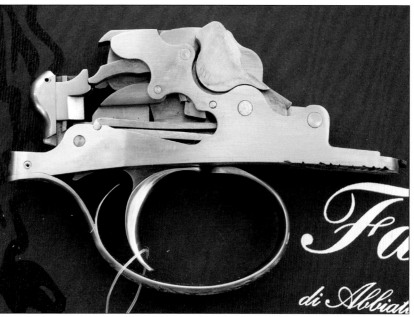

The gun's diminutive detachable trigger is a mechanical tour de force.

half the fun of a gun like this is show-and-tell time at the club.

The ejectors and monoblock appear to be of much the same mechanical design as the Perazzis'. Not identical, but similar. Considering the number of Olympic medals that have been won with Perazzis, a little mechanical similarity is not a bad thing.

But that's where it ends. The basic Perazzi is a tool, perhaps the best there is for certain things. This FAMARS is a jewel. It goes far beyond practical. This is art that works. The Dove Gun's receiver is a good example. It is formed by CNC from a chunk of steel and then hand-finished. FAMARS will make the receiver out of titanium if you prefer, but that will double the price of the gun. The receiver is no larger than absolutely necessary for the diminutive 28-gauge shell. Its underside is heavily rounded for a delightful look and feel. That curvature necessitated the relocation of the ejector trip rods farther up the sides of the action. This in turn required careful redesign of the forend metal. Beauty is not easy.

Our test gun's 32" barrels carried solid top and side ribs and fixed chokes.

The Dove Gun is available as a value-priced 20/28 two-barrel set. Our test gun was a 28-gauge with 32" barrels and solid top and side ribs.

Not to your taste? No problem. The Dove Gun comes with free choice of 29", 30" or 32" barrels, fixed or Briley screw chokes, and ventilated or solid top and side ribs. FAMARS also will let you select your barrel's weight. The company simply slightly increases or decreases the outside diameter of the tubes. You can have barrels as heavy or as light as you wish within reason and at no extra cost.

An extra set of barrels is a very fair $6,800. Most makers charge 50 percent of the cost of the gun for extra barrels.

The review gun's barrels had no ripples, and soldering appeared flawless. Cristina said that the barrels were soldered in-house using a combination of different-temperature solders to avoid warping the thin tubes yet securely anchor the ribs. Silvio noticed a subtle difference in the depth of blue finish between the monoblock and barrels along with a more obvious barrel/monoblock separation line. He felt that the latter should have been masked in a gun of this obvious quality. But it was a small point, and his overall opinion of the gun was very positive.

Subtle details abounded. For example, the forend hook soldered to the under barrel was less deep than usual. This allowed a shallow forend that was not only diminutive in keeping with the gun's scale but also allowed one's hand to be closer to the barrels for a better feel.

There is no point in discussing gunfit, as each stock is made to measure from "Select Quality 4" Turkish walnut. Exhibition wood is another $3,600. The wood on the show gun was heavily figured. It had strong straight grain through the head with good figure aft where it belonged. Wood-to-metal fit was excellent, with the wood just proud enough to allow a refinishing or two. Checkering was a simple borderless pattern, finely cut.

The finish was good but not perfect. A little bit of grain was not completely filled. The stock looked as though it might have been finished to a high gloss with something like Tru-Oil and then knocked down to a soft sheen with an abrasive. A slight streaking had not been buffed out. The inside of the forend showed a rough wood surface and was in stark contrast to the nicely finished interior forend metal. And that's the thing about handmade guns from small makers. You are buying a Ferrari, not a Honda. The occasional slip-up is all the more obvious by the beauty that surrounds it.

When you pay $20K for a gun, you expect functionality, but you also expect some glitz. Here the Dove Gun delivers in spades. It is simply gorgeous. Normally, I am one of those Philistines who couldn't care less about engraving. I've seen too many clumsy-looking guns all "scratched up" in a desperate attempt to make them look classy. It's like mixing Dr. Pepper and single-malt.

But this gun is different. The Dove Gun's delicious little rounded action accented by a Holland-style bolster would look nice enough

The Dove Gun's monoblock and ejectors seem to be much the same mechanical design as the Perazzi's.

lightly engraved, but it simply jumps with the 100-percent coverage offered as part of the package. Four different engraving motifs are offered: full deep ornamental, deep ornamental with oval game scene, double scroll with oval game scene, and full double scroll. Our test gun had the full deep ornamental, and it was very nice indeed.

The engraving is done by Accademia il Bulino, a group of 10 engravers led by Diego Bonsi. Cristina assured me that the engraving on the Dove Gun was all done by hand. It appeared to be of good quality, but understandably it was not as exquisite as that on some of FAMARS' much-higher-priced guns. Still, the engraving showed the gun to advantage and was actually quite a bargain when compared to similar embellishment from other makers.

SSM sponsored a "Have A Go" stand at the Southern Side-by-Side—this year a trap set to throw a single quartering-away target for those who wished to test-fire a gun they were considering. Vic Venters, two of his experienced shooting friends and I commandeered the Dove Gun, loaded up on ammo and proceeded with a much-abbreviated test.

Vic said that, in spite of its mere 6¼-pound weight, the Dove Gun had plenty of weight in the barrels but wasn't muzzle-heavy.

He thought it was just right. It was a lively gun that felt good in his hands. Vic's friend Peter Kolbe loved the look of the action. He felt that the Dove Gun was lighter and more responsive than his Browning 28. It fit him well, and he moved it to the target effortlessly and with great success. I don't remember him missing a target. Vic's other pal, Juan Marti, described the gun as feeling "like a little stick." It was lighter than anything he was used to, but he didn't feel that it was whippy.

I found the Dove Gun extremely responsive, requiring a different technique than when using a heavier gun. When I shot the target early with high gun speed and thus a good bit of upper-body inertia, things went very well. When I moved slowly and rode the bird a bit, it took a conscious effort to keep the gun going. A light gun does not move for you; you have to govern everything it does. The inertia of a heavier gun is like cruise control: It's sweet until something unexpected happens. Then the heavy gun becomes ponderous. The difference is not a question of good or bad; it is one of shooting technique and individual preference.

My personal dove gun is also a 32" 28-gauge, but it is built on the much heftier Perazzi MX8/20 action with heavier barrels. It handles

Cristina Abbiatico, President of FAMARS, pictured with the Dove Gun at the 2009 Southern Side-by-Side.

more like a light target gun than a game gun. For me, the FAMARS had somewhat the same weight-forward balance but, being 1¼ pounds lighter, it felt miniature. The show gun's barrels weighed 2 pounds 11.1 ounces. If I ordered one, I probably would have the barrels made with another ounce or so up front to add a touch more gravitas. But that's just me. Your mileage may vary.

An acquaintance of mine from New Orleans has a number of true scaled-action 28-gauge Perazzis. His weigh about what the Dove Gun does and are also long-barreled. He said that he had to relearn his shooting technique when coming from a heavier target gun, but once he did he found that he shot the lightweight 28s very well and came to prefer them.

Don Amos was kind enough to test the Dove Gun on his MOI turntable. Here's what he said: "I grabbed the Dove Gun off the rack and gave it a spin. In words, it is a lightweight gun with just slightly forward balance. It has swing efforts similar to a light pigeon gun a full pound heavier, and the weight is significantly disbursed from the center (not compact). It will be very light to lift and carry, and it will put a bit more of its weight in the front hand. The swings will require a bit more effort than a typical game gun, but will, in return, be more stable."

In short, the gun is quite light overall, but with some of the weight moved to the extremities, it shoots a bit more like a bigger gun. You will have to practice with it if you are accustomed to heavier target guns, but the potential is definitely there. If you are used to lightweight field guns, you will wallow in bliss.

Mechanically, the gun functioned correctly during our test. The ejectors were properly timed and quite vigorous. The gun gaped fully, and we didn't have to hold it open against spring pressure to insert a shell in the under barrel. The trigger pull could have used an extra touch or two from a stone but, to be fair, triggers on show guns aren't priorities. Our sample gun had classic-looking solid top and side ribs, but I would have picked the vent ribs all around for Argentina. The light, thin barrels combined with the solid ribs grew terribly hot after rapidly firing only a box of shells. When laying down a field of fire to defend yourself from a swarming horde of ravenous Argentine doves, a left-hand glove would be a must to avoid being branded. In just our little bit of testing, our barrels got so hot that the sliding forend release latch froze until things cooled down.

The FAMARS Dove Gun comes with a lifetime warranty on mechanical parts. Repairs are handled by the newly established FAMARS USA, in Rhode Island. The gun comes in a deluxe ABS case with accessories. The factory photos show extra leaf springs, firing pins and firing-pin springs plus five Thin Wall screw chokes if you choose the Brileys. FAMARS says that delivery time is four months.

This is clearly a heck of a gun. It is absolutely beautiful. Everyone commented on that. For $20,000 one expects a custom stock, nice wood and some other options, but the selection and quality of the engraving sets it apart from competition that is priced similarly. Fitting a removable trigger into such a tiny rounded action is a mechanical tour de force. The handling of the gun is more forgiving than its light weight would indicate.

Order the gun with vented top and side ribs, pack a heavy left-hand glove and head south to the land of endless doves. You'll enjoy this gun just as much when your friends genuflect to it as you will when the doves fall prey to its effortless lightning speed. The FAMARS Dove Gun is a functional work of art. Yes, you can have your caviar and eat it too.

Fausti Dea Round Body

They are "The Gun Sisters"—the shotgun industry's modern Dianas of the hunt. The three Fausti ladies run the Fausti Stefano Arms factory in the gunmakers' valley of Marcheno, Italy. They inherited the business from their father, Stefano, who founded it in 1948. Under the control of the sisters, the Fausti factory is a fully modernized, CNC-based, internationally marketed producer with about 40 employees.

Well known in Europe, Fausti's presence in the US has been variable until recently. In the past four years all that has changed. Fausti has opened its own US distributorship—Fausti USA—to market directly to retailers. The company continues as an OEM supplier, having replaced SKB in producing the over/unders and side-by-side shotguns for Weatherby. In the past Fausti made guns for Marlin (L.C. Smith) and for others in the US and English markets. Cabela's continues to carry a select line of Fausti O/U and side-by-side models. The latest side-by-side really caught my eye when I spoke to Giovanna and Barbara Fausti in the Cabela's booth at the Vintage Cup a few years ago.

It is called the Dea Round Body and, appropriately, "Dea" means "goddess" in Italian. Cabela's sells the Dea Round Body for $3,995 and currently stocks it in 20- and 16-gauge, 28", double-trigger versions with English stocks and splinter forends. Cabela's also handles the more-traditional-looking sideplated, non-rounded Fausti Dea SL boxlock side-by-side for about $1,000 less.

The Dea Round Body's scaled receiver is what catches your eye. As the name suggests, this Anson & Deeley boxlock is nicely rounded on the bottom edges. Fausti literature goes to lengths to say that this isn't just grinding off the sharp lower edges. The very action was built and redesigned to accept the rounded edges. As an interesting comparison to my 85-year-old 12-gauge Webley & Scott A&D action, the 20-gauge Dea's is actually a touch deeper in the water table but very much narrower thanks to its 20-gauge width. My guess is that the rounding of the Dea's receiver moved some of the internals in and up. You won't mistake the Dea rounded action for a Dickson, but the Dea Round Body certainly does have graceful lines and a comfortable one-hand carry.

Other than that, the action is pretty standard A&D. Inside, the

CNC machining is purposeful but not polished. There is no evidence of extensive handwork, but I have no issues with that as long as the gun works. The emphasis is on the outside, which mostly looks pretty good. I was surprised that our sample had faint machining marks on the front of the receiver shoulders where they mate with the forend iron. It is probably inconsequential, but you'd think that this one area would be baby-bottom smooth.

The manual safety is a simple trigger block. The hammers and firing pins are built as one unit. The firing-pin holes in the standing breech are not bushed, because failure of a firing pin will mean replacement of the entire hammer.

Hinge-pin employment is unique. There is a hinge-pin insertion/removal cap on the right side of the receiver but none on the left. Giovanna Fausti told me that "the hinge pin is not replaceable by the customers, but we have three different locking-bolt sizes for any problem connected to the wear of the gun after years of work."

The bottom action plate and triggerplate are one piece, unlike the two separate pieces in my Webley & Scott. The A&D action in the recent Robertson also used only one piece.

The automatic ejectors appear to be conventional Southgates but with a plus. There is a selector switch inside the forearm that converts the system from ejector to extractor with the turn of a lever. For some shooters this will be a convenience, but it is totally unnecessary for *SSM* readers, who already know how to keep our hunting fields pristine by catching and pocketing our empties . . . .

Although Fausti offers the Dea Round Body with a single trigger in foreign markets, the Cabela's guns all have double triggers. The blades are nicely cut, with the rear having a right-hand bias. The front trigger is not articulated, so you'll want to make sure your stock is long enough to avoid a dinged digit. Trigger pulls on our test gun were 6 pounds for the front and 5½ pounds for the rear. Both pulls were exceptionally crisp and free of creep.

Action lockup is by the conventional Purdey double underbolt. It works. It's proven. Everybody uses it. Case closed. The underbolt engages the two bottom lumps of the Fausti barrels' monoblock. As is often the case with A&D actions, one lump locks through the floorplate behind the hinge for additional strength.

Generally, metal joints on our gun were good. The bottom plate seam was well done. The monoblock seam was heavily engraved, but that's a stylistic decision, not a quality issue. The single locking lug that runs through the bottom plate wasn't as perfectly fitted as it could have been, though I'm sure it was adequate. The Browning Superposeds could give a lesson here.

Unlike the classic A&Ds, the Dea action has no visible screws on the outside. Three rounded solid pins on each side hold the internal bits in place. This gives the Dea's receiver a smooth look, especially compared to the 16 screw heads showing on the AyA 4/53 A&D boxlock.

The exterior of the action is silver. Fausti calls the coating Tecnifer. The result on the Dea Round Body is a classic silver coin finish that the company claims is highly resistant to rust.

The receiver engraving is a very fine rose & scroll with 100-percent coverage. It is applied by laser and, unlike some other examples of laser work, manages the curve of the rounded underbody quite well. Viewed through my unforgiving 10X loupe, the little laser craters and ridges were visible. Fausti said that the work was finish-

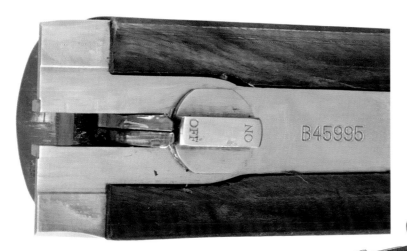

A selector switch in the forearm converts the system from ejector to extractor with the turn of a lever.

Outside, the barrels were free of ripples. The soldered ribs showed no quality holidays, and the barrels rang like wind chimes when struck. The dark medium-gloss bluing was well applied. The 11mm x 7mm tapered rib is flat and slightly raised in the European style. The top of the rib is machined to reduce glare. A simple steel bead adorns the front. The barrels weighed 2 pounds 8 ounces, an excellent light weight for 28" tubes with 3" chambers. Give thanks to those fixed chokes.

The Dea has a classic English stock and splinter forend. Dimensions are 14⁷⁄₈" x 1¹⁄₂" x 2³⁄₈" with a touch of right-hand cast. That's about as generic as you can get. The butt is

The Dea's action was redesigned to accept rounded edges.

chased by hand, but that was not obvious on our sample. The overall look of the engraving is a little hazy. Under the loupe, the definition is very clear, but to my naked eye some of it seemed to smudge together slightly in certain light. Perhaps that is the price of laser engraving that is so very fine. You'll have to judge for yourself when you see it.

The Dea Round Body's 28" barrels have 3" chambers and forcing cones that are longer than normal, in keeping with today's trends. The chokes are fixed, not screw-in. The right barrel on our test gun measured .625" with a Light Modified choke of .012". The left was .624" with a Light Full choke of .021". Nominal bore diameter for a 20 is .615", so these barrels were noticeably overbore. Both chokes were 3" long, including a short ³⁄₈" stabilizing parallel at the muzzle.

finished with a fancy figured wooden plate. It is a straight-line cut, so a pad could be added easily for extra length if needed. The stock was hollowed out as much as practicable to improve weight and balance.

Wood-to-metal fit on all exterior surfaces was quite good, with no gaps showing. The head of the stock and rear of the forend were just proud enough to allow a refinishing or two. This is as it should be. Inside the forend, the fitting of the Anson push-rod casing was a little rough on our sample, but you'd have to be some sort of anal-retentive gun reviewer to mention it. I did notice that the inside of the head of the stock did not have a protective coat of finish like the forend did. If it were my gun, I'd remedy that to prevent any oil soaking in the future.

The wood on our gun was nicely upgraded walnut—well and equally figured on both sides. It was a butterscotch color with a low-gloss hand-rubbed oil finish: very attractive. As on many other European guns, the wood pores were not completely filled. The checkering was excellent—too perfect to have been done by hand. Borders were correct, and there were no flat diamonds anywhere. My only slight aesthetic complaint was that the nose of the splinter forend was a little thicker than I like. That might be due to the extra wood support necessary because of the lack of a reinforcing metal escutcheon for the Anson push-button release. It's the same way on the RBLs.

Overall, the cosmetics of the gun are quite nice. The gun has a classic look. Nothing is out of place. Everything on the gun is steel or wood; no aluminum has crept in as it has on so many other new guns.

What comes in the box? Not much. In addition to the gun, you get some cloth sleeves for the stock and barrels, a very nice five-year warrantee, plus a generic manual. That's it. Well, not entirely. The "box" is actually a beautiful Negrini luggage case that wouldn't be out of place at the Plaza or on the *QE2*. Yes, it's sturdy ABS, but it looks as though it's trimmed in leather. Gorgeous. Negrini says it is suitable for air travel, but I wouldn't have the heart.

Sometimes you don't really need to shoot a gun to know what it will be like. You can just pick it up and tell that it will be good. This was one of those guns. At just under six pounds, the weight was ideal for an upland 20. Without the added weight of screw chokes and the thicker barrels they require, the tubes were properly balanced, giving the gun the neutral, lively feel so important for quick work in the field.

The grip area of the English stock was made with an oval cross-section. Although this may have been done to accommodate the draw bolt, it also lent a very welcome assist to the grip. This, along with the crisp and functional checkering, greatly contributed to a secure handhold when switching triggers.

Giovanna (left) and Barbara Fausti with the review gun at the 2008 Vintage Cup.

The stock dimensions were pretty much the 42 Regular of shotgunning. The RBL comes set up the same way. Personally, I like my side-by-sides set up a little higher than my over/unders, but that's just me.

The gun was an absolute delight to shoot once I figured it out. Side-by-side guns aren't aimers; they're pointers. I can try to be precise on long shots with an O/U but not with a side-by-side. When I tried to make sure of a shot with the Fausti, I often ended up disappointed because I lifted my head and stopped the gun. If you move the muzzles with the bird as you mount the gun and then fire as the stock touches your cheek, the Dea Round Body will shine. Being light and neutrally balanced, the gun has little inertia by itself. By bringing the weight of your arms and torso into the equation by swinging as you raise the gun, the Dea performs marvelously.

As to function, the ejector springs were a little uneven and threw different distances, but all else was fine. The triggers were a touch heavy, but they were so blessedly crisp that I hardly noticed. The manual safety was flawless, and that's important. And, no, I didn't try 3" shells in this lightweight gun. I'm sure that it can take them, but an ounce of shot from a 20 is plenty for me.

At $3,995, the Fausti Dea Round Body finds itself in a competitive market. It's priced in between the reliable, good-handling, but less-than-gorgeous AyA 4/53 A&D boxlock and the very nice Arrieta 557 and AyA No. 2 sidelocks. The Fausti is about the price of a well-optioned RBL 20 or Beretta's more industrial 471 Silver Pigeon boxlock.

The Fausti Dea Round Body holds its own among these competitors. The few flaws I found are more cosmetic than functional. The gun is beautifully balanced and handles delightfully under field conditions. A real effort has been made to make it attractive, with classic lines, nice wood and the rounded receiver. The Gun Sisters know what they're doing.

Franchi Veloce

I've always been leery of light guns, light beer and "lite" anything. Most shotguns less than six pounds feel whippy to me. I slash about and shoot them miserably. That's not true for everyone, of course. I have a pal at Ruger who is a marvel with a featherweight 28-gauge English side-by-side. He says he sort of pokes at the bird, rather than swings. I saw him take a triple on walked-up red grouse in Scotland—two with the first shot and one with the second. In expert hands, it can be done. In my hands the extremely light gun is usually the revenge of the PETAphiles and I go hungry.

Of course, I don't want a gun that balances like a nine-pound hammer just for the sake of stability, either. Some factory screw-choke 12-gauge guns have so much barrel weight that they ought to have an axle and a couple of wheels under the muzzle. We all want a field gun that's light to carry, smooth-shooting, good-looking and modestly priced. I may have found a candidate: Enter the aluminum-receiver Franchi Veloce 20-gauge over/under.

First some background: Franchi has been making shotguns in Italy's Brescia region since the 1860s. More recently the company has had a number of successful lightweight guns. In 1950 the first gun it sent to the US was the aluminum-framed, recoil-operated AL-48 autoloader. It's still in production. When I started hunting in the early '70s, I lusted after a ribless Falconet O/U with an aluminum receiver, certain that this would cure my ruffed grouse drought.

Beretta bought Franchi in the 1990s and changed the name from "Luigi Franchi" to "Franchi." The company is operated as a subdivision of Benelli, also owned by Beretta. Our O/U Veloce comes in 20 and 28 gauge, with either an English or pistol-grip stock. We tested 20-gauge versions in each stock style.

With a suggested price of $1,425 and retail reality a couple hundred less, Beretta is positioning the Veloce against the Weatherbys, Rugers and some of the Brownings. To prosper in this niche, the Veloce has been given an extra dose of glitz. If looks could kill, you'd have your limit every time with this gun. The Veloces I've seen have modestly upgraded wood with a good bit of figure under their subtle, real-oil finishes. The bright nickel-alloy receiver has decent-looking computer-generated "engraving." There's even a gold-washed ruffed grouse on one side and a quail on the other, in case you forget what the gun was intended for. The vented side ribs and finger-groove forend add more curb appeal. The opening lever is pierced and the right edge of the trigger guard rolled, just like the boutique guns. Even the sides of the monoblock and ejectors are jeweled. From five feet away it all looks smashing.

Under the makeup it's an honest gun. The aluminum-alloy receiver is bolstered by a stainless-steel insert dovetailed into the standing breech. The action is typical current CNC Italian, with steel Boss-type hinge stubs and a full-width steel Browning-type underlocking bolt. The rear of the receiver floor is recessed to accept two large locking lugs on the monoblock. This interface is steel to aluminum, but it's secondary; the main lock, of bolt to monoblock, is steel to steel.

The nickel-alloy receiver has a gold-washed ruffed grouse on one side and a quail on the other.

The interior of the action is very simple. Hammers are hinged on the triggerplate, whereas the sears hang down from the top strap. The hammers are driven by sturdy horizontal coil springs on guide rods. As befits a field gun, the safety is automatic, but it's operated by a wire that a gunsmith can disconnect easily. The safety/barrel selector is the familiar Browning U-pattern. The eight pins that hold the bits and pieces in place on the inside are nicely rounded solid

stainless steel, not some nasty roll pins. In all, the inside is a clean, modern design, presented well.

The triggers on our test guns were decent. One gun let off at $4^{1}/_{2}$ pounds and 5, the other at 5 and 6. I don't object to slightly heavy pulls on a field gun. A light pull is the danger when you stumble over that log. Besides, heavier triggers usually feel crisper. Both triggers certainly did feel crisp, and that's what counts. An additional bonus is that the triggers are mechanical, not inertia-operated, so you *always* get two tries.

Veloce O/U barrels have chrome bores, 3" chambers and abrupt forcing cones. Nominal bore diameter for a 20-gauge is .615", but one of our guns was .010" overbore and the other averaged .015" over. The chokes were no more consistent. Each of our two guns came with three flush-mounted chokes, lightly marked Cylinder, Improved Cylinder and Modified. The two Modified chokes varied by .008". With varying bores and chokes, it's almost impossible to know what you have unless you do your patterning homework. (Perhaps the factory should just stamp the chokes "More" and "Less.") The good news is that Franchi chokes use the Beretta/Benelli thread pitch, so replacements are available everywhere.

One of our test guns came with 26" barrels, the other with 27.5".

Both had ventilated side ribs for that racy look—"veloce" in Italian means "speed." Unfortunately, the vent side ribs also will collect rain, if you hunt in the wet. The top rib is narrow, ventilated and untapered. It's exactly what you would expect on a game gun. There's no useless middle bead, but the front bead is a large, white Bradley-style bead on a block. I found it very handy when shooting against dark-foliage backgrounds where a slender O/U barrel can become invisible.

Wood configuration was well suited to the guns' uses. Italian competition stocks tend to be clubby, but that country's makers understand field wood. Our stocks both measured about 14³/₈" x 1¹/₂" x 2", with 2" of pitch and slight cast-off. Sub-gauge guns often are stocked just a little higher than 12s. The Veloce dimensions suited a surprising number of shooters who tried the guns. The thin, hard-rubber recoil pad had a plastic insert at the top for friction-free mounting, but I'd grind off the sharp little toe on the bottom of the pad.

As mentioned, one of our guns had an English stock, whereas the other had a small, relaxed pistol grip. I slightly preferred the latter, but the English stock provided good right-hand control. The depth between the top and bottom receiver tangs is great enough to provide a deep oval cross-section at the wrist for good control. Stocks really come down to personal preference and aesthetics, but it's nice to have the choice. The forends on both guns were standard configurations with deep finger grooves. They're secure handles but not intrusive. Wood-to-metal fit was a little proud but adequate. The machine-cut checkering was perfectly fine, considering the price of the gun.

Our 26" English-stock Veloce weighed 5 pounds 9 ounces, whereas the 27¹/₂" pistol-grip gun weighed 2 oz more. That's more than a half-pound lighter than any steel 20 I hunt with. My two major concerns with any very light gun are recoil and whippy han-

dling. Bird season wasn't open when I did my testing, so I used the Veloces for FITASC, Five Stand, sporting clays and low-gun skeet targets. With standard ⁷/₈-oz target loads, free recoil came to about 18 foot-pounds. I'm no hero, but I easily shot 100 rounds per day with these shells. My more typical 6¹/₄-pound steel 20-gauge delivers about 16 foot-pounds with these shells.

As a very rough rule of thumb, calculated free recoil changes in a 1:1 percentage ratio with gun weight. If you lower gun weight 10 percent, you increase recoil more or less 10 percent. Changing the shell affects recoil even more than changing the gun weight. A shell velocity or payload change alters recoil in roughly a 2:1 ratio. Increasing the shot load from ⁷/₈ oz to 1 oz increased recoil in the Veloces to 23 foot-pounds. You wouldn't want to shoot targets all day with 1-oz loads in the Veloce, but for upland hunting these would be fine. In a masochistic effort to be thorough, I also ran some 3" 1¹/₄-oz No. 4 Remington Nitro Mags through the Franchis. Both the guns and I survived the 34 foot-pounds of recoil. That shell is occasionally usable but stout. Between you and the pheasant, the first one to get up wins.

What surprised me the most was that the handling of the Veloces was pretty standard. The use of alloy receivers had removed almost ³/₄ of a pound, but it was from the middle; the barrels and butts were normal weight. In addition, the factory screw chokes added an ounce or so right under the bead. The longer barrels added a bit more than another ounce. If these light guns had been center-weighted, like so many English doubles, they would have been whippy. With more of their weight at the extremities, however, they had the feel of regular 20s that just happened to be light.

My clay scores were about the same as I shoot with my heavier FN B25 28" 20. The Veloces were quicker-handling, but they weren't at all twitchy. I didn't even have to cheat by moving my left hand farther forward to artificially increase stability. The lighter carry weight is certainly noticeable. The English-stock Veloce with the shorter barrels was definitely faster than the longer pistol-grip gun. If you poke and pray in heavy cover when you hunt, you'd probably prefer the shorter setup. The longer barrels and pistol grip seemed to make for a slightly better all-around gun, with the balance point a bit farther forward. You can always get aftermarket extended chokes to increase muzzle bias if you wish.

The Veloce is a bargain at less than $1,500. It comes with a three-year parts guarantee. It's packed in a practical plastic takedown case with a pull-through cleaning gizmo, some oil, a decent choke wrench and three chokes. The gun definitely has upgraded exterior cosmetics, and the mechanicals are clean and solid; it does the job and looks the part. Alloy-receiver guns are more popular in Europe than they are in the US, but we're learning. If your gun doubles in weight from morning to evening and your last mile back

Modestly priced, Franchi's Veloce is a bargain for shooters looking for a lightweight over/under game gun.

to the car is always uphill, the Franchi Veloce will lighten everything except your game bag—and your wallet.

Update

The Franchi Veloce was imported from 2001 to 2005. The review was written early in 2003. The guns were fairly popular, so they ought to show up in the used market from time to time. Today the Veloce is still in production, but it has been placed on a pedestal. It is now called the Veloce SP and is part of the Benelli USA World Class Collection of upgraded guns.

Benelli, a division of Beretta, markets Franchi as well as Stoeger and A. Uberti.

The current Veloce SP differs from our reviewed Veloce in cosmetics and its $2,889 price but not in mechanics. The Veloce SP's aluminum receiver has been adorned with sideplates showing high-relief engraving setting off gold gamebirds and a pointer. The wood is also upgraded. The gun is now available only in 20 gauge with 26" barrels and a round-knob stock. But the good life hasn't chubbed it up, as it is advertised at a svelte 5$\frac{1}{2}$ pounds.

Grulla 217RB

❦

Grulla Armas is in the gun-making city of Eibar, in the mountainous northern Basque country of Spain. It started in 1932 as a group of a half-dozen gunsmiths calling themselves Union Armera. They made decent guns but weren't well known outside Spain. A few years ago I borrowed a pair of old Union Armeras when shooting driven partridge in La Mancha. Those were nice, workmanlike sidelocks that obviously had seen a tremendous amount of use, but they held up well during my stint.

In the mid-'80s, with most of the original founders gone, the company was sold to its workers under the directorship of José Luis Usobiaga. It was moved to a larger building in town and its name changed to Grulla Armas. "Grulla" is Spanish for "crane," and the bird had been the company's logo for some time. With the market for better Spanish guns improving, Grulla dropped its boxlock lines and concentrated solely on sidelocks, increasing quality and price as the market permitted. When this review was written in 2003, Grulla's dozen workers made around 250 guns plus a half-dozen

double rifles per year. For a full history of Grulla and other Spanish gunmakers, I strongly recommend Terry Wieland's definitive book *Spanish Best* (Countrysport Press, 2001).

Grulla markets Holland & Holland-pattern sidelocks in three levels. The basic guns are standard H&H-type actions with various embellishments as requested by dealers. Prices varied with the extras each importer wished to include. In 2003 prices were typically $3,500 to $4,500. The mid-range H&H-style assisted-openers sold for around $6,500, and the Royal grades, with top-of-the-line wood, finishing and engraving, cost twice that. That was then. Prices have doubled in the succeeding eight years.

Our review gun was the Grulla Model 217RB as specially made for Hi-Grade Imports. In 2003 it cost $3,898. By 2011 the price had doubled to $7,650. Blame a euro/dollar premium, inflation, an uncertain world economy or whatever, but there it is.

Also in that time period, Grulla's distributing retailers changed. Hi-Grade stopped carrying Grullas, and hence its custom-ordered 217RB version ceased. The Grulla line began to be carried by the distributors of Merkel. No more 217RB, but the very similar 216RB model was available. In 2011 things came full circle, and Hi-Grade Imports once again became a Grulla representative and its 217RB has resurfaced.

The 217RB has the basic H&H-type sidelock action, but it is "rounded" in the Boss style. Thus the "RB" for "rounded body." The bar smoothly melts into the hinge area, whereas the backs of the sidelocks flow seamlessly into the head of the stock, sans drop points. The underside of the action is slightly radiused but not nearly so much as with a true round-action.

I just love this treatment compared to the more traditional flat sidelock. You can close your eyes and run your hands over the Grulla without feeling any harsh angles. Everything blends. The hand fits naturally around the smooth receiver when carrying. Visually, I've never fully appreciated the juxtaposition of flat sidelocks and hard edges with the other curved parts of the classic game gun. Still, Grulla

Grulla sidelocks are based on H&H-type actions and come in a variety of models and grades. The 217RB has a round-bodied action.

makes guns both ways, so you can have what pleases you.

The locks of the 217RB action are made in the six-pin Holland style. H&H-type actions are by far the most copied because they work well, are durable and are easier to make to various quality standards than the fussier Beesley/Purdey system. This Grulla action is very nicely done. It's made from drop-forged steel. The only coil spring I saw was for a plunger in the intercepting-sear mechanism. All interior parts are machined and highly polished, with no tool marks visible. The insides of the lockplates are engine-turned. This gun did not come with hand-detachable locks, though I suppose you could

easily order a lever-head instead of a slot-head bolt. The intended anonymity makes the interior work even more impressive.

The trigger-block safety is automatic, with a nice raised bump on the top of the checkered catch. The front trigger is hinged for a little less digital abuse. Trigger pulls on our gun measured 2½ pounds in front, with no take-up or creep and just a hint of lateral play. The rear was 3½ pounds with no take-up, a bit of creep and no lateral play. I'd rate the triggers very good and a sure sign of extra shop time on someone's part.

The receiver has lots of little extras. The trigger guard has a rolled right edge. The firing pins are bushed, with gas escape valves on the fences. Trigger blades are gracefully cut. The "S," for "safety," and the cocking indicators are gold-lined. The fences are arcaded. The water table, barrel flats and lump bottoms are engine-turned. There were almost no quality holidays that I could spot. Even the awkward place where the back end of the under-rib butts into the barrel flats was fairly well finished.

Our 28" chopper-lump barrels reflected the quality of the action. Hot-blued a flawless glossy blue-black, they were nicely struck. The traditional swamped English game rib was unengraved, unobtrusive and fit neatly. There was the slightest possible indication of solder blush on one side of the top rib, but I had to use a magnifying glass to find it. These guns are proofed for modern loads at 900 BARs (about 13,000 psi), and the importer says the chromed barrels will handle steel shot up to a Modified choke. The chambers are 2¾" and the forcing cones traditionally abrupt, a possible advantage if using fiber wads.

Oh, did I mention our review gun was a 16-gauge? In medium to expensive side-by-side guns, at the time of our test Hi-Grade reported that the 20-gauge was the biggest seller, followed by the 16, then by the 28 and finally the 12. I guess that by the time someone arrives at this price category he already has most of the basic stuff and is seeking to fill in the gaps.

The test 217RB arrived with a classic straight English stock and splinter forend. You can custom-order any dimensions you want, and I'm sure that Grulla will accommodate pistol grips and beavertails if you wish. I was told that the wait for an ordered 217RB is four months. That's a good bit faster than some of the other makers.

The wood is properly oil-finished. You can shine it up with a therapeutic drop of linseed as you sit by the fire after a day's hunt. Our walnut was well figured but not quite equally grained on both sides. Still, it was nice, and Grulla is obviously trying to sate America's penchant for highly figured wood. The hand-cut checkering was appropriately fine but did show some faint overruns and blunt diamonds when examined very closely. The checkered butt was in perfect keeping with the looks of the gun and its field usage.

Little extra details abound. The metal escutcheon guiding the Anson pushrod at the tip of the forend is complex and requires meticulous inletting. The forend iron, held in place with simple wood screws on some Spanish guns, uses a sturdy through-bolt to

a slender engraved plate. The intricate inletting inside the head of the stock was perfectly done, with just enough wood removed to clear each functioning part. However, I was surprised that the wood inside hadn't received a protective coat of finish. If it were my gun, I'd take the 10 minutes to remedy that.

Wood-to-metal fit was first rate. Everything mated correctly, including the heading-up of the four stock horns and the sides of the very long lower tang. If there is an inletting failure or proud wood on a sidelock, it usually seems to be where the lower two stock horns abut the bottom of the receiver on either side of the trigger. Our gun was good here and elsewhere. The metal-to-wood fit of the slightly rounded sidelocks was flawless. I could run my hand along the sidelocks and, if it hadn't been for the engraving, hardly feel the transition to wood.

The 217RB was hand-engraved, not roll-engraved, with 100-percent coverage in a shallow rose & scroll pattern. The cutting was evenly executed. (I checked with a 10X loupe.) My impression is that the gun was engraved, and then the parts were hardened and the case coloring was polished to produce the bright coin finish this particular gun had. I'm sure that there are other engraving choices, depending on your preference and pocketbook.

The balance of this gun was spot on the hinge pin, as befits a field gun. In spite of this, the gun felt surprisingly stable, as though it carried just a little more weight at each end. It wasn't at all whippy, yet it was lively. It weighed just less than 6½ pounds on my electronic scale. That's a nice weight for a 16-gauge, though I have seen some lighter. I was told that the Grulla 16 is built on a receiver

The lockwork on our test gun exhibited excellent quality and finishing.

scaled to gauge, but darned if it didn't measure the same as a 20's from firing pin to firing pin and across the shoulders. All together the gun felt "of a piece." The weight, the dynamics and the looks were all in harmony.

You can tell a lot about the way a gun will handle just by waving it around, but you must shoot it a good bit to know for sure. I do most of my testing on clay targets because I simply can't put enough rounds through a gun in the field to form an opinion. Besides, it's another excuse to shoot more. I don't bother with pattern testing because you can order these guns with any chokes you want. I do test for barrel convergence. That's the ability of the gun to shoot both barrels to the same point of impact. Our Grulla was just fine.

After subjecting myself to unnecessarily brisk 1¹/₈-oz loads, I tracked down some more congenial 1-oz shells. That's really the ideal load for the 16. They were comfortable and effective. After a flat of ammo, the Grulla still worked perfectly. There were no failures, no hiccups, no nothing. OK, the auto safety was a touch stiffer than I would have liked, but that was it. The gun moved quickly without being precipitous. It was the kind of gun that was easy to shoot well. It was light for carrying but not too light for shooting comfort and stability. In this respect it had a slightly more Italian feel than British. I can understand why 16-gauge devotees are so enthusiastic.

As usual, I went on the Internet and solicited opinions from current Grulla owners. I was surprised at the number of responses, all favorable. Typical comments were, "Grade for grade, it seems just a little nicer than my other Spanish guns" and "I believe you get more with Grulla for the money." No owner reported any mechanical problems. These were happy campers.

Overall I was favorably impressed with the Grulla 217RB. It is priced about midway between AyA's Model 1 and Model 2 rounded-action guns and about the same as Arrieta's mid-level 871. It is not the bargain it used to be, but it is well made and definitely competitive at its price level. It's nice to see the Grulla crane flying high again.

Huglu Side-by-Side

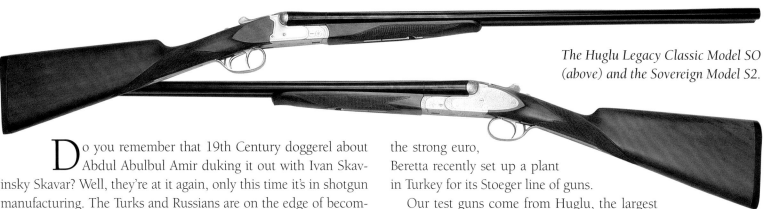

The Huglu Legacy Classic Model SO (above) and the Sovereign Model S2.

Do you remember that 19th Century doggerel about Abdul Abulbul Amir duking it out with Ivan Skavinsky Skavar? Well, they're at it again, only this time it's in shotgun manufacturing. The Turks and Russians are on the edge of becoming serious players at the less-expensive end of the market. Low-cost Russian Baikal shotguns currently are being imported by European American Armory Corp., Savage/Stevens and Remington/Spartan. The Turks are sending us Huglu (pronounced "Hoo-loo") guns through Huglu Armsco and Mark DeHaan Shotguns. This expansion into the US and other international markets has many European gunmakers worried. Within the past year, one fairly large Italian producer told me that he intended to stop production of his basic $1,500 guns to concentrate on his pricier models. He said that he couldn't compete at the low end with the quality of the guns that are and will be coming from Russia and especially Turkey. Even giant Beretta is being affected. In an effort to escape the cost structure imposed by the strong euro, Beretta recently set up a plant in Turkey for its Stoeger line of guns.

Our test guns come from Huglu, the largest sporting arms producer in Turkey. Huglu is a cooperative located in a town of the same name in the Taurus Mountains of southwestern Turkey. I read that the town of 3,500 has no restaurants or hotels, but it does have a clay target range. So much for priorities. From a modest two-man shop started during World War I, the gun trade in the town has expanded today to a modern CNC-driven 100,000-square-foot factory surrounded by hundreds of cooperative members doing outwork in home shops. Huglu production is around 50,000 shotguns per year and includes over/unders, side-by-sides, autoloaders and single-shots.

Previously, Huglu's road had been a little rocky. Building to a (low) price, quality often suffered. In past years many Huglus brought home by our servicemen after duty with our NATO ally were not of high quality. Some of the guns exported directly to the US some years ago were better but still not good enough. This was especially true of the single triggers, particularly on some side-by-side models. ("Double" is supposed to refer to the number of barrels, not what happens when you pull the trigger.) But things change. Modern CNC machinery, higher production standards and more-demanding US importers have changed the picture.

As mentioned, these days Huglus are being imported by Huglu Armsco and DeHaan Shotguns. Our test guns were provided by Mark DeHaan, who has his own line of guns and deals directly with Huglu. In addition to five O/U models, DeHaan stocks two side-by-sides. I had him send me one of each of the side-bys. The Legacy Classic Model SO is the base-model boxlock with an English stock, splinter forend, double triggers, extractors, 15-percent engraving coverage, and screw chokes in the 12-, 20- and 28-gauge guns. The .410 and 16 have fixed chokes. I got this gun in a 28" 28-gauge version. The Sovereign Model S2 is the same except for false sideplates, more scroll engraving and a single trigger. The S2 comes in a 28" 20-gauge version. Sixteen-gauge fans take note: Both models come with proportionately sized receivers for all five gauges. In addition to the standard SO and S2 models, DeHaan offers a custom SGr Deluxe side-by-side or O/U series built to your specifications, with high-grade engraving, wood and finishing but not ejectors.

The actions on our test guns were typical Anson & Deeley boxlocks. When I pulled the stock on the 28 to look inside, I thought the company had forgotten some parts. Extractor guns are like that. All you see are the two long wire springs for the trigger-blocking safety detent, the flat spring for the opening lever and the two long sear lever bars riding above the double triggers. You can just glimpse the rears of the hammers. The leaf hammer springs are out of sight in the action body. I can't conceive of anything simpler.

Two cross pins through the action locate the hammers and mainsprings. In typical A&D style, there are two screws securing the bottom plate for lock access. Like the archetype Webley & Scott A&D, the hinge pin is built in and not replaceable. Eventually, your grandchildren may have to TIG or dovetail the hook to snug it up.

Workmanship is basic but perfectly fine. The receiver is CNC machined from a block of steel. There were some faint tool marks on the inside but no more than I typically see on an old Model 21 or Superposed. The opening lever and safety switch appear to be cast. The cast checkering on the opening-lever handle wasn't very sharp. All of the other parts appear to be machined. I have no idea how hard the metal on the sears and hammers is, but I saw nothing to indicate any undue softness when I examined things after my test period.

These actions have more locks than a chastity belt. On the 12s, 16s and 20s there's a Greener crossbolt plus Purdey double underbolts plus a single barrel lug through the bottom of the receiver plus sideclips. The 28s and .410s skip the crossbolt but have the rest. Our test guns locked up like vaults and had no slop when hung open.

The triggers on both guns were heavier and had more creep than I like, but they weren't too bad. I'd invest in trigger jobs if they were mine. On the plus side the triggers worked reliably. I expect that from double triggers, but single triggers on many side-by-sides can be problematic—and, as mentioned, those on the early Huglus were no exceptions. The mechanical single trigger on my Model S2 20-gauge worked perfectly, so maybe that genie is back in the bottle.

The barrels on the DeHaan Huglus are monoblocked in the conventional manner. There's an engraved line disguising—but not hiding—the monoblock/barrel seam. The barrel flats and lumps are well machined but not polished. The always awkward underpart between the forend hook and the monoblock was nicely polished and far cleaner than I've seen on many more expensive side-by-sides. The bluing was deep, bright and quite well done, with some slight carding lines showing only on the sides of the rib. A flat matte finish is also available. The rib is the raised flat type reminiscent of many American side-by-sides. The top of the rib has the appropriate glare-reducing matting machined on it. There's a single stainless bead at the muzzle.

Held up to the light, the chrome-lined bores appear correct, but the outside of the barrels showed the slightest amount of waviness. I had to look hard, but it was there. Far more noticeable is the swelling of the muzzles where the screw chokes are accommodated. I didn't find it objectionable, but you certainly notice it. Ruger went to great trouble and expense to eliminate this bulging on its side-by-side Golds by using Briley Thinwall chokes. Huglu took the less-expensive route with thicker screw chokes and jugged barrels.

The screw chokes in the 20- and 28-gauge were similar in appearance to Beretta Mobil chokes, but they aren't interchangeable with Mobil chokes. My test guns came with five chokes. They were marked with 5, 4, 3, 2 and 1 rim notches but no writing. The manual said that the notches corresponded to Cylinder Bore, Improved Cylinder, Modified, Improved Modified and Full constrictions. In the 28 the chokes had correct dimensions, and the bore size was spot-on at .550". In the 20 the bore was .620" instead of the nominal .615", yet the chokes were more open than indicated.

The wood on the test guns was plain walnut with a subdued straight grain. Yes, it's Turkish. No, it's not fancy. DeHaan told me that the wood on the test guns was somewhat plainer than what usually comes through. Wood-to-metal fit was very nice, especially in the critical areas of the top and bottom tangs. Checkering was hand-cut. It was quite good on the 20 and adequate on the 28. I was told that the wood finish is an oil/urethane blend that is hand-finished. It's a non-glare matte and fully fills the pores. Like the

finishes on many Japanese shotguns, it's a bit muddier than I'd like and there needn't be quite so much finish in the checkering, but it's all quite acceptable.

As mentioned, the base DeHaan SO model comes with an English stock, and there is a $1/2$" rubber butt pad with a plastic horseshoe insert at the top. The sideplated S2 is available with either an English stock or Prince of Wales grip. The forends on both are splinters with the slightest hint of a Schnabel tip. The forend is held on with a well-fitted Deeley pull-down latch. Both forends on our guns were tight with no slop. The stocks are attached with the European-style drawbolt rather than the English-style vertical bolt between the tangs. Stock measurements for both guns were $14^3/8$" x $1^1/2$" x $2^3/8$" with about $1/4$" cast-off at the toe and 3" of pitch.

All of the engraving is done by hand. Rare among the builders of inexpensive guns, Huglu has refrained from covering the receivers with acres of tacky-looking roll-engraved scenes. The modest border engraving on the basic SO model is restrained and, if not elegant, in subdued good taste. The more ornate engraving of the sideplated S2 is an open Arabesque scroll done in a shallow cut. The Huglu double-eagle crest on the top of the S2's opening lever is less successful in its execution.

Speaking of less success, the major visual drawback to both guns is the matte-chrome receiver finish. It looks like silver Rustoleum was sprayed on. I'm sure it is very durable, but all who saw it felt that it was unattractive and cheap-looking. The blued or case-colored receivers offered on some of the O/Us would be so much nicer. On the plus side, if this is your rainy-day gun, it sure won't rust.

Mechanics and cosmetics aside, it's the weight and balance that make or break a field gun. Everything else is really secondary. The balance, feel and handling of the DeHaan SO 28 are exceptional. At 5 pounds 10 ounces, the little 28 is well served by some weight forward to avoid being whippy. The balance point is about 1" in front of the pin, and the weight is distributed evenly along the barrels. I think that the little bit of extra weight from the screw chokes is a plus in a gun this light. This Huglu was one of the best-handling 28 side-by-sides I've ever used. It is rare that a featherweight gun handles this smoothly.

At 6 pounds 10 ounces, the 28" 20-gauge is more of a handful. Like the 28, it also balances 1" in front of the pin, but it feels very much more nose-heavy. It weighs a full pound more than the 28, and it feels as though that weight is all in the barrels. I have no explanation for the same balance point yet radically different feel for the two guns other than the difference in total weight. I even tried waving the gun about without the 1.2 oz of screw chokes installed, but it still had more weight up front than I want in a 20-gauge field gun. It was noticeably more weight-forward than the 20-gauge Beretta 470, A&F Zoli/Rizzini, Webley & Scott and Sauer I compared it to. That said, the DeHaan S2 20 was extremely

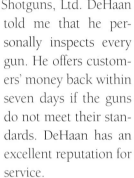

easy to shoot on clays. With a weight-forward bias, it had a nice swing and follow through. For hunting it's a bit slower than I'd like for grouse or quail. For wild pheasants, where there is a little more time and heavier loads are useful, it might be very nice indeed.

Both guns were completely reliable with all types of ammunition. Barrel convergence seemed correct, and points of impact were 50/50, flat along the ribs. The heavy triggers weren't great, but I could live with them. The manual safeties worked crisply and were easy to operate. The extractors were no handicap. Besides, if you use your DeHaan garniture at Studley Royal, it will be the loader's concern, not yours. The absolutely perfect balance of the 28 made it a delight to shoot. The weight-forward bias of the 20 made it easier on clays than it would be on short-range jinking gamebirds.

The gun packages come with the five chokes, an instruction manual and a two-year guarantee. They are sold directly by DeHaan Shotguns, Ltd. DeHaan told me that he personally inspects every gun. He offers customers' money back within seven days if the guns do not meet their standards. DeHaan has an excellent reputation for service.

The sideplated S2 has hand-engraved Arabesque scroll and Huglu's double-eagle crest atop the opening lever.

Oh, yes, the price. The double-trigger base-grade DeHaan SO is $640 in 12, 16 and 20 gauge, $795 in 28 (our test gun) and .410. The fancier sideplated single-trigger DeHaan S2 is $795 in 12, 16 and 20 (our other test gun) and $995 in 28 and .410. At these prices, the guns are amazing values for the quality and performance delivered. It's no wonder that Spanish and Italian makers are looking over their shoulders.

Update

Things change but still remain the same. This Huglu review was written in early 2005. Since then there is new distribution, but the

Turkish Huglu remains. Stronger than ever, too. In late 2005 Huglu's main gun sales were assumed by CZ-USA; www.cz-usa.com. The company carries the broad line of Huglu's O/Us, side-by-sides and autoloaders. The names are different and so are the current prices, but the guns reviewed remain in the lineup. Mark DeHaan's Website, www.dhshotguns.com, lists his line of SGr Deluxe model Huglu sideplated O/Us made to custom order. DeHaan also offers service and repairs to all Huglus.

Ithaca Model 37 Featherlight 28

The Ithaca Model 37 Featherlight 28 (above) and the Ithaca Model 37 Grade AAA 28.

I just love pumpguns. They are so participatory. So very American. So macho. Popular, too. The pump is the largest-selling shotgun action in the US. Mind you, I have nothing against the less physically demanding actions, but watching someone really handle a pump brings an extra something to our sport. For the most part, pumps are inexpensive, reliable and extraordinarily durable. The better pumps can be made to balance quite well. They are virtually maintenance-free, and they function in the worst possible weather conditions.

When we think of classic pumpguns, it is usually of Winchester Model 12s and 42s, Remington 870s and Ithaca Model 37s. The Ithaca M37 has been around since 1937, and it had an interesting start. John Browning may not have invented water or fire, but in the

gun world he might as well have. The Ithaca Model 37 was mostly one of his.

In 1913 Browning filed for patent protection on a new bottom-loading, bottom-ejecting pumpgun. He sold the rights to Remington, which named it the Model 17 but didn't start production until 1921. In the intervening time, Remington inventor John Pedersen patented some improvements to the design. Remember Pedersen? He was the one whose "Pedersen Device" converted the 1903 Springfield bolt-action military rifle to a semi-auto. He also invented the .276 Pedersen cartridge, which almost replaced the .30-06. Remington sold 73,000 Model 17s before production ended in 1933, when the company went to the new side-ejecting Model 31 pump.

Ithaca was looking for a pump about then. The company intended to introduce a slightly modified Model 17 as the Ithaca Model 33 when the Browning patents expired in 1933. When Ithaca learned about the additional Pedersen patents, it held off until those expired in 1937. The Ithaca Model 37 has been in production ever since, longer than the run of the Winchester Model 12 or Remington 870.

But Ithaca's road hasn't been without its detours. Founded in 1883, the company changed hands in 1967, 1987, 1996, 2005 and 2007. In 1987 Ithaca Acquisition, Inc., changed the name of the Model 37 to the Model 87. In 1997 Ithaca Gun Company, LLC, changed it back. Today the new Ithaca Gun Company, Inc., located in Sandusky, Ohio, owns the rights and continues the manufacture of the Model 37 on modern computerized machinery.

The company currently produces M37 pumpguns in numerous configurations. There is a short-barreled ribless Defense model plus two Deerslayer slug guns—one for a scope and one for iron sights. For bird hunters the company makes the Model 37 in 12 and 20 gauge with either Featherlight steel or Ultralight aluminum receivers. There are also Trap, Waterfowl, Turkey and shorter-stocked Ladies' versions.

Our review gun was introduced at the 2009 SHOT Show as the latest addition to the line: the 28-gauge Model 37 Featherlight. It is the first 28-gauge in M37 history. It has a true 28-gauge-sized receiver that, according to Ithaca COO Mike Farrell, has no parts interchangeable with the 20-gauge receiver. Ithaca says that each M37 Featherlight 28 is made to order, with a delivery time of four to six weeks. It comes in three grades. The A grade, with plain wood and modest machine engraving, costs $999. The AA grade has nicer wood and full-coverage, hand-chased engraving for $1,589. The AAA version has full fancy wood and full-coverage hand-chased engraving with gold inlays for $3,499. We were sent three test guns, all A grades, but one had upgraded wood.

The 28-gauge Featherlight receiver is solid steel machined from a single billet. Other than the brass front bead, recoil pad, plastic butt cap and magazine plug, I couldn't find any part on the gun that wasn't walnut or steel. The action appears identical in function, if not in size, to those of earlier 37s. It is bottom loading and bottom ejecting, lacking the customary side port that most other pumps have. Lefties and the usual duck blind "peltees" on the right can rejoice.

Mechanically, the gun is intriguing. The M37 shell carrier has two spring-steel prongs. They rest at the top of the action on either side of the bolt when the gun is in battery. After firing, the pump stroke pulls back the bolt. The dual extractor claws on the bolt engage the rim of the fired shell and extract the hull from the chamber. As the hull comes free, the split carrier prongs sweep downward, ejecting the hull out the bottom of the receiver. The action is timed so that the loaded round in the magazine is released just as the carrier bottoms out below the magazine. The magazine spring pushes the new shell out and it is cradled between the two carrier prongs. Pushing the forend forward sweeps the carrier and shell upward to the entrance of the chamber, where the closing bolt pushes it home. This process has been working well for more than 70 years, but it does require properly regulated timing.

The M37, like the Winchester Models 12 and 42, uses a single action bar. Remington uses two, claiming less binding. In practice, I found the M37 smoother than the recent 870s I've tried, though not as smooth as my well-worn Winchesters.

The triggers on the three sample guns varied. One had a 2- to 3-pound pull, which is much too light for a pumpgun. One was $4^1/2$ to 5 pounds, and the other a touch heavier at $4^3/4$ to $6^1/4$ pounds. These last two felt about right. All were marvelously crisp with no take-up and almost no overtravel. The trigger-blocking safety in the rear of the trigger guard was a little sticky but worked correctly.

M37 28-gauge barrels come in 26" or 28" lengths, and an extra barrel costs $249. The barrels are heralded as "solderless." The rib supports are machined integrally with the barrel tube, not soldered on. Ithaca claims that this method avoids the heat warpage common to soldered rib posts. The rib slides over the posts and is held on with a single Torx bolt about 6" from the receiver and by a stop at the muzzle. The flat, steel, $^9/_{32}$"-wide untapered rib has an upper surface machined to eliminate glare. At the muzzle you can choose a simple brass bead or Ithaca's own $^1/_2$" red glowworm.

Ithaca claims "lengthened forcing cones to reduce recoil and shot deformation." When I measured them against the Connecticut Shotgun RBL 28 and the Perazzi 28, I did, indeed, find the M37 cones to be about $1^3/_8$", a good $^1/_2$" longer than the Perazzi's and RBL's.

The M37 barrel is attached by inserting it into the receiver and giving it a quarter-turn to engage $^1/_2$" of machined receiver threads. This secure mounting is required because the bolt locks into a notch in the top of the receiver, not into a notch in a barrel extension as on the 870. The Winchester M42 uses somewhat the same approach as the 37, but it has the advantage of a replaceable threaded section that can adjust for wear.

The M37 28 comes with three Briley screw chokes designated Improved Cylinder, Modified and Full. A Skeet choke is available but not included. The chokes are 2" long, with the designation notched on the rim and printed on the body. All were conical to about $^1/_2$" of parallel at the muzzle. I measured three sets of chokes, and they were very consistent, more so than the barrels. One barrel bore was .548" and jibed perfectly with the chokes to provide nominally correct constrictions. The other barrel IDs were .005" larger, making all the chokes about one designation tighter than their markings. The chokes threaded into the barrels very smoothly but, when seated, all protruded about $^1/_{64}$" for an odd cosmetic effect.

The stocks on our three guns all measured $13^7/_8$" x $1^5/_8$" x $2^1/_4$", though Ithaca's own Website claims 14" x $1^1/_2$" x $2^3/_8$". The test stocks had no cast and very little pitch. Although this height is about "average American production gun," the length is short by today's standards and even shorter than the $14^1/_4$" listed for the 12- and 20-gauge Featherlights. However, the large, fairly tight pistol grip moves the hand forward and makes the

The minimal machined engraving on A-grade guns is a restrained scroll pattern.

stock seem a touch longer than it is. The butt is finished with a black 1" Pachmayr Decelerator pad. The pad was efficient but sticky, and it was not particularly well fitted on any of the guns. It appears that the pad is compressed during the grinding process and then puffs out slightly when finished.

Wood-to-metal on the guns was fine at the stock/receiver joint but a touch too proud on the forends. The 10 lpi mechanical checkering was borderless, simple, clean and correct. The stock finish appears to be a matte synthetic with an appropriate stain and complete filling of the grain. Farrell said that surface nicks were easily repaired.

The wood figure on our first two A-grade samples was quite plain. As mentioned, the higher AA and AAA grades get fancier wood. One nice thing is that you can order your Grade A with the upgraded wood used on the AA and AAA guns for an extra $175 and $350. Our third A-grade had the fancier walnut, and it transformed the gun. Get the glitzy wood. You deserve it.

The forend on the M37 is a relatively tiny 6" in length. That's even shorter than those on the original Winchester 12s and 42s and a good bit shorter than the extended forends on the 870s. The short length forces the left hand to stretch quite far forward. Some will find this uncomfortable; some won't notice. It is a matter of personal preference, but that's the way the 37 has been doing it for more than 70 years.

The engraving on our A-grade guns was appropriate for the price. The minimal machined receiver engraving was in a restrained, tasteful scroll pattern. The AA grade has upgraded wood plus distinct full-coverage woodland hunting scenes with a setter and flushing birds on each side of its blued receiver. The AAA grade has full fancy wood and the same engraved scene, but with the dogs and birds in 24-karat-gold. Farrell said that he and CEO David Dlubak told master engraver Bill Mains, "Do anything you want. Just get our dogs on there."

The sides of our A-grade receivers were medium-gloss blue, whereas the top was an anti-glare matte blue. The gold-colored trigger inside the dainty trigger guard was a nice touch, as was the engine turning of the cast-metal slide inside the action. The medium blue of the barrel set off the matte low-glare rib. However, when held to the light, the outside of all of the test barrels were anything but smooth, clearly showing machining waves under each of the integral rib posts.

The Model 37 28-gauge Featherlight package includes the aforementioned three screw chokes, a flat stamped choke wrench, a Torx wrench for rib removal, a separate Hoppe's trigger lock, a magazine plug to reduce capacity from four to two, a one-year guarantee and the most basic two-page manual I've ever seen.

The shooting performance of the M37 28-gauge was interesting. The first two guns we were sent didn't work. The timing was off on both but in different ways. One would eject the fired hull and the second cartridge at the same time. The other usually would fail to fully eject the fired hull. Farrell said that he was aware of these issues on some guns and that it was due to slightly incorrect parts sizing from outside suppliers. The third gun we were sent functioned perfectly.

Frankly, I would not be too concerned about these issues, as there is always a bobble or two in a new production gun. The design is proven beyond a shadow of a doubt—and there *is* that one-year warranty.

The third gun was everything you could ask for mechanically. The action was slick and fast. It does have a disconnector, meaning that you can't just hold the trigger back and pump the way you can on a Winchester Model 42. Still, it doesn't hinder quick pumping the way the disconnector on the Browning Model 12 reproduction 28-gauge does. Our M37 could be cycled quickly, and it was much smoother than the actions on the Browning BPS and recent Remington 870s I've tried.

Loading was even more of a pain than it is on 12- and 20-gauge M37s, because the bottom loading/ejection port is 28-gauge size and thus even smaller but my fingers have stayed the same size. The loading drill on the 37 is to put two into the magazine and then pump to chamber the first round. On an 870 you just throw one in the side port, close the action and put one in the magazine. Much easier. For hunting it won't matter, but for volume practice on clays, wear gloves or you'll get blisters trying to fit those shells into the magazine.

Shooting the gun was a mixed bag. The gun was difficult for some shooters to control. At 5¾ pounds on my digital scale, its light weight and neutral balance made for extremely responsive—some might say whippy—handling. One tester commented, "It feels like I'm shooting my kid's gun." Another fellow who owns one reported that he ran a straight at skeet the first time he shot his, so it really is an individual thing.

The 28" barrel weighed 1.6 oz more than the 26" and made things a bit steadier. If it were my gun, I'd experiment with adding some weight inside the magazine tube. The short stock and sticky recoil pad also caused issues for some shooters.

Ithaca does offer complete customization of this gun. For an added price, the company will custom-make a stock to your requirements in any grade of wood you can afford. Custom engraving is also available.

Shooting lightweight guns, especially with the added movement of a pump, is an acquired skill. This isn't a case of good or bad. It's a preference issue. It is what you get used to and train with. If you put in the practice, this gun would be lots of fun for small upland birds. The Ithaca 28-gauge Model 37 Featherlight is certainly an attractive gun, and it is built on a true 28-sized action. It offers enough options to set it up the way you wish, and the design certainly has stood the test of time. As production settles in, it would be worth a look if you are man enough to handle an American pumpgun.

Kimber Valier

(Seth Goltzer)

The first thing you'll notice about the Kimber Valier (pronounced "Va-leer") side-by-side is that it doesn't look Turkish. There are no odd double-headed birds, no Byzantine engraving patterns, no gilded sideplates, no strange carvings or shapes. It looks English. In fact, it looks suspiciously like someone copied a Holland & Holland sidelock. Pretty darn well, too.

The realities of an inflated euro have driven many gun companies to explore countries with gunmaking traditions yet low labor costs. For the past decade Turkey has concentrated this value advantage toward the economical production of lower-cost guns, much as the Spanish and Japanese did before it. The surprisingly nice $795 Turkish DeHaan Huglu 28-gauge side-by-side boxlock I reviewed is a case in point. In 2005 Kimber took it up a notch with its mid-priced Valier 20-gauge sidelock. Retailing at $4,299 for the Grade I and $4,999 for the Grade II we tested, the Valier competed directly against mid-range Italian boxlocks and Spanish sidelocks.

You know the current iteration of the Kimber company as the producer of a wildly successful version of the 1911 .45 ACP pistol and high-quality production rimfire and centerfire rifles. In 2002 it also began importing the Augusta over/under from Investarm S.p.A, in Marcheno, Italy. It received a calm reception.

The Kimber Valier was made by the Hatfield Gun Co. in the town of Huglu in southern Turkey's Taurus Mountains. This is not the same plant that produces the modestly priced Huglus marketed by CZ and DeHaan. The Hatfields have a long history of making guns in the US. (Ted Hatfield showed the prototype of an interesting little 28-gauge Turkish side-by-side at the 2004 SHOT Show.) The Valier was named for the Montana town of that name, a favorite bird hunting locale of Kimber employees.

The Valier's action is a close copy of the classic seven-pin Holland-type sidelock. Lockup is by the traditional Purdey double underbolt. It's all the time-tested stuff that we have grown to know and respect. The H&H-type action dominates the sidelock world just as the Anson & Deeley action is the paradigm for the boxlock. Cynics have said that the Holland-type action is popular because it will work properly even when poorly made, whereas the Purdey/Beesley self-opener works only when well made. One look inside the Kimber and you'll know this is all irrelevant. It's a jewel.

A hand-detachable sidelock thumbscrew is as much a temptation as an unguarded cookie jar. The first thing I did when I got the gun was twiddle that screw lever and pop off the locks. They came off smoothly—not too sticky, not too loose. Every internal part bore evidence of personal attention. The surfaces that weren't engine turned were carefully polished or nitre-blued. The nitre-bluing on the hammers and pins reminded me of the iridescent blued hands of an old Patek Philippe pocket watch. There were no gouges or rough spots on the interior metal. All of the springs are classic leafs, no coils. The cocking indicators are gold lined. It was very impressive. I took the liberty of comparing the interior of the Kimber action to that of a $7,000 upper-middle-grade Spanish Arrieta rounded-body sidelock. The workmanship on the Valier was at least equivalent, with even a little more hand-finishing evident in places. Thanks to the plant's CAD/CAM and CNC machinery, Kimber claimed that the lock parts are drop-in interchangeable from gun to gun. That doesn't mean that they are raw off of the CNC machine. All the parts I saw bore evidence of hand-polishing, too.

The double triggers on our Valier were very good. Pulls were light and crisp. There was virtually no creep, slop or drag. There was only the slightest side-play of the trigger blades. The front trigger is articulated to prevent a rapped knuckle. An articulated trigger is a nice little extra. The manual tang safety was positive but easy to flick on and off. (That's significant, because in a field

gun the feel of the safety is as important as that of the triggers.)

The standing breech is solid, without the little extra of disc-set strikers found in some other guns. If you break a firing pin, it will take a few minutes longer to change it. There are gas-vent races cut into the breech face in case you pierce a primer. The action exterior has the classic "square shoulder" look, not the currently popular rounded-action contour. Perhaps Kimber will offer that as an option.

The Valier's 20-gauge barrels are 28" long and have 3" chambers. No other barrel lengths are offered. The tubes are of chopper-lump construction and are joined by brazing. You don't have to worry about hot barrels loosening soft

The traditional and understated engraving stands up well to close inspection.

solder. The barrels are chrome lined—a boon to the slothful among us—but they are not proofed for steel or HEVI-Shot. Forcing cones appear conventional in length. Valiers are listed as coming with Improved Cylinder and Modified fixed chokes. There are no options there either. Our test gun's right barrel miked .625" with .002" choke. Nominal 20-gauge bores are .615", so our gun was slightly overbore. Two points of choke is a lot closer to Cylinder than Improved Cylinder. As befits a very open choke, the design is a 1" taper to a 1/4" flare with no parallel. The left barrel miked .626" with a choke of .012", about a Light Modified in a 20-gauge. The choke is about 2" long with a straight taper and no flare or parallel. The bores looked smooth when held up to the light, and the bore gauge slid through without any catching. Kimber claims that each gun is individually tested for pattern and convergence at the factory.

The automatic ejectors on our Grade II were the tried-and-true Southgate-type design, and the workmanship was excellent. They operated smoothly without binding, even though there was almost no visible separation of the ejector rims at the breech of the gun. It was very close machining. Timing was perfect. For do-it-yourselfers, the Grade I Valier is supplied with extractors.

On the outside, the top rib is of the tapered and slightly raised flat style so popular on older American side-by-sides. It's attractive, but there is no option for those who prefer the more elegant swamped game rib. The rib surface is machine-cut to reduce glare. Up front there is a single brass bead. An awkward part of many barrels is the short under-rib between the forend hook and the ejector heads. If there has been a shortcut taken, you often see it here. Like the Arrieta I compared it to, the Kimber was properly finished in this area. The exterior of the matte, rust-blued barrels was very nice but not perfect. There was the slightest hint of a ripple or two near the muzzles when I looked long and hard enough.

Our Grade II had about 50-percent-plus engraving coverage. In the past I've seen some overly fancy Turkish guns fall down in this area due to Byzantine-style engraving motifs. Like some Germanic engraving, it's not so much a question of quality but of taste for a particular market. Kimber took no chances here. The Valier engraving is hand-cut in a subtle, attractive and very traditional foliate scroll. I looked it over with my 10X loupe and found it to be flawless.

The receiver and forend metal are case-colored. Ours was well-enough done for a modern chemical process that can get blotchy, but it had the faintest brassy look, which wasn't present on the Spanish gun. You may prefer it or not, but it is very subtle.

Not so subtle was the wood. The walnut on our Grade II was Turkish (naturally) and very nice. I don't know how many "A's" or "stars" to give it, but the three Grade II guns I've seen all have had snappy lumber. Surprisingly, Kimber told me that the only difference between the Grade I and the Grade II is extractors versus ejectors. The firm said that the engraving and wood grade on both guns is the same. If you don't mind extractors, you can save a quick $800.

Our test gun came with an English stock measuring 14^{13}/$_{16}$", with drops of 1^5/$_8$" x 2^7/$_{16}$". Kimber's literature said the stock had no cast, but our sample had conventional ^{1}/$_4$" cast-off for a right-handed shooter. The wrist of the stock is slender but fairly round. I prefer a more oval wrist, as it promotes better control without additional bulk.

The forend is the one bit on the gun that isn't straight out of Ye Olde England. At 9^1/$_2$" long, it's a couple of inches longer than the conventional splinter game-gun forend. It also has the slightest vestigial Schnabel lip. One of the reasons the company may have fit a longer forend is that the Valier uses the larger Deeley pull-down latch, as opposed to the more common Anson pushrod found on most English and Spanish side-bys. Still, the Deeley latch was well made and locked perfectly.

Wood-to-metal fit was generally excellent, except that the forend iron was slightly below the wood surface. In a hot-barrel situation, this could be advantageous, so it may be intentional. Or not. The fit of the sidelocks was flawless. Checkering is claimed to be 24 lpi, and I'll take Kimber's word for it. If I were really fussy, there was some diamond-flattening near the edges, but I had to look hard in just the right light to see it. The butt is checkered, and there are cleanly cut teardrops behind the locks. Kimber also claimed that the wood got 30 hand-rubbed coats of oil. Ours should have gotten 31, as there were a few finish spots on the forend and underside of the stock that were a bit thin. Other than those little holidays, it was a nice stock-finishing job with a deep luster and good color in the highly figured wood.

The gun carton didn't contain any extra knick-knacks other than a couple of flannel bags for the barrels and butt. For an additional $405 you could have a fitted canvas & leather takedown case. Kimber's warranty was one year on parts and labor, but in practice the company has been very generous in its interpretation.

Our test gun weighed 6 pounds 8.8 ounces. This is right at the upper limit of what I would accept in a 20-gauge side-by-side field gun. Some Spanish 20s weigh that much, but most are 4 to 6 oz lighter. English 20s are usually closer to 6 pounds, and some weigh even less. Still, weight isn't nearly as important as balance. That's what defines a gun, and the Valier is a well-balanced gun. The pivot point is about ½" in front of the hinge pin, but more important, the weight is evenly distributed throughout the gun. It's not whippy. It's not muzzle heavy. You can feel the weight, but it doesn't fight you. I'd be happier if the Valier were a little lighter, but I'm not complaining.

Because it was early summer and bird season was closed when we tested our gun, a number of us put a good many rounds through the Kimber at clays. Target shooting isn't as reflexive as upland hunting, but the gun felt moderately agile with just a hint of stateliness due to the weight. When shooting multiple doubles or a flurry, the barrels became too hot to hold, but the gun just shrugged it off. Even when cooking, the action never felt looser or stickier than it had when I'd taken it out of the box. There was no bubbling of flux, no sticking of ejectors, no sign of hairline cracks, no flattening of the heads of the firing pins, no nothing. The gun simply ignored the usage. Obviously, a few flats of ammo don't make for a long-term test. The Hatfield Gun

Co. claims to have run 250 proof loads and 15,000 shells through a sample gun during a three-day hot-barrel marathon without any problems. Your mileage may vary, but it seems promising.

The Valier was an easy gun to shoot, but it shot very flat for me and I had to cover the targets. Normally, I set my side-by-sides to shoot a little high. This could be corrected easily with a higher stock but, alas, Kimber doesn't offer stocks to customer dimensions. You have to take what comes. As I run my double-trigger guns about ½" to ¾" longer than my single-trigger guns, I also needed more length. Alas again. If I owned the gun, I'd have to bend it, cut off the checkered butt and add a pad. Yes, it fit a number of other shooters just fine, but that's not enough. Socks and shirts come in different sizes. So should $5,000 shotguns.

As far as I could tell, barrel convergence was good, though it was hard to be sure with such a large pattern from the open right barrel. Kimber tests each and every gun for barrel regulation. The left barrel added another 10 yards of range with most ammunition, and that's about right. My favorite upland chokes are right around .005" and .015" in all gauges, and the Valier's were close enough. Since the gun had 3" chambers and was obviously very strong, I ran some 1¼ oz Remington Nitro Mags through it. Both the gun and I survived. Recoil wasn't awful at all, perhaps because of the gun's weight. With standard loads, the gun was a delight to shoot. The crisp triggers and tactile safety encouraged instinctive shooting. The slightly forward bias helped follow-through and kept the muzzles down for the second shot. The ejectors dealt easily with even steel-head promo loads.

The Valier's action is a close copy of the classic seven-pin Holland-type sidelock.

I admit that I have been excessively nit-picky in my review of this gun. Kimber should take that as a compliment. The Valier is so darn nice that there aren't any meaningful manufacturing flaws. I have to sink to carping about little stuff that is probably correct in another sample. Yes, this was a new manufacturing facility and, yes, Kimber was among the first to charge so much for a Turkish gun. But when you look closely at the Valier, the quality and value are there and then some. This is an excellent example of the beneficial union of CNC machining and hand-finishing. I do think that it would have been nice had one been able to specify chokes, barrel lengths and especially stock dimensions, as you can on Spanish guns. But, for a first try, I thought the Valier was an exceptional entrant in the mid-priced side-by-side derby.

NOT QUITE POST MORTEM

Well, shows you what I know. I felt that the Kimber Valier was a very nice gun. That, of course, was the kiss of death. Importation started in 2005, and Kimber ended it in 2008. Perhaps the company was too busy selling its 1911 pistols. As I write this, the *Blue Book* value of secondhand Valiers in excellent condition is only about 10-percent less than their original MSRPs, probably equal to the actual purchase prices, so time has been kind to them when they crop up on the used-gun market. That speaks well of the gun's quality.

But it's not over. As I write this, what appears to be the same gun is listed as an available model by Commando Arms (www.commando-arms.com). It is shown in both Commando's version and the Webley & Scott version. W&S lists its gun as the 3000 Series Premium seven-pin sidelock.

Kimber Marias

It's gorgeous. It's exotic. It's a relative bargain. But will that be enough? I'm speaking of the new Kimber Marias sidelock over/under. Introduced in 2006 and following close on the heels of Kimber's Valier sidelock side-by-side, the Marias also relies on modern machinery combined with a non-Euro pay scale to recreate a classic game gun. The Marias is made in the same Hatfield plant in the town of Huglu, Turkey, that produces the Valier. It is a continuation of Kimber's effort to provide Anglo-classic game guns with all the bells and whistles at very competitive prices.

Like the Valier, the Marias is named after a bird hunting area of Montana favored by Kimber employees. The name obviously is meant to emphasize that this gun is by and for hunters. I sympathize with the advertising gambit, but it will take a hard-hearted hunter to drag this beauty around the harsh world of talus slopes, beaver ponds, barbed wire and briers. The Marias looks so much more at home next to a leather armchair by the fire with a glass of Oporto's best nearby. It's that kind of gun.

It is important to remember the price of this gun as I discuss it. The Marias is a true sidelock O/U. Six-figure British "bests" aside, other sidelock O/Us that come to mind are the Beretta SO series, the Merkel 303 and the AyA Augusta. All three start around $25,000. The Grade I Marias lists for $5,379, and the Grade II is $5,799. Grade Is all come with Prince of Wales stocks and "grade three" Turkish walnut. Grade IIs come with either Prince of Wales or English stocks and "grade four" Turkish wood. All the Marias models have Schnabel forends. The Grade I is available only with 28" barrels, whereas the Grade II will be available with 26", 28" and 30" barrels. The guns currently are imported in 20 gauge, with 12 gauge soon to follow. Our test gun was a Grade II 26" 20-gauge.

In most gun reviews I start with a discussion of the action. Although I don't think that the action is as important as the barrels in most cases, with the Marias it is the back-action sidelock O/U receiver that gets your attention. It certainly has the look of a timeless masterpiece from early in the last century.

The boxlock action, not the sidelock, dominates the O/U market. There's a reason. Sidelock O/Us are extremely difficult to design and make compared to sidelock side-by-sides. Think about the relationship between the barrel chambers and the hammers in the sidelocks of a side-by-side. They are sort of in a line, allowing a direct and powerful firing-pin strike to the primer. Not so in the O/U sidelock. The chambers are stacked on the centerline of the gun. This demands that the hammers of the sidelock O/U drive one firing pin in and acutely upward, whereas the other is driven in and acutely downward. This geometry can result in light strikes. The Brits tried all sorts of O/U sidelock designs involving off-center spindles, different-length hammers and upside-down locks to get around this before Boss and Woodward got it right, albeit at the cost of exquisitely careful fabrication.

The Marias action has a single trigger, but it is not selective and does not have the intercepting sears common on many sidelocks. I don't know whether these omissions are design issues, cost issues or both.

The sidelocks are easily hand-detached with a conventional thumbscrew. Inside you can see that the bend of the hammer mainspring runs toward the rear of the sidelock rather than to the front, hence the back-action designation. In theory this placement does not require removal of metal along the highly stressed sides of the O/U's receiver, thus making a stronger or thinner receiver possible. In theory six angels can dance on the head of a pin, too. With the modern 4140 steel used here, strength certainly isn't the issue the way it might have been once.

The hinges are Boss-style replaceable side-stub hinges that you see in Berettas and Perazzis. The action has three locks. Two of them are passive monoblock lugs that engage holes completely through the receiver floor. The active lock is a low-locking full-width tongue similar to that used by Browning. Flat cocking rods are located in the bottom of the action. The leaf mainsprings look easy enough to replace when the inevitable happens. The inside of each five-pin lock is very simple, as it should be on a sidelock that lacks the

complexity (and added security) of intercepting sears. It's noticeably less busy than the sidelock of the H&H-style seven-pin Valier side-by-side. The firing pins are not bushed, so access must be through the rear of the action. The safety is manual, with a properly raised bump and a nice "clicky" feel. It blocks the rebounding hammers, not just the trigger. A nice touch is that the Marias's single trigger is mechanical, so you always get a second shot even if the first barrel fails. It is not selective and always shoots the lower barrel first. There is no double-trigger option.

Everything inside the action is case colored, polished, engine turned or nitre blued. The screws, hammers and trigger blade have the gorgeous iridescent nitre bluing we saw on the Valier internals. The insides of the lockplates are engine turned. All moving parts are polished. There are no sharp edges to indicate that they were just pulled raw off of the CNC machine. Nitre-blued gold-lined cocking indicators are added as an elegant touch. It's all nicely done.

Farther forward, the monoblock is strictly modern Italian rather than English. Conventional ejectors and ejector springs are built into the monoblock just like several current mid-range Brescia O/Us. This isn't a bad thing, as it is a good system, but it seems a little removed aesthetically from the olde-tyme action of the gun. The monoblock sides are jeweled, as are the ejectors, and little effort is made to disguise the monoblock seam on the barrels.

The barrels have 3" chambers with relatively short forcing cones. The tubes measure about .622" ID. Nominal 20-gauge bores are .615", so the Marias has a bit of an overbore. The bores of the barrels are chromed, and Kimber assures us that they are suitable for steel shot. The gun comes furnished with five screw chokes: Cylinder (.620"), Improved Cylinder (.610"), Modified (.600"), Improved Modified (.595") and Full (.588"). The IC, M and IM are a little tighter than I'm used to seeing in a 20 but are close enough. The chokes themselves are a bit less than 2" long and use a straight taper, not the parallel/conical form often seen with longer tubes or fixed chokes. The jury is still out on whether one configuration is better than the other, but the straight taper lends itself to shorter chokes. Choke designation is marked on the barrel of the choke, but there are no notches in the rim to indicate choke when in place.

The barrel tubes are smooth and show no outside ripples when held to the light. There is no bulge to announce the screw chokes, which are just about invisible when in place. On our gun there were two registering pinholes on the side-rib ends at the muzzle used to align the choke installation, but they will be filled on future guns. Ribs are soft soldered. Side ribs are solid and full length, from muzzle to monoblock. The ventilated top rib is flat, .31" wide and machine scribed on the top for a non-glare finish. There's a single brass bead up front.

Yes, I would have preferred the classic looks and strength of a solid top rib. No, you can't have one right now, but it is being considered for the future.

The Marias is a stunning, nice-handling gun—at a price a quarter that of other sidelock O/Us.

The Schnabel forend locks on with a well-fitted conventional Deeley pull-down latch. Other than that—and the fact that there is currently no other forend choice for those who loathe the Schnabel—it is unremarkable. At least this Schnabel has a relatively modest Hapsburg lip, but a plain slender field forend would have been so much more in keeping with the classic lines of the gun. There is also a vestigial Schnabel lip on the otherwise classic Kimber Valier side-by. Maybe it's an Austro-Turkish thing. I'm not the only one

who feels that a Schnabel is out of place on this gun. Kimber is looking into offering a more traditional forend.

I did not see an example of the English stock offered on the Marias Grade II guns. The Prince of Wales ("round knob," to you old Browning fans) grip on our test gun was well executed and properly proportioned. The trigger-guard tang runs halfway down the front of the grip. Our stock measured 14^5/16" x 1^1/2" x 2^1/4", with minimal cast and about ^{1}/4" right-hand toe out. Pitch was about 2". All pretty standard stuff. The stock is not attached with a lengthwise drawbolt, as is done on most boxlock O/Us today. This sidelock action offers no interior vertical surface suitable to receive a drawbolt. Instead, it uses tang screws typical of a side-by-side sidelock. One screw descends from the top tang, and the other is underneath the trigger guard going upward.

The Kimber Marias is stunning at a distance and equally so up close. Indeed, it will stand close inspection. Wood-to-metal fit on our gun was very good. Around the locks the fit was perfect, with just enough proud wood to allow refinishing down the road. Same with the inletting of the forend iron. The Turkish walnut on our Grade II Marias was very nice, bordering on excellent. The forend and stockwood matched. The stock had the same figure on both sides. Checkering was a simple pattern and stated to be 24 lpi. It was well—but not perfectly—executed, with a little diamond flattening near some edges. The teardrops behind the sidelocks were cleanly cut. The butt was completely covered in the same fine checkering. Stock finish is said to be oil. It was a flawless high-gloss application with all wood pores completely filled. The oil maximized the butterscotch background and dark-chocolate streaks of the wood.

The barrels carry an attractive rust blue, neither too shiny nor too matte. Kimber states that the receiver, forend iron and sidelocks are case colored by the bone-charcoal method. The colors are mottled dark blues and ambers. It is absolutely beautiful. The bright glossy bluing of the trigger guard clashed slightly and might have looked better were it more subdued. The good-quality hand engraving is listed as 50-percent coverage, but I'd guess it was more like 20-percent. It's a tight floral scroll that is perfectly in keeping with the overall appearance of the gun. So often tasteless over-engraving can destroy the "mood" of an otherwise gorgeous gun. They got it right on the Marias. The subtle engraving, case-colored

The monoblock sides and ejectors are jeweled, and little effort has been made to disguise the monoblock seam on the barrels.

sidelocks, rust-blued barrels and stunning wood make this a gun that even a New York Senator would covet.

But looks don't bring home the birds. A short-barreled 20-gauge field gun is meant to be carried all day. My electronic scale grunted under the 7-pound 2.2-ounce heft of the Marias. I reweighed it. Still 7 pounds 2.2 ounces. For a 20-gauge field gun? Well, other than that, Mrs. Lincoln, how did you enjoy the play? None of my O/U 12-gauge upland guns weigh that much. A field 20 O/U ought to be closer to 6 pounds. Maybe a touch more, but not much. What's the

point of spending the entire day lugging around a gun that weighs as much as a 12 but has the payload of a 20?

I'm willing to lay some of the blame on *Juglans regia*. Fancy wood is heavier than kindling. The receiver profile is also quite large for a 20. Although smaller than the tall 12-gauge Browning O/U action, it's within a few thou of the 12-gauge Beretta receiver and a good bit larger than the 20-gauge Beretta. I also think that the Marias sidelock action weighs more than a conventional 20-gauge boxlock, but I didn't pull it off to weigh it, so I'm just guessing.

The balance fulcrum of the Marias was 1/2" behind the hinge pins. In a 6-pound 20 this rearward bias would make the gun uncontrollable, but in a gun that is more than 7, it actually made it handle quite well and feel nicely responsive. The balance may be farther to the rear than is common, but the weight is well distributed throughout the gun, and that's important.

It's said that one advantage of a sidelock is that it centers the weight between the hands better than a boxlock, but I think that's just a cover-up because so many sidelock actions are heavier than their boxlock counterparts when built to equal quality. In addition to our test gun's 26" barrels, you can get lengths of 28" or 30". Because the Marias barrel tapers do not change with length, the longer barrels will move the balance farther forward. This will gain stability and smoothness at the expense of responsiveness. Good for pheasants. Less so for grouse and quail.

Of course that's if the gun actually works. Our test gun was one of only two available at the time, so obviously they still were learning things about production. Still, that's no excuse for our gun running 30-percent light strikes on factory Remington Sport ammo. Maybe it was just a bad lot with low primers, but maybe not. The Marias did function perfectly on factory Remington STS and Federal shells, but it also occasionally misfired with reloads using PMC, Remington or Fiocchi primers. What wasn't affected by shell brand was a sticky lower ejector that failed to pop out the shell, regardless of make, about every fifth time.

And then there was the trigger. Sidelock single triggers always have been an issue on British and Spanish guns but not so much on Italian and German ones. The Marias single trigger did not double, but it had absurdly heavy pulls for a gun of this purported quality.

In theory back-action locks do not require removal of metal along the sides of the receiver, thus making a stronger or thinner receiver possible.

The trigger pull on the lower barrel varied between 6 pounds 10 ounces and 7 pounds 6 ounces. The top barrel was consistently 7 pounds 6 ounces. There was a little bit of scratchy creep on the bottom barrel but none on the top. The manual says, "The trigger pull on this shotgun is set at factory and should not be altered." Gimme a break. In a lighter gun these heavy pulls would have been more noticeable. As it was, due to the heft of the Marias, they were disconcerting but not debilitating. While on the subject of the manual,

here's another gem. When firing, the manual warns you to "Be prepared for loud noise and recoil." Well, most of the time.

Considering the obvious careful handwork throughout the gun, I am tempted to ascribe the light primer strikes, sticky ejector and heavy triggers to a glitch in quality control in a single early sample. However, candor—and consultation with a friend steeped in British gun design—forces me to mention the inherent design difficulties of the sidelock O/U as a possible culprit for the light strikes. As to the trigger, a cynic might say that heavy pulls were the cheapest way to keep a sidelock single trigger from doubling even after the selective-trigger feature has been deleted for simplicity. Someone with a rosier view would say that a few more file strokes would have set it all to rights. At least it shows that the company doesn't cherry-pick the review guns. It also should be noted that the Kimber Valier side-by-side I tested some months ago had no quality issues. Clearly, Hatfield has the ability to do it right.

The disadvantage of a non-selective trigger is partly overcome by changeable screw chokes. I didn't pattern the chokes, but I did check barrel convergence. It seemed fine. The notchless flush chokes are inserted and removed with a friction wrench. Chokes without wrench notches may be prettier, but relying solely on friction combined with the lack of a leverage bar on the wrench has its risks. The lower-barrel choke threads were a little scratchy, and I would have liked more grab than the friction wrench provided when inserting and removing the chokes. One time the choke in the lower barrel was recalcitrant enough to require the tender ministrations of my burly shop assistant Forza Bruta.

Our Marias came in a cardboard box complete with legalese manual, choke tubes, velvet gun sleeves and chamber locks. The warranty is for two years. Kimber will sell you a fitted takedown case for $340. That's about it for extras right now. When I questioned the lack of a custom-stock option on a $6,000 gun, I was told that this was a possibility down the road. I learned that Kimber may establish a custom shop so that you can order a personalized gun. The Marias deserves this.

So what's the bottom line? Our early production sample had some functioning issues. They may be easily remedied quality holidays or more serious design flaws. I suspect the former but would be less than honest if I didn't at least mention the possibility of the latter. These problems should have been caught before the gun was released. There isn't much that can be done with the excessive weight. Depending on the type of hunting you do, it may or may not be a deal-breaker.

On the plus side the Kimber Marias is gorgeous, stunning and delicious. It handles well and has good shooting balance. It has an exotic action that is sure to create comment. Its price is a quarter that of other sidelock O/Us. Although I think that the gun is heavier than necessary for aggressive field carry, with longer barrels it would be ideal for driven birds, dove shooting or even fun sporting clays. The weight will smooth the swing and lower recoil. Besides, the killer good looks of this buxom beauty are surely worth an extra bird or two.

POST MORTEM

As Robbie Burns said, "The best-laid schemes o' mice an' men gang aft agley." Kimber imported the Marias from 2006 to 2008 before retiring completely from the shotgun business. While not as popular as the Kimber Valier side-by-side, the Marias shows up occasionally on used-gun Websites.

But it also has a future or, at least, a presence. It shows up as a current Webley & Scott model on the Commando Arms Website (www.commando-arms.com) and also as a separate Commando Arms house model. At this writing, Commando Arms does not have a US dealership.

Kolar Sporter

It's so incongruous. In my gun safe the massive Kolar sporting clays gun stands between a petite Winchester Model 42 .410 pump and a lightweight 1920s Webley & Scott side-by-side. It's like parking a D9 Caterpillar tractor between a Ducati and an MG TC. If ever the phrase "horses for courses" were apt, this is an example.

Since sporting clays started in the US in 1986, the game has followed skeet and evolved from a test of field shooting with field guns to one of specialized presentations and even more specialized guns. Today's usual over/under sporter has at least 30" barrels and weighs in around 8 pounds. But if some is good, more is better. Right? Kolar thinks so, and the company may be correct.

It all started in the early 1970s in Larry Kolar's machine shop in Ithaca, New York. At the urging of a skeet-shooting friend, Kolar developed a set of skeet-tube inserts with integral extractors. Don Mainland, who owns a large machine shop in Racine, Wisconsin, bought the rights to the tubes and began making them in the late '70s. The Kolar skeet tubes continue to be popular to this day. In

1988 Mainland started making the 90T single-barrel trap gun for Remington. There were 3,500 guns made before production ceased in 1994. Toward the end of that run, Mainland's key personnel decided to design and build competition over/unders under the Kolar Arms name. Our review gun is the AAA Competition Sporting Standard model of 2008. Its name recently was changed to the Kolar SC. A new version called the Kolar Max Clays was introduced in 2011. The difference is that the SC has a traditional fixed rib, while the Max has a raised adjustable rib. The Max also comes in trap and skeet variants. Other than that, the guns are the same.

Most clay-target guns are converted field guns, which makes sense when you consider the general demands of the gun market and where the volume sales are. Not the Kolar. This over/under was designed from the ground up as a no-compromise competition gun.

One look at the receiver will convince. It looks like a Perazzi on steroids. Machined from a billet of 4140 chrome-moly steel, its Boss locking system allows a shallow but very wide action. It's one of the widest I've seen. The huge, squared, twin locking lugs protrude from high on the receiver face. This allows a more direct and less flexible connection between the opening lever and the locking plate.

The action pivots on two easily replaceable side hinge stubs. The bottom of the receiver is solid, with no Browning-style lower lumps piercing it. In fact, the entire receiver is cut from one chunk of steel. Unlike many other guns, the top and bottom tangs plus the rear vertical support are hewn from the same single chunk of steel as the main body of the receiver. It simply can't flex. CNC machinery sure has come a long way. The opening lever is the only cast piece on the entire gun.

Like guns by Perazzi, Zoli and some others, the Kolar has a removable trigger group. It's held in with one Allen screw to forestall inadvertent detachment. Hammers are driven by coil springs centered on guide rods. The trigger is selective via a toggle behind the trigger blade. The trigger is mechanical, not inertial, so it will work with sub-gauge tubes. The trigger group and action have been awarded a number of US patents. The current State II trigger was redesigned to be particularly resistant to fan-firing. Kolar paid a lot of attention to the little details, too. Most of the cross pins in the trigger are tacked in place with a tiny center punch just to make sure. Sears are heat treated and titanium-nitrited for long life.

The trigger blade is adjustable for length of pull for about $1/2$" along a track. It has notch detents and is secured with an Allen bolt. Adjustable triggers are fine until they come loose. These shouldn't. Like any proper competition gun, the top-tang-mount-

Recesses in the Kolar monoblock allow for spacers of variable thickness to keep the gun locking vault-tight, as may be needed to adapt for wear or mounting additional barrel sets.

ed safety is manual. As an interesting plus, it also can be locked out entirely should a competitive shooter wish to do so.

Barrel structure follows the usual tube-and-monoblock method. After the tubes are fixed in the monoblock, the joint is magnafluxed to make sure it is perfect. The monoblock carries easily removable ejectors almost identical to Perazzi's. High on each side of the rear of the monoblock are the large squarish receptor cavities for the dual locking lugs. They are like Beretta's, only larger.

The side of the Kolar monoblock has an interesting patented feature. Like Perazzi, Kolar uses the Boss-style bifurcated lumps on each side of the action to engage recesses in the sides of the monoblock. Kolar has added replaceable inserts at the rear of each monoblock recess. Different-size inserts can be used as barrels wear in to maintain full contact and take pressure off of the hinges. This feature also is very helpful in fitting a second barrel to the same receiver. Boss used the same arrangement, but the replaceable inserts were on the receiver walls not the barrels. The sporter is available with an additional lightweight tubed carrier barrel for NSCA sub-gauge competition.

Kolar buys its barrels as raw hammer-forged tubes, which are then machined to specification. Our sporter barrels were the "Semi-Lite" .750" bores. This is a good bit more of a 12-gauge overbore than Krieghoff, Browning or Beretta. Twelve-gauge nominal is .729", so you get the picture. Kolar's bores are big. And heavy, too. The emphasis is on the "Semi" not the "Lite," as these Kolar barrels weigh about 4 oz more than the typical Perazzi sporter's. If for some reason you want even heavier barrels, Kolar will ream the bores to only .735" to add 1½ oz. As would be expected in a state-of-the-art target gun, the chamber forcing cones are a long 2". The bore interior is not chromed; it is nicely polished with a computer-controlled Sunnen hone.

The Kolar sporter is available with fixed chokes of your choosing or with screw chokes. Our test gun came with five screw chokes from .000" Cylinder Bore to .020" Modified, but you can get whatever constrictions you want. The chokes were polished stainless, .6" extended, and the constriction was clearly marked on the extension for easy reference. Choke tapers are the popular conical/parallel design, with .010" bore relief at the rear and ⅝" parallel at the front. The chokes are just shy of 3" long—long enough to permit effective gradual tapers. Currently, Kolar is experimenting with total-taper, no-parallel, Teague-style chokes as well.

Although most of the action comparisons are to Perazzi, Kolar looked to Krieghoff for barrel inspiration. Krieghoff made split ribless barrels a hallmark in competition guns. The huge advantage to this approach is the adjustability of barrel convergence. Kolar uses replaceable hangers to attach the barrels at the muzzle and replaceable spacers to separate them in the middle. The barrels end up being joined at the monoblock, middle and muzzle, not along their entire length by side ribs. Because the spacers and hangers can be replaced by those of different sizes to force the barrels apart or bring them together, barrel convergence is easily adjusted.

You would be amazed at how many guns with soldered side ribs do not print both barrels to the same place. Barrel convergence is the first thing I test on a new gun. Kolar's convergence adjustments can be made by the owner, which is very interesting and very useful. This is indeed a high-tech machine.

Kolar's engineers clearly took inspiration from the designs and mechanical elements of the best Italian, German and English guns for this sporter, then innovated a number of them for a no-compromise competition gun. The patented detachable trigger group offers reliability and all the functions a clays shooter could want.

Barrel options abound. Sporter lengths can be 28", 30", 32" or 34". Barrel weights can vary depending on the bore size selected. Our 32" test sporter came with a "ramp taper" top rib that was silver soldered in place. It was raised .4" at the rear and sloped down to .15" at the muzzle. (A flat-taper rib also is available if you prefer no built-in vertical lead, or an adjustable rib can be had in the Max model.) The width of the rib tapered from .44" at the breech to .33" just beneath the usual Bradley white-bead-on-a-block front bead. There was also a small steel center bead. Mercifully, the barrels were not ported, but porting is available if you must.

Our barrels were high-gloss blued, but the rib was machined

on top with a channel down the middle to cut glare. Although the action is available in "black-iron bluing," ours was the matte silver color of electroless nickel plating. The contrast was quite attractive. The trigger group was done in the same electroless nickel with a gold trigger blade. The nickel will neither wear through nor rust.

There was little engraving on the receiver of our standard-grade gun. It was just enough to break up the flat areas. The Kolar lion rampant crest was on the bottom. Heavily hand-engraved French gray receivers are available on the higher grades.

Off-the-shelf Kolar stocks emphasize heavy vertical Italianate competition pistol grips and Krieghoff-style Monte Carlo combs. The Kolar catalog shows three different sporting stocks, three skeet and more than a dozen trap. Not to your taste? No problem. Kolar will make a stock to your dimensions on its state-of-the-art CNC stock machine. If you don't have your dimensions, Kolar will do the fitting at its 45-yard indoor test range. The stocks also are carefully shaped for width to govern weight for proper gun balance. The stock-bolt assembly even has a set of conical washers to permit contraction and expansion of the stock without cracking.

The single-border checkering on our gun was hand cut to a purposeful 22 lpi, which provided a good grip. Slick, ultra-fine checkering has no place on a competition gun. A practical black Pachmayr Decelerator sporting clays pad with the plastic non-stick horseshoe insert at the top adorns the butt.

The Kolar sporter's standard forend is a sleek, attractive "Eurostyle" forend reminiscent of the English-spec Perazzi sporters. A fuller beavertail is also available.

The stock finish used on our gun was a high-gloss polyurethane. On the plus side, it is durable, waterproof and immune to my universal-solvent sunscreen. On the negative side, it is harder to fix the inevitable dings. Both the stock and forend were properly finished inside to prevent oil seepage. Wood-to-metal fit was excellent, with no gaps of any kind. The wood was left just proud enough to permit a refinishing or two.

The walnut was really nice on our sample. It had good figure, color and contrast. Of course you can get even fancier wood as you move up the scale of the five engraving upgrades. It all depends on how much glitz your station in life requires. Our basic test model, the Nickel Standard, now the Kolar SC, sells for $8,995, while the Kolar Max with the adjustable rib and comb is $10,795. This is right in with the basic Perazzi or Krieghoff. At the top of the Kolar ladder, the Select engraved model runs $24,990, whereas the Custom Grade is priced on request. The basic sporting clays model comes with a sturdy aluminum Americase that is quite suitable for airline abuse. The case contains the five chokes, a proper notched choke wrench, a tube of grease, a surprisingly informative instruction manual, a wrench for the stock and also one to remove the trigger, and a three-year guarantee.

Shooting the Kolar sporter was a real eye-opener. When I first put it together, I kept looking for an axle and set of wheels. At 9 pounds, it was a load. At first I struggled with it. My sporting clays shooting style is a combination of field and clays. I swing through a lot of birds. I generally prefer lighter and more facile clays guns. My favorite personal over/under sporters are FN Superposed target guns weighing just less than 8 pounds with 30" barrels. They move quickly and are easy to make corrections with, but I have to remember to drive them through the birds. The Kolar was balanced right at the hinge pin, but the greater weight gave it a higher moment of inertia than those of my FNs.

With the heavy Kolar, my timing was all wrong. The inertia put me in front of quartering-away targets and behind fast crossers. At the suggestion of a Master Class shooter who shoots a Kolar, I changed my lead method. Instead of coming from behind the birds and firing as I swung through, I started the muzzles well out along the flight paths ahead of the birds for a sustained lead. This way I was able to match muzzle speed to the speed of the birds while always staying in front. This requires very little muzzle movement if you start the gun in exactly the right place. That's just what the Kolar wanted. I was able to hit many of the targets with virtually no effort. The weight of the gun made it very steady during the short swing. Because the gun was moving slower than it would have been if coming from behind, there was less chance of overswing and overleading. Yet the gun's weight made it easier to follow through and not stop the swing. This horse had indeed found his course.

Clearly, changing my shooting style to adapt to a gun like this would take several thousand rounds. But it might be worth it. Many of the very best competition shooters use sustained lead on clays, and a heavy, precise gun like this Kolar makes this method easier. Concerning the heft of the gun, one very knowledgeable shooter remarked, "It shoots better than it feels." How very right he was.

On the functioning side, the gun was flawless. Everything worked. The trigger was a little lighter than I'm used to, at $3^1/4$ pounds lower and $3^1/2$ pounds upper, but it was very consistent. There was more creep than I like but no overtravel and, most important, no variation at all in pull weight. The chokes stayed in tight but were easy to remove. The gas seal between the choke skirt and barrel effectively eliminated carbon deposits. The trigger and stock detached easily

The removable ejectors appear similar to those on Perazzis. The barrels, while joined at the monoblock, are ribless like Krieghoff's, though with spacers at the muzzles and in the middle that offer user-adjustable convergence.

but were never loose. Ditto the forend. Everything fit properly.

Between the overbore barrels, long forcing cones and well-designed chokes, the patterns were more efficient and hotter in the center than I am used to for a given constriction. Fewer pellets were being deformed. With the Kolar, you can open up your chokes a bit to gain the widest effective pattern possible. The manual mandates that the gun be used only with "lead factory target loads." That seems restrictive when so many clays shooters reload. Steel shot is not recommended.

A number of people who shot the gun commented on its low recoil. Obviously, heavy guns kick less than light ones. Adding a pound (12 percent) to an 8-pound gun reduces calculated free recoil by about the same percentage. Some feel that overboring and long cones reduce perceived recoil, but you can't calculate that.

The Kolar sporter is a no-compromise gun. It is built to do one thing very, very well and for a very, very long time. I doubt that the gun could be worn out, but if it needs attention, Kolar's service department has the highest reputation. This gun certainly isn't for everyone. If you shoot sporting clays to practice for your days afield, this is probably too much gun. But if you are an analytical competitive shooter and are willing to adapt your style to the gun, the Kolar sporter may allow you to achieve scores you thought impossible.

Krieghoff Essencia

After the second bottle had been opened, dinner discussion turned to "best" guns and who makes them today. We were at the 2006 Vintage Cup and had been wallowing in the finest doubles extant. Two of our party suggested that these days the Germans are making better English guns than the English. Although the next evening my dinner table full of English gunmakers declined to share that opinion, there's no doubt that the Germans are producing some stunning classic game guns.

In the past I'd always felt that German and Austrian guns were built like bank vaults—delightfully complex, yet visually odd. I could never get past the heavy engraving of open-mouthed ducks or the rifle-like stock configurations complete with sling swivels and cheekpieces. I still can't fully forgive the country's gunmakers for inflicting the Schnabel forend on us.

It was never a question of quality; it was a question of taste. German makers built for German customers and gave them what they wanted. But so many others worldwide admired the British game-gun paradigm that it was only a matter of time until some German craftsmen turned their substantial abilities to producing guns for that market too. One only has to look at the current production of Hartmann &

Weiss or German native Philipp Ollendorff to find British-style sidelock game guns the equal of any.

And then there is Krieghoff. In America we think of the German K-80 over/under as a competition gun. It is the most desired O/U for American-style skeet and is extremely popular for ATA trap. It also picked up speed in sporting clays by winning the 2006 World FITASC championship in the able hands of Brit Ben Husthwaite. Heavy, durable, extremely soft-shooting and with the best trigger in the business, it has come to epitomize what many Americans want for domestic clay target games. A chauvinist might note that this isn't surprising, as the K-80 stems from the Remington Model 32, but that's unfair, as today's K-80 is greatly improved.

Although Americans think of Krieghoffs in terms of clay target guns, it is very different on the Continent. There, Krieghoff markets a variety of consummately Germanic double- and treble-barreled rifle/shotgun combination guns as well as single-barreled rifles and even some new Parabellum Luger-style pistols.

In the early '90s Krieghoff commissioned a single boxlock from

Ivano Tanfoglio at Ferlib to test the interest in marketing a side-by-side game gun, but it went no further for a decade. The introduction of the Essencia side-by-side sidelock at the 2003 Vintage Cup caught us all by surprise. I was stunned when I first saw it. How could a company whose aesthetics centered about practical slab-sided clays guns and complex Drillings come up with this smooth, seductive sidelock classic? Shows you what I know.

Steve Phillips, Krieghoff's director of sales, told me that the Essencia sidelock and its boxlock sibling are both made in Germany through a partnership with German master gunsmith Jens Ziegen-hahn. Ziegenhahn is a fourth-generation gunmaker and is well known for his double rifles as well as his classic custom shotguns. At its introduction, the Essencia received the *Shooting Sportsman* Award as an ideal custom-fitted game gun at the Gold

Most recently, the Essencia sidelock has become available with hand-detachable sidelocks or with an optional sidelever.

Our test gun was a 28" 20-gauge with double triggers. This price range puts it significantly above the run-of-the-mill side-by-sides and significantly below the British "best" and top Italian efforts. For those who choose to invest $25K in a field gun, it's not so much a question of absolute cost as it is relative value. If $2,500 will buy a nice 20-gauge side-by-side, what makes another

Beautiful lines, gorgeous coloring, excellent performance— the Essencia is what a shotgun is all about.

Medal Concours. I was impressed by the gun, and when one became available for testing, I snapped it up. But first, to keep my comments and expectations in perspective, I should mention the bottom line. The current list price of the Essencia sidelock before options is $29,895. It comes in 12 gauge with 28" or 30" barrels or in 16, 20 or 28 gauge—all on a 20-gauge receiver—with 26.5", 28" or 30" barrels. Three years after introduction, the company added a true 28-gauge scaled-frame model in 28 gauge or .410 for $33,950.

20-gauge side-by-side worth 10 times as much? Well, let me tell you.

The Essencia action is a seven-pin back-action sidelock. Back action means the mainspring faces rearward as opposed to the forward-facing spring of a bar action. A back-action design allows the action bar to be rounded for a slimmer, smoother look. The Essencia's interior design is a little different than what I'm used to, but it is certainly clean and well executed. All the springs are leaf. The locks and bridles are case colored, the springs are polished and everything else is gold plated. The firing pins are disk-set for easy removal from the face of the standing breech. The disks have the usual twin holes for removal-tool purchase, but each one also has a perfectly indexed set screw as an extra Teutonic touch. The sidelocks are screwdriver

removable, but the Krieghoff manual warns owners not to try it themselves. *Verboten!* They say that the locks and stock should be removed only by factory-trained personnel.

Lockup is by the classic Purdey double underbolt. The standing breech also is recessed to accept what Krieghoff refers to as a Purdey third bite for additional lateral stability. The locking lumps that engage the bolt do not protrude through the bottom of the receiver—something that some feel is the sign of a "better" gun—but the bottom of the receiver is removable via a small and a large screw-on plate. The latter plate holds the triggers. The hinge pin, with cap-screw access, is replaceable. Cocking indicators are the classic gold-washed tumbler pivot stubs protruding through the sidelocks. Between the pin-heads and numerous screw heads, the outside of the action is busy but not visibly so, as many of the heads are obscured by the case coloring. All screw-head and plate-alignment seams on our gun were flawlessly flush.

The case coloring on the Essencia's action is stunning, and the standard engraving pattern is a fine scroll.

Our test gun came with gold-plated double triggers. The front trigger is articulated to save knuckle dinging. Pulls were crisp and consistent at 4¾ pounds front and 6 pounds rear. As the Essencia is a bespoke gun, you can order whatever pulls you wish. If you prefer a single (non-selective) trigger, that is available for an additional $1,450. The trigger guard has rounded edges on both sides.

As important as the triggers are on any gun, on a field gun a smoothly operating safety is just as important. The safety action on our gun had just the right feel to it. The Essencia comes with your choice of an automatic or manual safety. The safety button has a high, aggressively checkered bump. Your thumb will positively not slip, but a lot of use will put a hole in your glove.

The automatic ejectors appear to be the tried-and-true Southgate system. Ejector mating to the face of the breech showed flawless machining. They functioned flawlessly too, without needlessly hurling the empties into the next time zone the way some guns do.

Our test gun was one of the original prototypes. It was a 20-gauge with 28" barrels and 3" chambers. Forcing cones were of normal length, unlike the lengthened cones so long a feature on K-80 target guns. At .624", the bores were slightly over the .615" standard. The fixed chokes were of the conical parallel type and were listed as Improved Cylinder and Modified, but you can order anything you want, including Briley screw chokes, for an extra fee. The fixed chokes were carefully cut, with the tighter choke showing an increase in length of the conical and parallel sections compared to the more-open choke. It is this flexibility of choke length that gives fixed chokes an advantage over screw chokes, especially in tighter constrictions. Many choke designers feel that tighter chokes require longer cones and parallels than more-open chokes. Fixed chokes permit this extra length, whereas the uniform lengths of screw chokes do not. The Essencia manual suggests that if you must use steel shot, use it in steel-approved screw-choked barrels with Modified or less. Surely a gun like this deserves a more-benign nontoxic-shot load.

The barrel rib is flat, concave and slightly raised. It's a nice compromise between the raised rib and the swamped game rib. There's a tasteful metal bead up front. The rib surface is plain, with what seems to be a slightly duller finish than the flawlessly rust-blued barrels. It was all beautifully done, with one exception: Our test gun clearly showed the solder seam where the main rib met the 2" stub rib at the breech end. As our test gun had been shot a good bit, I wouldn't mention it except that I saw the same seam exposed in some product photos of another Essencia. The rest of the gun was so exquisite that this flaw really stood out.

The Essencia is a seven-pin back-action sidelock in which the locks and bridles are case colored, the springs are polished and everything else is gold plated.

The 20-gauge-frame Essencias can be had with extra 16- or 28-gauge barrel/forend sets for $10,450 each. Extra 20-gauge barrels are $8,450, because you don't need an extra forend.

What isn't uniquely Teutonic is an appreciation of gorgeous wal-nut. It's always difficult to describe the wood on a gun like this, because you can order pretty much what you want. The dimensions are up to you, as they should be. The quality of walnut on our sample was simply stunning. I don't know whether this was the "Grade II" standard wood or the "Very Best," at an optional $2,000. I couldn't imagine someone ordering a $30K gun and not springing for the best wood.

Checkering was a whole lot of lpi—about as fine as you can get and still provide a gripping surface. It was perfectly cut, too, with no errors at the corners or edges. Ditto on the checkered butt. The stock was finished in Tru-Oil, as so many of the best European stockmakers do. Krieghoff advises that you rub down the stock with a drop or two of Tru-Oil every now and then to keep it fresh.

The forend is listed as a semi-beavertail, but it is so "semi" that it could pass for a splinter, with just a touch more depth in front where the Anson pushbutton is. The interior of the forend is finished to the same level as the exterior. Even the visible parts of the ejector mechanism are gold plated.

Which leads us to the gingerbread. The action of the gun is available in coin silver nitride or blue if you don't wish the standard case coloring. But if you don't get the case coloring, even your dog shouldn't come when you call. The Essencia's case coloring is stunning, exceptional, breathtaking. The blending of vibrant blues, straws, purples and other hues are beyond description. I understand that it was done in Germany by Joerg Schilling. I've not seen better from St. Leger or Turnbull. I was told that Krieghoff uses a proprietary clear-coating process that should immeasurably extend the life of the colors. Our test gun was several years old and had been through many hands. The gold wash on the front trigger was just starting to thin, but even the case coloring of the much-handled edges of the action had not thinned.

Unfortunately, there is a pimple on the nose of perfection. Each side of the action is inflicted with large gold letters screaming "Krieghoff." I know that the company is justly proud of its gun but, in an offering so otherwise tasteful, this is a bit much. Something a little subtler might be in order.

You can have any kind of engraving your wallet will tolerate, but the standard pattern is just about perfect. It's about 10-percent coverage of nicely executed fine scroll, mostly along the borders and receiver bottom. It's a beautiful less-is-more look that fits the restrained and classic overall appearance. It doesn't fight with the rest of the gun for recognition the way the engraving does on so many over-embellished sidelocks.

This is important, because it is the shape of the Essencia action—not any particular added embellishment—that imparts its grace. I'll be frank with you and commit a little heresy. Although I always have admired the quality of a classic traditional sidelock, the juxta-

position of the flat sidelock plate with the rest of the curved surfaces of the gun has always seemed to clash. The Essencia is mechanically a sidelock, but it has a dainty rounded action. The sidelocks flow into the stock with just the slightest curve on the edges. There is no drop-point transition. There are no abrupt edges. The underside of the action is substantially curved to fit the hand for comfortable field carry. Yes, I know that everyone is rounding sidelock actions these days, but not like this. The Essencia's smooth curves are echoed by the slightly convex double-indent outline at the rear of the diminutive sidelocks reminiscent of an 1880s British gun like a Scott, Blanch or H&H Dominion. It's gorgeous. It's sensual. It passes the "close your eyes and run your hands over it" test. No rough segments. No awkward angles. Just smooth-flowing perfection.

The Essencia isn't all just good looks either. It's a shooter. At 6 pounds 6 ounces, it is about right for a 20-gauge. Balance was on the pin. I didn't measure moment of inertia, but the gun feels as though it carries just a little bit more of its weight at the extremities than some more-center-weighted British 20s I've shot. Not too much, but just enough to impart some stability while permitting rapid movement. Of course this is all a matter of personal taste, but I really think that in spite of its extraordinary looks, this gun was designed by a shooter for a shooter. Sometimes you can have your strudel and eat it too.

Barrel convergence, ejectors, triggers and safety all worked as they were supposed to, though, as mentioned, I might lighten the trigger pulls just a touch. They were certainly crisp enough and gave instant response. The barrels and action were also easy to clean—a sign of smoothly machined surfaces.

As befits such a gun, the Essencia comes with a first-class all-leather Emmebi case with separate canvas cover. It contains snap-caps, which Krieghoff advises you use to relax the springs before storage. There is a one-year warranty. I should also mention that the Krieghoff service in the US is among the best you will ever experience.

I have written gun reviews both here and elsewhere for a number of years. During that time I have shot junk and gems. This little 20 touched me in a way that few others have. It's one of those fortuitous combinations of form and function. It is stunning to look at, very well made and delightful to use. The Essencia name was well chosen. It's what a shotgun is all about.

McKay Brown

~~~~

While we generally think of side-by-sides as either sidelocks or boxlocks, there is a third type. It's the triggerplate round action. Compared to the others, it's a smaller and more elegant mechanism, which many consider the strongest of all.

The basic design of the Scottish round action was a Dickson improvement of the MacNaughton triggerplate action. Dickson patents spanned the 1880s, and today the guns are made by John Dickson & Son and by McKay Brown. They are little changed in design.

David McKay Brown used to work for Dickson, and he used the knowledge gained there to make his version of the Dickson round action when he started his own shop in Glasgow in 1967. Today he is recognized as one of the foremost gunmakers in the world.

On the other side of the Atlantic, Lee Leone retired in 2003, and when he did, he wanted more than the usual gold watch. He hunted a lot and wanted a really good upland bird gun. Lee has been a grouse and woodcock hunter all his life. He lives in the Northeast Kingdom of Vermont a few miles from the Canadian border. He has

bred, raised and trained his own setters for hunting. He literally could send the dogs out his back door and chase ruffed grouse.

Lee sought the advice of *Shooting Sportsman* writers Michael McIntosh and Douglas Tate, both of whom recommended a McKay Brown Scottish round-action side-by-side. He went to Scotland with Doug, who introduced him to David.

Lee ordered his 20-gauge round-action in 2003 and received it 21 months later, in 2005. Since then he has shot it a good deal on New England grouse and woodcock, as well as on numerous trips to the Dakotas for pheasants, Huns and sharptails. It definitely has been used as it was intended. As this is a bespoke gun made to suit Lee's requirements, as I discuss it I'll talk about why Lee set it up the way he did.

Much has been written about the Dickson-style round action, but examining and shooting one gave me an even greater appreciation of what the Scots have contributed to shotgun development. At a casual glance, the uninitiated might think it a common Anson & Deeley boxlock. Nothing could be further from the truth.

The McKay Brown side-by-side round action is petite yet tremendously strong. The heavily rounded bar of the action tucks well underneath the 20-gauge barrels. The action is only 1.4" wide at the replaceable hinge and .87" deep. It is so small and dainty yet, with the mainsprings aft and the ejector mechanism more centered, the action bar is more solid than in other designs.

This is because the McKay Brown is a triggerplate action. It places all the action bits on one integral central stanchion on the narrow triggerplate. The long arching single-arm bow springs (as opposed to the usual A&D and sidelock hairpin springs, with their vulnerable 180° bends) appear to be extremely robust. The bow springs even have roller bearings where they attach to the hammers. David told Lee that it's not necessary to dry fire the gun to relax the bow springs before storage; it's just fine to leave them under tension.

The action of the gun also contains the ejector mechanism. The forend metal is devoid of anything except the cocking stud, which on opening drives back the action rod, which cocks everything. The forend has no ejector hammers as you see in the Southgate system. It is all very simple and very clean.

The ejectors are powered by large coil springs in the action that operate projecting cams on the water table. These cams are compressed when the action is closed and act to assist in opening the gun. From the outside, it looks a bit like Purdey's Beesley self-opener system.

Lockup is by underbolt engagement of the two barrel lumps in the style of Purdey. As an indicator of action strength, the McKay Brown's lumps are wider than usual. With a dash of Scottish practicality, there is also a rib extension third fastener engaged by the Scott spindle, somewhat akin to that on my old Webley & Scott 500. Other than the notch for the third fastener, the breech face is plain, showing only the firing-pin holes. Firing pins are separate from the hammers. The gun does not feature disk-set pins, so a broken one is removed from the rear of the action.

Cosmetically, the action interior is a Technicolor clockwork of

gold plating, burnished steel, nitre bluing and case coloring or soft silver, all carefully finished. To see all of this, you remove the triggerplate by unscrewing it from the bottom. It doesn't pop out like a Perazzi, but it does come out as a single piece.

Machining on the gun is a combination of old and new. Where needed, basic parts are sent out to be CNC machined and then returned to the shop for final fitting by hand. As one of my betters once said, only the last file stroke counts.

Lee ordered his gun with double triggers, though a non-selective single trigger is available for those who must. The front trigger blade is not articulated, something you shouldn't need if the stock length and wrist are correct. Lee has quite a large hand, and I noticed that the front trigger blade on the gun was made with less curvature than usual to provide a bit of extra finger room for him. Nice touch. And that's the problem with reviewing a gun like this. It is truly bespoke. Just about everything except the basic construction of the action is built to the buyer's taste.

The engraving of the action was described as small Scottish scroll done in a

The wood-to-metal fit was excellent—as was Creative Art's small Scottish scroll engraving.

coin finish. The hand engraving is by the Italian guild Creative Art and, as expected, it is absolutely first class. Of course you can order any engraving you wish. Two of my favorite McKay Brown round-actions are the "Woodcock Gun" and the "Crocodile Gun," engraved by Scotsman Malcolm Appleby. Both are museum quality. Lee picked a coin finish rather than case coloring because the coin finish would hold up better when the gun was carried a lot in the field.

This is also a good place to mention metal-to-metal fit. The main seam where the trigger-plate fits into the bottom of the action was so finely fitted that I needed a 10X loupe to find it.

The classic chopper-lump barrels were 29" long with a proper swamped game rib. McKay Brown will make the gun with a raised rib if you prefer that sighting plane for high driven birds. To me, that would introduce a hard line on an otherwise gloriously curved gun, but it's your money. The bluing on the barrels was a soft rust blue and, as you can imagine, properly done.

Interestingly, the 20-gauge bore diameters were .624", about .009" overbore from the nominal .615". There are those who view a slight overbore as a ballistic enhancement. The fixed chokes Lee selected were .007" and .014", about Improved Cylinder and Modified. Teague's excellent custom screw-ins are available for those who can't make up their minds. Chambers were 2³/₄". Forcing cones appeared conventionally short. The London proof was marked 950 bar, or 13,775 psi. With these chokes, Lee prefers 1-oz B&P No. 7¹/₂s or 8s for grouse in the East and 1-oz nickel-plated B&P or Fiocchi No. 6s in the right barrel and No. 5s in the left for South Dakota pheasants and sharpies.

While McKay Brown will make the 20-gauge round-action at about 6 pounds, Lee requested a weight of about 6¹/₄ pounds to go with the longish 29" barrels. When the gun came in at 6 pounds 4.6 ounces, David apologized but said that the balance was absolutely correct, so he didn't want to touch it. Needless to say, Mr. Brown is a perfectionist. He told Lee that he wouldn't sell the McKay Brown name when he retired. He didn't want someone else making guns under his name that he couldn't oversee and supervise.

Wood dimensions are to the customer's order. Lee selected a classic English stock and splinter forend to complement the lines of the gun. When visiting the shop to order the gun, he was shown a number of highly figured stock blanks and said that he took an unconscionable amount of time to select between the two finalists. He wisely chose one with straight grain from the action head to the wrist, where strength is needed, before it turned on the charm behind the wrist. An advantage to the round action is that the head of the stock is not cut away as much as it is on a sidelock, so it is stronger. Wood-to-metal fit at the head was excellent and just proud enough to allow a refinishing or two.

Simple, strong, small and beautiful, David McKay Brown's modern take on the Scottish triggerplate round action is an icon of fine gunmaking.

As an anal-retentive gun writer, I looked hard for flaws on the gun. Fortunately, I found a few flattish diamonds in the hand checkering along one edge of the oil-finished forend. Thank goodness. Reviewing a perfect gun would be so boring, not to mention fawning.

In the five years that Lee has owned the gun, he figures he's taken it afield more than 100 days. The gun has experienced no breakage or failures of any kind. I've hunted with Lee in South Dakota and seen him use it to great effect.

I was only able to shoot the gun at clays for one day, but it was long enough to get a sense of it. Were I so fortunate, I would have ordered the gun exactly as Lee did, with perhaps slightly different stock dimensions to suit my build and shooting style. Barrel length, weight and balance were spot on. The gun had that rare balance between stability and agility. As Lee is primarily a grouse hunter, I knew the gun was built for speed, but it also handled longer targets in a steady fashion. At least it did until I started to aim, and then I got what I deserved. This gun was really set up right and reflects what a knowledgeable shooter wanting a reactive gun would select.

Both triggers were set at 4³/₄ pounds, and there might have been just a touch of creep on the front after five years. Ejectors were perfectly timed, and they hurled the empties a full 15 feet. Spectators beware. Barrel convergence appeared correct, as one would

The retirement gift that keeps on giving.
Lee Leone with the review gun—his pride and joy.

expect on a handmade—and hand-regulated—gun of this quality. The assisted opening was just that. If the gun were cocked and closed, simply moving the lever over would open the gun fully. If it were just fired, moving the lever over would open the gun only about halfway, not enough to eject the shells and recock. By the way, moving the opening lever was greasy smooth, with absolutely no drag from the spindle or bolt. This shows flawless machining and finishing. Another indication of proper joining is that after shooting, the high polish on the standing breech and barrel faces stayed free of carbon.

The current price for the Round Action in 12, 16, 20 and 28 gauge is £29,000, £1,000 more in .410. Engraving is extra and runs from £3,375 up (way up). In dollars, as I write this, a 20-gauge with very nice basic engraving would start at about $50,000.

If I wanted a sub-gauge double and price were not a concern, I would unhesitatingly pick a McKay Brown Side-by-Side Round Action. While not as famous as a Purdey, H&H or Fabbri, the McKay Brown has a certain charm that I have not found elsewhere. The rounded action, the triggerplate bow springs, the subtle curve of the top tang, the marvelous balance, the inherent strength and the obvious quality all draw me to this classic Scottish gun. And it has little to do with the fact that my middle name is Campbell.

Merkel 2116ELC

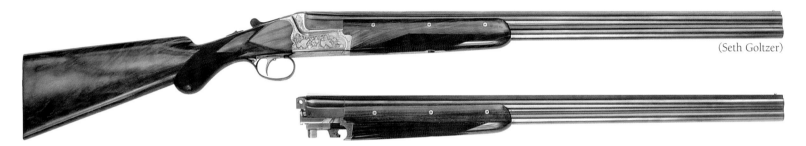

(Seth Goltzer)

Merkel without a 16-gauge over/under is like *Weiner* without its *Schnitzel*. It's just not right. Merkel has a 16 side-by-side, but the 16 O/U ceased in the late '90s, when Merkel changed its O/U line from the 200 series to the new 2000 series and the 16 didn't make the cut. Five years later, in 2005, the 16 O/U returned. That fall *Shooting Sportsman* Ed-in-Chief Ralph Stuart mentioned that he would be hunting with the Merkel 2116ELC 16- and 20-gauge O/U two-barrel combo and that I would be welcome to test the gun afterward. I jumped at the chance.

I'll start this review with the barrels, because they're the most important part of any shotgun, and Merkel's are exceptional. The tubes are made by cold-hammer-forging, which is reputed to impart a higher surface hardness than other methods. Rather than use a conventional monoblock, each barrel is sleeved into its own small block, and then the two blocks are brazed together. Merkel refers to

this as a "demibloc." The upper barrel's block has the twin Kersten lock tabs machined into it, whereas the lower barrel's block has the two underlumps. Otherwise the barrels and ribs are soft-soldered together.

The interiors of the barrels are traditional but with a difference. The 16-gauge has a slight .007" overbore, whereas the 20 is oversized by a more significant .012". The forcing cones are traditionally short. Even though the modern trend is toward longer cones, in a field gun some makers still prefer short cones. They believe that a rapid transition from chamber to bore may produce a better gas seal with fiber wads or in cold temperatures when some plastic wads can harden.

Merkels come with fixed chokes, not screw-ins. Chokes in both barrel sets of the test gun were listed as Improved Cylinder and Modified. Both ICs measured .008", whereas the Modified on the

20 was .016" and on the 16 was .018". These measurements are certainly normal. What was a little different is that Merkel uses relatively short conical chokes with no parallel section. Many chokemakers feel that a parallel section at least equal to the length of the shot column helps stabilize the shot just before it exits the barrel. I've seen excellent performance from chokes cut both ways, but I thought that I should mention it.

Both barrel sets are 27⅞" in length. The side ribs are solid, as is the top rib. I'm a fan of solid top ribs on O/U field guns because they can't pick up brushy detritus the way vent ribs can. A solid rib is also easier to clean after a rainy hunt. The solid top rib—actually an inverted U-shaped piece of metal—is stronger and more resistant to dents than most vent ribs, too. Besides, I think it looks cool. The top rib is completely flat, with no ledges, steps or swoops to destroy the line. It has a graceful taper from breech to nose and a modest brass bead at the front. It's just right.

The 20-gauge barrels weighed 3 oz more than the 16s. One wag told me that it was obviously because of the smaller hole, but the barrels had different outside diameters, too. Actually, it's common for the smaller-gauge barrels to be heavier on combo guns, especially some 20/28 combos.

Merkel offers only 12- and 20-sized actions in the 2000 O/U series. Our 2116 20/16 combo is built on a true 20-gauge action. Merkel describes the lock design as a "modified Anson & Deeley" where the hammer and sears are mounted inside the frame. This contrasts to the Blitz triggerplate action of the previous 200 O/U series. The Merkel-trained service-department head at the US distributor said that the new action is more rigid. The Merkel action is easily identified by its Kersten crossbolt locking mechanism. Twin locking lugs from the upper barrel demibloc are engaged by a transverse crossbolt. The crossbolt is visually and physically intrusive when the gun is open. If you carry the gun broken, it can snag on things. Some find that the protruding locking lugs interfere with hasty reloading. But Merkel actions are strong, that's for sure. Handsome is as handsome does.

A standard Browning-type hinge pin combined with a Kersten crossbolt produce one of the taller O/U receivers. (Seth Goltzer)

The crossbolt with its two locking extensions is the sole active receiver lock. The bottom-barrel demibloc has two huge lugs that passively engage cavernous recesses in the bottom of the receiver. It's interesting to note that one of the locking-lug recesses in the bottom of the receiver has a replaceable shim block. According to Merkel, this was used to precisely mate the barrel lug to the receiver at the time of manufacture. You'd think that Merkel's extensive use of CNC and EDM technology would obviate such a fitting adjustment. Perhaps the Germans simply are being meticulous.

Hinging is via a standard replaceable, full-width Browning-type pin. This and the crossbolt contribute to one of the taller O/U receivers. The Merkel's action is $1/3$" taller than that of a Beretta 686 20-gauge and $1/8$" higher than that of a Browning Superposed 20. Fortunately, the bottom of the Merkel receiver is nicely rounded, so it has a comfortable one-hand carry (when closed) in spite of its height. Merkel actions always take a little firmness to close. The manual advises you not to feed the opening lever closed by hand. Let it snap shut. Earlier Merkels I tried were much stiffer when new.

The 2000-series Merkel O/Us also differ from the 200-series guns in that the new guns use coil springs, replacing the leaf springs of the older line. Coil springs seldom break, but they do degrade over time. Leaf springs work at 100-percent efficiency until they snap. Leaf springs are reputed to produce faster lock times and crisper triggers, but I'd be hard pressed to prove that. The mechanical single trigger on our 2116 was exceptional. It had zero slop, creep or overtravel. The sears broke like glass at 4 pounds each and were better than most of the leaf-spring Perazzi triggers I've used. The Merkel trigger blade can be moved about $1/4$" fore and aft as an accommodation for hand size. Double triggers are available if you prefer. The manual top tang safety is a simple fore-and-aft on/off switch. It operated crisply and had a nice bump on it, so your thumb won't slip. An auto safety is an option.

The 2000-series O/Us have a new barrel selector, replacing the 200s' trigger-based sliding selector. The new one is an odd-shaped toggle set within the trigger guard just behind the trigger blade. It's sort of neat, and hunters with double-jointed fingers might actually be able to select a barrel with a bird in the air.

The receiver has Merkel's version of disk-set strikers. A large oval plate Allen-keyed into the face of the standing breech is removable for servicing firing pins and springs. Both the demibloc and interior of the receiver are carefully finished and polished where appropriate. It's beautiful interior work and definitely shows that you are dealing with a better class of gun. (Unfortunately, when it comes to cleaning time, the receiver area also has more nooks and crannies than an English muffin.) In keeping with the German penchant for extra gizmos, the automatic ejectors can be disabled and used as extractors by simply turning a small slot-head screw on each side of the rear of the forearm.

They really got the wood right on this gun. The traditional Merkel three-piece forend is there in all of its slender glory and complication. The two upper sidepieces are permanently attached to the lower barrel with three screws each, whereas the lower unit is detachable via a perfectly fitted Deeley pull-down latch. The advantage of the more expensive and complicated three-piece forend is that the top pieces are mated to the barrel as though they grew out of the metal. The downside is that they are hard to remove for cleaning or for disassembly of the ejectors. Merkel's forearm is one of the smallest and sleekest available on any O/U. It is a major contributor to the gun's fine sense of handling.

Stocks on this gun are available with an English grip or the relaxed, rounded half-pistol grip that was on our gun. The latter is virtually identical to the "long tang, round knob" grip on the Superposed 20-gauge, which means it's about perfect. Relaxed enough not to cramp the hand in field conditions, the round knob allows extra purchase with the lower two fingers for better gun control. The grip seemed to suit everyone who tried it. The off-the-shelf stock dimensions of our test gun were $14^5/16$" x $1^3/8$" x $2^3/8$", with about $1/4$" cast-off and 3" of pitch to a plastic buttplate. The stock is attached with a standard drawbolt. If the standard dimensions don't suit you, a custom stock is available for about $2,000 more. Where practical, buying the standard stock and then bending it to your dimensions could save you a lot of money.

Our gun came with nicely figured wood showing striking contrasts in light and dark tones. The oil finish was glorious. The color was just right and glowed with a soft matte sheen. Pores were fully filled. Everything was smooth and correct. Merkel's stockmakers had finished the wood properly on the inside, too. Wood-to-metal fit was very good even at the convoluted line where the stock heads up. The hand checkering (20 lpi) was suitably fine for a gun of this class, but it also provided enough grip to be practical. Few things are more useless on a field gun than checkering so fine that it's slippery.

The 2116ELC is midway between the 2000EL and 2002EL on the Merkel scale of Teutonic magnificence. Our test gun came with a game-scene-engraved receiver and a silver nitrite finish. No one ever argues with pretty wood, but receiver decoration is open to opinion. Some don't like silver receivers on game guns, no matter how durable the finish. German game scene engraving is also an intensely personal thing. The engraving on our gun was done by one of Merkel's 14 in-house engravers. The grouse, quail and setter scene was nicely hand cut, if you like the style. I've seen some German engraving that looked as though it had been squashed in with the tread of a Tiger tank, but this was pretty good. Still, most of the people I showed the gun to said they would have preferred a blued or case-colored receiver with a simple Arabesque pattern. Merkel anticipated this, because the

The action is locked with a Kersten crossbolt, and the bottom-barrel "demibloc" has two lugs that engage recesses in the receiver bottom.

(Seth Goltzer)

gun also comes as a less-adorned Model 2016, with a case-colored receiver and modest scroll engraving.

General workmanship on the gun was excellent. A couple of niggling "quality holidays" did show up: There was a minuscule gap where one end of the hinge pin fit the receiver. In the right light the bluing on the trigger guard seemed slightly speckled. This is clearly nit-picking, but I have to find something wrong with each test gun, and this is all I could come up with. Besides, for the price, you should expect perfection.

Our test 2116ELC, with its mid-range engraving and two sets of barrels, retails for $14,195. With just the 16-gauge barrels, it would be the 2116EL and sell for $9,995. It's also available as a 20-gauge. I know of one specially ordered 2116ELC with the combo of 16- and 28-gauge barrels so, if you request it, Merkel will oblige. If you'd prefer a case-colored receiver and modest scroll engraving, as I do, ask for the 2016EL. You'll save a few thousand dollars. These prices reflect the havoc caused by the decline of the dollar against the euro, but they also reflect the obvious first-class quality of these guns. Merkels all come with nice Emmebi Italian cases, and there is a five-year factory warranty. Since 2005, Merkels have been imported and serviced by Merkel USA, located in Trussville, Alabama.

In 2010 Steyr Arms acquired Merkel USA, but Merkel remained in the same facility.

With the 20-gauge barrels, our 2116 weighed 6 pounds 11.2 ounces. That's pretty heavy for a 20-gauge field gun. It's also a lot more than the 6 pounds 4 ounces advertised in Merkel literature. My 28" FN Superposed 20 weighs 6 pounds 4 ounces, and the difference is noticeable. Our Merkel was beautifully balanced and hid its *avoirdupois* well, but you would be carrying around a half-pound more than necessary. Fortunately, the barrel weight is distributed all along the tubes, not in a glob at the end the way it is with some modern screw-choke barrels. (If you want screw chokes in the Merkel, send the gun to Briley for aftermarket work.) The extra weight made the gun very smooth to shoot on clays, yet it is clearly fast enough for gamebirds. It has 3" chambers and was manageable with 3" 1¼-dram Remington NitroMag buffered No. 4s—my favorite Neanderthal 20-gauge shells for birds that bite back.

I confess that I haven't been a 16-gauge fan. It has nothing to do with the gauge's performance; it's an ammo-availability issue. When you descend from the puddle jumper onto the deserted tarmac of Frozen Nose, Montana, or Possum Bottom, Arkansas, and ask for a box of 16-gauge 1⅛-ounce copper No. 5s at the local hardware store, you'll be treated like the space alien you are. Yes, on most domestic airlines it's possible to check five kilograms (or four boxes) of carefully packed ammo, but the TSA at JFK went berserk the last time I tried it, so it can be a pain. Sixteen-gauge reloading components are also harder to come by than those for 12s and 20s. (Addicts who need group support can go to www.16ga.com.)

That said, with the 16-gauge barrels in place, the Merkel certainly did handle well. At 6 pounds 8.2 ounces, the setup was 3 oz lighter than the 20 and felt it. The 16 seemed a little faster and a little easier to shoot. In spite of the fact that both barrel sets were equally choked at IC & M, on clays it seemed I only had to be close to the bird to get a good break with the 16, whereas I had to be spot on with the 20. Paper patterns, especially with the Modified barrels, showed the 16 to be tighter. Go figure. It makes me wonder whether all that drivel about the "square shot column" and mythically short shotstring of the 16 may not have a grain of truth to it. There's no question that I shot the 16 better. The gun just felt so completely right. Even the Merkel receiver, which seemed oversized on the 20, was in perfect proportion for the 16.

The bottom line is that the 2116 is good in the guise of a 20 but positively perfect as a 16. This Merkel has everything I like in a gun—flawless handling and balance, vault-like construction, first-rate assembly quality and supreme complication with enough quirkiness to be fun. If ever a gun could win me over to the whimsy of the 16, this would be it.

Perazzi MX8/20 28-Gauge

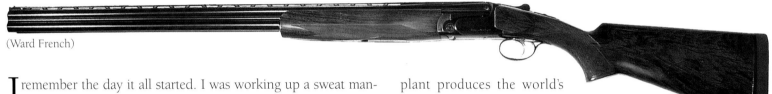

(Ward French)

I remember the day it all started. I was working up a sweat manfully defending some Argentine winter wheat from air assault by the bird of peace. I was using a 12-gauge anti-aircraft battery and had fired enough shells to be pounded into the ground like a tent stake. The outfitter was going to have to dig me out of the dirt or just cover me over and mark the site. I knew there had to be a better way. I needed a softer-shooting dove gun.

A long-barreled 20-gauge auto was too easy and made too much sense. I wanted—no, *needed*—a 28. Through the years I've owned a number of 28s, but they've been mostly the short-range, fast-reacting guns appropriate to the gauge. This time I wanted a longer-range 28 with a long sighting plane. I wanted it to have enough weight to be stable but not so much as to be tiring. And it had to be strong, able to shoot a ton and not disintegrate. It was time to "build" a Perazzi.

The first incarnation of the Perazzi firm was started in 1960 in Brescia, Italy, by Daniele Perazzi and Ivo Fabbri. In 1965 Fabbri left to pursue perfection in gunmaking; Perazzi stayed to emphasize the competition gun. Both succeeded. Today Perazzi's ultra-modern plant produces the world's most successful competition guns. The company has won more Olympic, World and European championship medals than all other manufacturers combined. In Sydney in 2000, half of the Olympic shotgun medals went to Perazzi. In Athens in 2004, Perazzi won 66 percent of all shotgun medals. In Beijing in 2008, it was 75 percent. Perazzi also offers an excellent line of durable field guns. With the ability to combine parts to order, the maker can produce a truly custom gun if you know what to ask for.

For years I'd been impressed by the long, lean feel of Perazzi O/U competition sporters built for the British market. These emphasize lengthy but light barrels with thin forends and slender stocks. Because I was passing through London in the fall of 2001 on the way to shoot in North Yorkshire, I took a side trip to a Perazzi dealer in Wales. There I was able to try a large selection of Perazzis at the Treetops shooting grounds. My wife and I stayed in a charming little country inn while I designed my dove gun.

The barrels would have to be long, to avoid the whippiness of many 28s, yet of reasonable weight. A 34" Perazzi 20-gauge I tried was too much, so we settled on 31½" barrels. The total gun length would be about the same as a 28" auto. The side ribs were to be solid from the forend to the muzzle but ribless under the forend, to shift weight forward. Of the several top ribs available, I chose a vented, flat, tapered one with a single brass bead up front. I'm not a fan of raised ribs and center-bead clutter.

Perazzi offers three action sizes for its 28s. The dedicated 28-gauge action was too light for what I wanted and, at twice the price, too dear for my purposes. Twenty-eight-gauge barrels hung on the 12-gauge action would have been too heavy. The midsize 20-gauge action would be just right. It came with either a selective, non detachable trigger or the traditional Perazzi removable trigger. The fixed-trigger action weighs a couple of ounces less because it is narrower, but it just wouldn't have seemed like a real Perazzi to me unless I could yank the trigger out to show my buddies. I picked the removable-trigger MX8/20 action.

Perazzi detachable triggers can be selective or non-selective, leaf spring or coil. Because I already had decided to go with a pair of fixed tight-Modified (.016") chokes, the simpler non-selective trigger would be appropriate. In the melee of dove shooting I've never had time to fuss with swapping barrels and chokes. I just want to jam in the shells

The MX8 monoblock has side cheeks bearing on the receiver's lugs, permitting a shallow action.

and fire. Besides, Perazzi really knows how to cut fixed chokes. Because of their "one length fits all" design, screw chokes were a compromise I didn't want when trying to make the little 28 perform. Also factory screw chokes often concentrate weight at the muzzle, not along the barrel, where I wanted it.

Coil springs versus leaf springs is a multi-beer discussion. Leaf springs have the reputation of being a little crisper. I can't prove that, but they do work 100 percent until they don't work at all. Coils are the old soldiers and just fade away over time. In the field coils are probably more reliable, but the Luddite in me opted for the traditional leaf. Besides, Perazzi includes a neat little kit of extra springs, a fitting tool and firing pins with each gun.

The insides of the trigger and action of the MX8s are beautifully machined but not hand-polished. Edges are razor-sharp. The MX8/20 is just a miniature of the classic 12-gauge Perazzi MX8 action. It employs Boss hinge stubs and a split locking tongue engaging shoulders halfway up the rear of the monoblock. There are no lumps under the monoblock, but its sides have cheeks that theoretically bear on side lugs in the receiver. This permits a shallow action, the durability of which is beyond question. Ask any Olympic shotgunner.

Wood dimensions are to your preference. Perazzi will build just about anything you can describe. Someone simply punches your numbers into the CNC machine and goes to lunch. I wanted a long, slender forend. No trendy Schnabels, with their Hapsburg lips, thank you. But not some bulky beavertail either. I settled on a minimalist field-style forend, but one about 1½" longer than usual to be in proportion to the long barrels.

Italian competition stocks can be chunky with massive vertical pistol grips—totally out of place in the field. Perazzi's slender field stocks were better suited to my needs. I had the pistol grip relaxed slightly to suit my hand and sent the rest of my dimensions. Standard Perazzi wood comes with a lacquer finish and perfectly nice checkering suitable for a gun that's meant to work for a living. In a nice touch the MX8/20 stock is instantly removable with the supplied tool. I ordered a very thin recoil pad so that I could replace it with a thicker one if I needed more length. Sub-gauge guns usually seem to need more length than standard bores. I wanted to be ready if I'd guessed wrong.

As with any Perazzi, engraving and wood quality are up to you. You pay; the company provides. I felt that the plain blued action was just fine but ordered a modest wood upgrade to improve my chances in the walnut lottery. Perazzi is notoriously chintzy with its standard-grade wood when you compare it to what you see on some much-less-expensive brands. All told, the gun, as ordered to my specs, would cost $4,500 delivered to my US dealer. This 2002 price included all delivery and import taxes and fees. I began to count the days. It was 300-plus before I got the call.

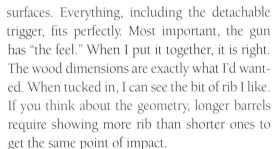

Perazzi is famed for its detachable trigger group.
(Ward French)

The Perazzi arrived in an attractive, practical gun case suitable for many trips to Argentina. The first thing I always notice is the wood. I should have bought more walnut lottery tickets. There is some grain, but it is oddly angled and not equal on both sides. Bluing of the metal is a flawless low luster over immaculate surfaces. Everything, including the detachable trigger, fits perfectly. Most important, the gun has "the feel." When I put it together, it is right. The wood dimensions are exactly what I'd wanted. When tucked in, I can see the bit of rib I like. If you think about the geometry, longer barrels require showing more rib than shorter ones to get the same point of impact.

The gun weighs exactly 7½ pounds, with balance at the hinge. The barrels are stamped at a weight of 1.490 kg, which translates to 3.28 pounds. As a frequently practicing oenologist, I would describe the balance as "moderately dignified," or "smooth with a hint of exuberance." You can sense the full weight if you hold the gun vertically by the barrels, but in the shooting position it comes to life. It has the stability you can only get from long barrels. Heavy short barrels don't feel the same. It certainly isn't a suitable carrying gun for grouse or quail, but for standing still and shooting a ton, this gun is the berries.

At least it would have been if it had worked. It wouldn't set the second trigger. Some genius at Perazzi had fitted the trigger with a 20-gauge inertia block. The lower recoil of the 28 needs a different block. Because I didn't have a single-shot 28 in mind, the gun went to Giacomo Arrighini. If you own a Perazzi in the US, you should know Giacomo. His shop, Giacomo Sporting USA, is in the old Lefever Arms building in upstate New York. When Giacomo strips a Perazzi, his hands move faster than a Times Square sharpie hustling Three Card Monte. The offending inertia block

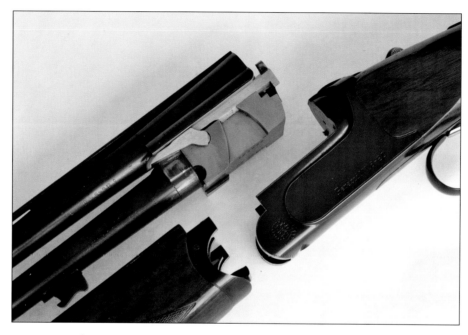

The MX8/20 is not the fanciest gun, but it can be made to the owner's specs for maximum performance. (Ward French)

was exorcised and the correct one installed, tuned and tested while he discussed the fine points of Perazzi maintenance. Giacomo urges easing the opening lever closed by hand rather than letting it snap into place. He also prefers using modern oils like Tri-Flow, Slip 2000 or BreakFree CLP on the bearing surfaces rather than grease. He feels that grease can get squeezed out of the high-pressure points,

whereas oil will always remain. Giacomo also advises relaxing the Perazzi leaf springs during storage.

The gun now functioned perfectly. The hammers dropped at 3$\frac{1}{2}$ and 3$\frac{3}{4}$ pounds, crisp as Peking duck. As with any new O/U, I first tested for barrel convergence. Over/unders often shoot the top barrel high because of the geometry of the action. Fortunately, my gun printed both barrels in perfect overlay. The .016" chokes produced patterns that were 24" wide at 30 yards using $\frac{3}{4}$ oz of No. 8s. That's a very useful pattern for a 28 and can stretch close to 40 yards with good effect on soft birds like doves if everything is right.

I made one final adjustment to stock fit. Effective stock length really should be measured from the middle of the pistol grip to the butt, not from the trigger to the butt, because a trigger finger can easily flex an inch or so. Guns with a fairly relaxed pistol grip can take more length than those with tight-radius grips. After experimenting for a while, I ended up removing the $\frac{1}{2}$" original recoil pad and substituting a 1" pad.

No doves being handy, I opted for clays. The handling of the gun was everything I'd hoped for. It was precise enough for shallow quartering-away targets where the slightest overswing would cause a miss. Close crossers like skeet birds required some muscle to get the gun moving. As I said, it wasn't built for quail.

It shone on longer targets. The long skinny barrels encouraged precision and required less apparent lead. Clay breaks well past 40 yards were impressive, but I had to be absolutely spot-on. There was no forgiving fringe. I've noticed that often doves start to jink when they get inside 30 yards. I wanted this 28 to surprise them a little farther out before they could plan evasive maneuvers.

The entire project was great fun. I had the privilege of dealing with some wonderful people and ended up with what I hope will be a killer dove gun and a fun clay sporter. The gun shoots "bigger" than it is. It moves with a paced but fluid lethality. Its shape is pleasing to my eye. The mechanics are beyond reproach. Best of all, recoil is almost nonexistent. The next time my dove outfitter sees me submerged behind a mountain of hulls, he won't have to dig me up like a turnip.

UPDATE

I got that MX8/20 28 almost 10 years ago. At this writing, it has 23,325 logged rounds through it. (Yes, I log every round I fire. No, I can't help doing it.) That's not all that much for a target-quality gun. There are some very-high-mileage Perazzis in use among the target-shooting fraternity. I've used mine much more for fun clays than serious doves, but it has proven to be a marvelous dove gun when it has gone afield. The gun remains one of my favorites and never fails to please when I take it out for an airing.

Repairs have been modest. Since the gun was first set up with the correct inertia block and a nice trigger job, it has suffered one broken lower-barrel mainspring, one broken ejector and one worn opening-lever spring. Not flawless but pretty good.

That's the good news. The bad news is that today's 2011 retail price from Perazzi USA is $11,270. You might get a bit of a discount from a retailer, but expect to be in the $10,000 range for a basic MX8/20 28. I paid a bit less than the going American price when I bought my gun in England, but a decade has taken its toll.

It's not the fanciest O/U or the most expensive. But if you know enough about how you want to spec it out, for sheer shooting ability this gun has no peer. There is a reason that the best shooters in the world insist on the Perazzi.

Remington 105 CTi

The embossed silver metal grip cap proudly proclaims "Remington—100 years of autoloading shotguns 1905-2005." Founder Eliphalet and his son, Philo, would be proud of the company. It has been almost two centuries of occasional kitchen appliances, typewriters, bicycles and lots of guns. Not the least of the achievements was Remington's popularization of the ubiquitous gas-operated semi-automatic shotgun.

Remington's venture into the semi-auto arena did not start auspiciously. Just after the dawn of the 20th Century, gun-designing genius John Moses Browning approached Winchester with a revolutionary design for an autoloading shotgun. Winchester's powers that be lacked his vision and turned it down, to their eternal regret. Browning next went to Remington in 1902. The company was interested, but negotiations fell through due to the death of one of the Remington principals. Next in line was Fabrique Nationale, in Belgium. FN snapped it up, starting what was to be a long and prosperous Browning partnership that endures to this day. The gun involved was the one we know as the Browning A5 humpback recoil-operated shotgun. Remington quickly bought a license and in 1905 began producing it as the Model 11. It was the first autoloading shotgun produced in the US.

The Model 11 (1905-'45) sired the Sportsman (1930-'47), the Model 48 (1948-'68) and the Model 11-48 (1949-'68), all of which were recoil operated. In 1956 Remington started cooking with gas and produced the Model 58 Sportsman (1956-'63), quickly following it with the gas-operated Model 878 (1959-'63). Together these two guns sold nearly 50,000 annually. But the blockbuster was the justly famous Model 1100. It was introduced in 1963 and continues today in various iterations.

And that's been part of the problem. Good as the Remington 1100 was and is, a lot has happened in gas-gun design in the past 40-plus years. Companies like Beretta have produced superlative, durable semi-automatic gas guns with frequently updated designs. Remington slightly modified the 1100 by adding a spring-clip gas bleed to the 11-87 in an attempt to keep up, but the company still was selling a 40-year-old gun in a rapidly evolving market and a declining market share showed it.

Until now. The new 105 CTi is positively, absolutely new. Remington says it is the first bottom-load/eject autoloader ever. It's the first factory semi-auto I'm aware of with a titanium receiver, roller-bearing trigger sear and oil-filled recoil absorber. The gun currently is available only as a field-grade 12-gauge with a 3" chamber. It is made in Illion, New York, alongside the 1100 but, like most other gunmakers, Remington outsources a number of parts and processes.

The action of the 105 CTi is where most of the innovation is. The "CTi" represents the elemental symbols for carbon and titanium. The action is machined from titanium. Although expensive, it's a great metal for some gun applications. It also gives the PR boys something to trumpet. I don't know if it saves any more weight than the aluminum-alloy receivers used on Berettas and the like, but it is strong. The titanium part of the receiver is coated with blue/black TriNyte, a trademarked tungsten-carbide layer with amorphous carbon overlay that Remington refers to as "tough as diamonds." The woven carbon-fiber insert is cosmetic, but it is eye-catching and gives the gun a new look.

Remington calls the bottom-feed/eject system Double-Down. You and I can just call it Ithaca Model 37 pump. It uses the same kind of split-finger lifter. It combines with the TurboFeed (every feature has a trademarked name) loading system, wherein you just push the

One of the innovative features on the Remington CTi is a rotating collar that locks the bolt in battery.

Rotating Collar

Extractor Claw

first shell partially into the magazine, let go and it is whisked into the chamber. The name may be new, but this feature is shared with Browning Gold autoloaders.

The bolt is unusual in that it locks by rotating like a Benelli's but with a difference. The cast metal bolt has a body, a non-rotating head and a rotating collar between the two. This collar is cammed to rotate into a notch of the barrel extension to lock the bolt in battery. The firing pin is held in the bolt body with a common cotter pin. On the bottom of the front of the bolt is a huge, $1/4$"-wide extractor claw. The charging handle—the piece that used to always fly off your 1100 at the wrong moment—is now firmly anchored to the bolt body. It can be released only with a counter-clockwise quarter-turn when the bolt is closed. Nice touch. At the rear of the bolt is the 5" action link. It connects the bolt assembly and the hydraulic absorber in the stock. The link is one of the parts that used to break all the time on the 1100s, but now it is made from heavy cast metal that looks quite durable.

The trigger is also innovative. The substantial body is cast aluminum alloy with a serviceable black coating on the trigger guard. The interior parts are steel stampings. Unlike the 1100 or Beretta auto trigger, it's fairly complicated, with many tiny hair-width springs and little itsy parts. But it's ingenious too. It doesn't have an ordinary sear. Instead it uses a little roller bar to engage a notch in the hammer. It looks like the link of a bicycle chain. In theory this allows a crisper trigger pull with less acute machining. As with the 1100, the trigger unit is easily removed for cleaning with two punch pins.

Attached to the back of the action is the new Rate Reducer. It looks like the usual tube housing the main spring, but it isn't. Part of it is actually a small oil-filled shock absorber. The harder a heavy shell pushes the bolt back, the more resistance it provides. This normalizes bolt speed and aids parts longevity. This unit also helps somewhat to dampen recoil. With the Rate Reducer handling the rearward bolt movement, bolt-closing energy is supplied by a coil spring wound around the magazine tube like the Benelli or A-5 Browning.

The gas system is somewhat similar to the 1100's in that it uses gas-sealing rings that encircle the blue TriNyte-coated stainless-steel magazine tube. There's one ring in the action sleeve and a second at the front of the under-barrel gas chamber. This time, though, the gas-sealing rings are captive. There is no little rubber O-ring to mess with, but there are a number of fixed rubber buffers in the trigger group and receiver. The action bars are stamped stainless and are held to the action sleeve by Allen screws for easy individual replacement if needed.

Our 12-gauge test gun came with a hammer-forged 28" barrel (26" is also available, but not 30" initially). At .736" in diameter, it is fashionably overbored. The 2"-long forcing cone is also in keeping with the current trend. The bore is polished, not chromed. Three flush-mount stainless screw chokes are included. They are the new Remington ProBore style also seen on the most recent 1100 Competition guns and will not interchange with previous RemChokes. The Improved Cylinder has .010" constriction, whereas the Modified has .020" and the Full .035". These numbers are spot-on nominal.

The chokes are about 2" long and have a ½" stabilizing parallel in front of the taper. The front rims are notched to accept the adequate choke wrench provided. They also have smaller notches to indicate choke constriction. Remington does it backward from just about everyone else in that the tighter the choke, the more notches.

The untapered vent rib is a touch more than ¼" wide. It's made of carbon and aramid fiber and is glued in place. This no doubt saves a little weight over the traditional steel rib. Unfortunately, our rib wasn't on perfectly straight. It also was slightly frayed at the edges when we looked closely. The front bead is the traditional Bradley white-bead-on-a-block competition design. There is also a center steel bead, an odd addition for a field gun.

The outside of the barrel is untapered over the front 20". There is no jugging for the choke. This barrel is nicely balanced and weighs about the same as a 28" Beretta 391 barrel. It's a far cry from Remington's first thick screw-choke barrel, which had all the subtlety of a sewer pipe. Barrel finish is a bright hot blue that is well applied. The exterior on our gun was ripple-free.

The gas chamber hanging under the barrel looks vaguely like that of an 11-87. It has the usual two gas holes connecting the chamber to the bore. Like the 11-87, it also uses spring-clip-stopped vent holes to the outside of the chamber. The 105 has four holes and two such circular clips to regulate excess gas venting. This might have been a running design change, as the photo in the manual shows no such vent clips.

Although the inside is definitely innovative, Remington wisely avoided the ultra-modern disco-dementia exterior design that has plagued some other guns. From the outside, the 105 CTi looks sort of like an 1100. You'll quickly notice the woven-carbon-fiber look atop the receiver. You may even notice the bolt slot without ejection port on the right side.

The wood is standard Remington autoloader. Our stock and

forend had a little figure in the walnut. It was overlaid with a matte version of Remington's durable—but dentable—synthetic finish. The head of the stock and inside of the forend had enough finish to prevent oil absorption. Wood-to-metal fit was typical 1100, though the forend didn't seem as loose. Checkering on our gun was a far cry from the "impressed," or squashed, checkering inflicted on 1100s of the '70s. Today's effort is mechanically applied and very nice indeed. Speaking of cosmetics, the gun has more logos on it than an Indy car. There were nine—count 'em, nine—bits of graffiti on the gun. There was even an embossed "R" on the rear of the operating handle.

Stock dimensions are cataloged as 14¼" x 1½" x 2½", but our test gun was ³/₁₆" lower at the nose. Very low indeed. There was no cast and moderate pitch. This may be fine for the average guy, but because all our readers are above average, it would be nice to custom fit the stock with a shim set like those provided by Beretta, Benelli, Browning and others. Nope. No shims. No adjustment. No hope. What did Remington save in not providing shim adjustment? Fifty cents? Come on, guys.

What's worse, as part of an effort to reduce recoil, the butt of the stock has been forced to endure an extremely convex pad like the Browning Cynergy and Franchi I-12. This Limbsaver brand R3 super elastomer pad has a slightly protruding toe to stick into the pectoral muscles of some shooters. It also bulges forward into the stock. It's supposed to really reduce recoil, but what do you do if

you want to lengthen that short stock? Other pad lengths aren't offered. A standard pad won't fill the concavity. This stock is like buying a suit that can't be altered. Some people will be happy. Many won't. It makes you wonder if the people who make the guns actually shoot them.

Our gun weighed 7 pounds 6 ounces—6 ounces more than stated in the brochure. Its balance was distinctly nose heavy but not terribly so. Like all Remington autoloaders, it performed great as a target gun, and I'm sure it would be ideal in the duck blind. I'd want it to be a little quicker for upland hunting. Still, with the 26" barrel, it would be pretty close. For a 12-gauge autoloader, it certainly is light enough, thanks to that titanium.

Roller-Bearing Sear

Another feature is a roller-bearing trigger sear.

The trigger was an absolute delight. Marvelous. First rate. That roller sear absolutely works. Pull was a consistent, crisp 4½ pounds. Even the trigger blade was a comfortable ergonomic casting. The cross-button safety was in its usual Remington location at the rear of the trigger guard. It can be reversed for left-handed shooters. This was the best factory trigger I've ever used on an autoloader.

And lefties are going to love the bottom ejection. Ejected hulls pitched down and a few feet forward. No more putting red-hot 3" hulls down your partner's neck in the duck blind. Remington promo literature claims that the 105 is easier to load and unload. Every one of my testers who tried it found it difficult and awkward at first.

There was definitely a learning curve, but once that was mastered it was only slightly less convenient than a standard "button closer" autoloader. True, on loading with the TurboFeed feature there is no button to push but, as with the Browning Gold, the first round had to be pushed an exact distance into the magazine before it would be magically whisked up into the chamber without jamming. Learn to deal with the Turbo-Feed, because the 105's bolt-closing lever near the front of the trigger group is really stiff to operate.

Speaking of jamming, our gun averaged two or three jams per 25 shells. Remington says that the gun is designed for 1^1/$_8$-oz 2^3/$_4$" shells through 3" hunting loads. Fair enough. It didn't like mild 1-oz loads, but it would cycle hot 1-ouncers and even the 1,350-fps 24-gram Olympic shells.

The malfunction issue with the 105 was not due to shell strength. It was due to the razor-sharp extractor-claw recess at the bottom of the chamber mouth. Shells that weren't lifted up quite enough got hung on the recess and had quarter-inch-wide strips scalped back from the fronts of the hulls. It occasionally happened on all brands of shells we tried. Perhaps a little judicious stoning would cure it, but it definitely needs addressing.

So too does the non-replaceable recoil pad. The convex pad obviously has more recoil-absorbing material in the middle where you want it. That's good. Remington claims that the rate reducer, recoil pad, overbore barrel and long cone reduce recoil by a whopping "up to 50%." In this relatively light gun, this might make shooting 1^7/$_8$-oz turkey loads bearable. Many who shot our test gun commented on the light recoil. Taller shooters struggled with the non-adjustable gun fit and were unable to appreciate the supposedly lower recoil.

What I didn't fail to appreciate was the incredible Velcro-like grab of the pad. I don't know what miracle techno-polymer Limbsaver uses on that pad, but it's so sticky that it could put the hook-and-loop people out of business. I have never used a pad that wanted to grab my hunting coat like this one. It might work if you mount your gun by pushing it out and then hauling it back, but that's hardly good form. You actually could see some shirt fibers stuck to the back of the pad after my friend used the gun. A couple of turns of electrical tape solved the problem, but Remington should deal with this.

When shooting a fair amount, as you would at doves, the 105 CTi's barrel really got hot. Perhaps the carbon-fiber rib and the barrel expand at different rates, but the slight bend in the rib that was just noticeable when the barrel was cold curved a good bit more when things heated up. Several shooters commented on it. The IC choke tube also kept loosening up.

The 105 CTi is shipped in an FAA-approved molded green-plastic takedown case of average quality. Our gun came with the three chokes, an adequate choke wrench, a manual that you actually should read to learn disassembly, the largest trigger lock I've ever seen, and a magazine plug. Remington's warranty is for two years. Suggested list price is $1,399.

Whether the gun catches on or not remains to be seen. The frequent jams, lack of stock adjustment, bent rib and PETA-approved recoil pad should be easy enough to fix if there is the corporate desire. There is no question that the gun is innovative. Whether or not you consider bottom ejection a major deal, the lower recoil and superlative trigger are pluses.

The big question is whether the gun actually functions better, not just differently, than the competition. Among gas guns, that competition isn't the 1100. It is the class-leading Beretta 391. The 391 is less expensive, well balanced, easily adjusted for fit and has a proven track record of extreme reliability. I was told that future plans for the 105 CTi include a competition model and perhaps sub-gauge guns. I hope that future also holds some fine-tuning of the existing model.

Post Mortem

I wrote this review in 2007. The Remington 105 CTi's lifespan was from 2006 to 2008. Speak no ill of the dead, unless they are politicians, but I told you so. However, peaceful eternal rest was not in the cards. A "New! Improved!" CTi-II briefly surfaced in 2009. It offered a revamped gas valve, bolt improvements and other hopeful engineering changes. It also finally offered an adjustable length of pull. Too little. Too late. It lasted only a few months before mercifully being put down.

Remington Model 332

(Seth Goltzer)

The legend of the phoenix is that of a supernatural creature that lives for 500 years. Nearing death, it builds its own funeral pyre and self-immolates. As it burns, it is reborn from the ashes to live for another half-millennium. Maybe it's a stretch in a shotgun review, but Remington is definitely in the "rising from the ashes" business with its new Model 332 over/under.

It all started with the Remington Model 32, an O/U made from 1931 to 1947 and noted for its separated barrels and hood-style latch. Like Harry Truman, the Model 32 seems more appreciated in death than it was in life. Whether the Model 32 was the victim of the Great Depression and war-time shortages or couldn't compete with John Browning's Superposed masterpiece is your call, but only about 6,000 were made. In a semi-phoenix lateral resurrection, after World War II a modified Model 32 design was produced by Krieghoff, in Germany. It has now morphed into the latter's ubiquitous K-80 target gun.

Remington's phoenix rested from 1947 to 1973, when it rose again as the Model 3200. This had the Model 32's signature split barrels and hood latch plus a very good trigger. It was a decent gun but too ponderous for most field duty. The clay shooters loved it. Matt Dryke used one to win International Skeet gold in the Los Angeles Olympics in '84, one year after the gun was discontinued. That kind of timing ages a PR department.

In 1993 Remington rose again with a totally new O/U design optimistically called the Peerless. Gone were the locking hood and split barrels; in were false sideplates and mediocre quality. The market yawned. After five years the Peerless phoenix lit the match and was reborn as the Remington Model 396, a cosmetic revamp aimed more at the skeet and clays markets. The 396 lasted from '96 to '98 before Remington mercifully put it down. Never a company to rest on its ashes, in 2000 Remington came up with the new 300 Ideal. Like the Peerless before it, the name was inapt. It only lasted a year before rising again, in 2001, as our current phoenix: the Remington 332.

The Remington ad hype pushes the similarities between the 332 and the original 32, conveniently omitting mention of the interim guns. Because the 32 came and went before many of our current readers were born, I wonder about comparing the 332 to a gun most have never seen. The 332 has to be judged against today's guns. At a list price of $1,624, it's up against Ruger, the plainer Citoris and Berettas, various Franchis, Veronas and a host of other phoenix-eaters. The Remington folks swear that they have devoted considerable effort to improving the quality of this new gun—and I believe them.

Our test 332 was a 12-gauge with 28" barrels. As I write this, Remington makes only one model and one gauge in its Ilion, New York, plant. It has a modern design, with nothing mechanically in common with the 32 or 3200. Like all Remingtons— and most other makers' guns in this price area—it was designed to be mass-produced on modern machinery. The steel receiver uses trunnion stub hinges and a Perazzi-style split locking tongue engaging two small shoulders in the lower monoblock. There are also two vestigial lugs at the top rear of the monoblock fitting in the upper sides of the receiver.

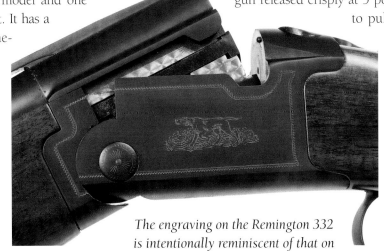

The engraving on the Remington 332 is intentionally reminiscent of that on the Model 32. (Seth Goltzer)

The action is quite compact—about the same size as that of a Beretta 686—and is all machined from a solid chunk of steel, including the integral rear brace between the upper and lower tangs that makers usually insert as a separate piece. Most of the interior bits are stamped or cast metal, with minimal machining. Cutting and casting marks are evident on the inside but not on the outside. The mechanical trigger (something I prefer on a field gun) adds a touch of complexity to an already busy interior. The wire connecting the opening lever to

the safety appears Rube Goldbergian, but it works. The 332 is not as complex inside as a Krieghoff, but it's no Perazzi either.

The safety, as important on a field gun as the trigger, is of the Beretta style, with a lateral barrel-selector toggle inside the safety-switch body. The safety on our gun operated with a satisfying *click* and just the right resistance. It also can be locked in the "fire" position for target shooting. Remington always has been known for decent triggers. After a small bit of take-up, both sears on our gun released crisply at 5 pounds. I like both my O/U triggers to pull the same, because I often shoot the top barrel first for incoming waterfowl and doves.

Barrels are Remington's "Light Contour" profile. As mentioned, our test barrels were 28", but 30" and 26" tubes are available too. The barrels are thin in the middle, to control excessive weight, but jugged at the muzzle, to accept the 2" flush-mounted screw-in RemChokes. Improved Cylinder, Modified and Full chokes are supplied, but anything is available in the aftermarket. Bore diameters were an almost-nominal .727", so Remington has shunned the current overbore craze. The chambers are 3", as befits a field gun with waterfowl potential. The forcing cones are a moderate in-between length that works well with both large nontoxic shot and/or fiber wads.

The rib—non-tapered and 0.3" wide—is raised slightly at the rear. There's a white bead up front and a useless little steel bead in the middle for those who like to aim really hard. The side ribs are solid, full length and brazed in place. In one of the few cosmetic flaws on our gun, there was a slight skipping in the braze line. The barrels are joined at the rear in a conventional monoblock, which also houses the ejectors. For those who don't know how to catch their hulls, the ejectors can be deactivated quickly by easy removal of the ejector sears.

The conventional walnut stock measured 14" x 1½" x 2¼" with zero cast. The pistol grip is relaxed and very comfortable for a variety of hand sizes. The stock is noticeably less deep at the butt than it is on some other guns. This reduces weight and gives the gun a slimmer look, but it also lessens the area—and thus the efficiency—of the 1" black recoil pad. The forend, secured with a Deeley-style pull-down latch, is relatively short with deep finger grooves. It has a very pleasing feel. The forend iron has an adjustment screw for tightness. Our test gun's forend had the slightest amount of lateral play but was otherwise solid.

Cosmetically, the plain American walnut is enhanced by exactly the right shade of dark-brown stain and satin high-tech synthetic finish. The well-executed 20-lpi machine-cut checkering is attractive and aggressive enough to do what checkering is supposed to do. Both the receiver and barrels have the look of classic satin rust bluing—though it's actually done by high-tech bead blasting. Intentionally reminiscent of that on the Model 32, embellishment is a tasteful roll-engraved pointer on one side of the receiver and a setter on the other. Other than the side-rib braze-line gaffe, the outside fit and finish on our gun was excellent. It all looked smashing. Everything comes in a plain cardboard box with the three chokes, a decent choke wrench, an Allen key to adjust the forend, and a confident two-year guarantee.

Obviously, off-the-shelf gunfit is highly subjective. A 14" stock, including the pad, doesn't leave today's taller man many options. Remington and Ruger continue to insist on the short stocks our grandfathers preferred. Still, I shouldn't be so picky, as most of the people I loaned the gun to shot it well. In bulky waterfowl clothing or in the awkward suddenness of a field shot, a short stock has its place.

Our test gun weighed an actual 7 pounds 8 ounces with a nose-heavy bias and high moment of inertia. A 30" version I shot balanced 2" in front of the hinge, and our 28" test gun was close to that. That's the weight penalty you pay for screw chokes in most mass-produced O/Us. In 26" the gun might work for grouse if you don't mind the total weight. With longer barrels, it would shine as a waterfowler or open-country field gun where longer shots emphasize steadiness. The extra muzzle weight did keep the muzzle down for a fast second shot, though it made correcting for erratic flight more difficult. The excellent trigger and crisp safety were real pluses. Remington well understands that weight-forward guns are more forgiving for the average shooter. Perhaps the company does have the golden mean and I'm just being a meany.

I hope that Remington stays with this gun and maintains its considerably improved quality. The phoenix bit has been done to death, and the new 332 deserves to stick around. The model is neither peerless nor ideal, but it is attractive, carefully assembled, easy to shoot and fairly priced. Remington gets credit for keeping the fire burning until it got things right.

Post Mortem

The Remington 332 lasted from 2001 to 2006. If you find one used for much less than $1,000, it might be worth a look. It was a decent gun, though a bit clunkier than its foreign competition. Eventually Remington also offered Peerless, Premier and F Grade embellished 332 models.

The 332 was Remington's last attempt to make an O/U. The company imported an Italian-made Peerless model by Sabatti for a few years after discontinuing the 332, but at this writing Remington does not offer an O/U.

Robertson Side-by-Side

The provenance of the Robertson side-by-side begins with the 1839 birth of John Robertson to a Scottish family of gunmakers. Robertson subsequently worked for Joseph Whitworth and Westley Richards. In 1891 he purchased "best" gunmakers Boss & Co. Wishing to offer a more modestly priced gun in addition to the Boss bests, for a while Robertson had boxlock side-by-sides made under his own name in Birmingham.

Fast-forward one century. At the 2005 SHOT show, Graham Halsey, the boss of Boss, showed me early examples of a reborn Robertson boxlock side-by-side being made in the new CNC-fitted Robertson shop in Birmingham. He introduced me to Gary Clark, designer of the gun and manager of the shop, who took me through the gun. The plan was to start with the sideplated boxlock 20-gauge, then do an over/under 12, and then add a side-by-side 12 and an over/under 20.

Progress has been slower than expected, as it usually is in the British gun trade. To date, only the 20-gauge side-by-side has been produced. Cabela's Gun Library received a half-dozen of the guns made in 2007, and the folks there were kind enough to send me a highly engraved 30" version. It retails for $17,000.

The Robertson action is a blend of classic design and a bit that is modern. The purely decorative sideplates may fool you for a moment, but it is a basic and proven Anson & Deeley boxlock, the most copied side-by-side action in the world. Company literature says the action is "semi-rounded," but the underside looks pretty square to me. It has been brought up to date with a replaceable hinge pin, disk-set firing pins that can be replaced from the breech without removing the stock, and a tightening "draw." Clark noted that this latter bit is an insert behind the rear lump inside the action, similar to one in the 1909 Boss O/U. It is a replaceable block that can be simply changed to tighten the gun if eventually required.

Like my own faithful 1920s Webley & Scott A&D boxlock, the bottom action plate is removable to grant access to the leaf trigger springs, but on the Robertson the plate includes the lower trigger-plate too. And quite a trigger it is.

Though double triggers are available on order if you prefer, the guns that Cabela's received all have single triggers. Single triggers and British guns go together like Cleopatra and asps. True, Boss did and still does make a functional single trigger for its sidelock. In fact, it was John Robertson who invented the Boss single trigger in 1894. The A&D action lends itself more to a single trigger than a sidelock because of the A&D's more centralized lockwork, and our test gun's single was very nice. Pulls were 4$\frac{1}{4}$ pounds right and 4$\frac{3}{4}$ pounds left—both crisp with no creep. Well done. To keep things simple and reliable, the trigger is inertia operated and not selective. Like it or not, the right barrel always fires first.

Opening and closing is by the usual Scott lever. Lockup is courtesy of the proven double underlug. The action was well fit, and it operated with the greased slickness expected of a better gun. Floorplate and sideplate seams were flawless.

The usual top tang safety is automatic, engaging each time the gun is opened to protect us from ourselves. The selective ejectors are pure Southgate, with their flat V springs and hammers in the forend. The forend itself is held on with the classic self-adjusting Anson pushbutton. All the bits and pieces are precision CNC'd, as you would expect today.

The sideplated-boxlock action's cosmetics were stunning. Our gun was the top-end 90-percent-engraved version with hand engraving by Geoff Moore or Chris McEvoy. It featured an exceptionally attractive tight scroll that was flawlessly executed. It was absolutely first class, even under an unforgiving 10X loupe. Well done, indeed. It was further enhanced by some of the better case coloring I've seen. The engraving and coloring certainly reflected the price of the gun. (A less-costly $10,000 Robertson was offered with 50-percent engraving and a lesser grade of French walnut.) The fact that the screws on the bottom and right side of the action weren't properly indexed probably reflected someone's haste to leave early for a cuppa.

It's the action that gets the attention, but the barrels are the most important part of any gun. Not only do the barrels govern the pattern but, more importantly, they also define the gun's balance and thus handling. Handling is everything.

Our test gun had 30" barrels, as did all of the Robertsons imported by Cabela's. These 20-gauge barrels have 3" chambers and are choked Modified/Full at .019" and .025" on .629" bores. With .615" being the nominal bore for the 20, these barrels have a trendy overbore. The choke dimensions are normal for the stated designation, but the choke profile is not standard. Today most European fixed chokes, particularly

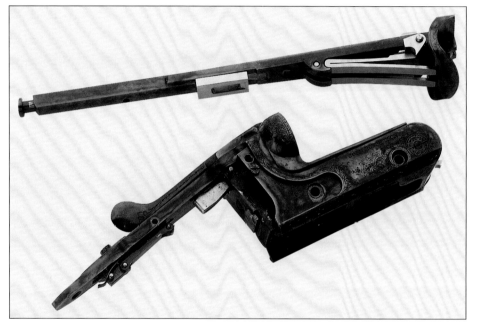

The Robertson has an A&D action and Southgate ejectors. (David Grant)

tighter ones, have a taper leading to a parallel section at the muzzle. The theory is that the taper tightens the shot load and then the parallel section stabilizes it before exit. The Robertson barrels have no parallel section. They have purely conical tapers measuring 1.5" long for the Modified and 2" for the Full, tapering right to the muzzle. The forcing cones in front of the 3" chambers are also the traditional short length.

I asked Clark why they used this choke design. His answer was as interesting as it was inclusive. "The barrel stock is purchased from the German HK-JS group and is quite unique here, being hammer forged. The same process is used for military machine guns and such. Our idea was to produce a 3"-chambered gun that offered the best weight and balance, as many magnum guns, in my opinion, are just too sluggish.

"The interesting thing is that the choke and chambers are forged as well, and in just eight minutes the tube is created and has a very high tensile strength. The choke profile lends itself well to forging and creates good, even patterns without the need to increase wall thickness.

"Another big issue here is the legal proof requirement, which states now that all 3" guns must be magnum proof tested. This is a multi-shot, very tough test, particularly for lightweight guns, so a gradual cone profile, in my view, reduces the possibility for pre-choke bulging resulting from heavy loads.

"However, choke can be adjusted to customer requirements and work goes on into supplying a discreet interchangeable choke-tube option. Interestingly, the UK proof houses only recommend the use of up to Half-choke with steel shot as an industry standard here."

The barrels are joined at the rear by saddle, or shoe, construction.

This differs from the traditional British chopper lump and typical European monoblock. It is basically a plate, with the hooks incorporated, upon which the barrels are set. Clark felt that it made sense for the gun. "Using the hammer-forged tubes therefore lends itself to a shoe lump," he said, "which offers a stronger joint than dovetail and a more attractive joint than monoblock."

The rib is described as a "Boss-style concave rib." It's a compromise between the raised flat European rib and the classic swamped English game rib. The profile is a good bit above the barrels for the rear half and then runs roughly parallel to the barrels to the muzzle. It's a nice choice for those who like a little bit of rib but not so much that it

The Robertson features beautifully engraved and finished sideplates, an Anson & Deeley action, and innovative barrels hammer-forged in Germany. (David Grant)

thickens the svelte profile of the gun. The surface is plain bright blued and concave, with a proper brass bead up front. The top rear of the rib sports a little engraving and is inscribed "J. Robertson 16, Mount Street, London." This was the Boss shop address before it closed in 2008. As I write this, Boss is based outside London at its factory in Kew. Nothing on the Robertson mentions Birmingham unless you count the crowned "BNP" Birmingham nitro proofs on the barrel flats. In all, the barrelwork on our gun was flawless, with blemish-free bluing, perfect solder lines and well-fit ejectors.

Our particular gunstock was a traditional English configuration and measured $14^{11}/_{16}$" x $1^{13}/_{32}$" x $1^{31}/_{32}$" with 1" of pitch and a bit of right-hand cast. A fitted stock takes an extra four weeks for delivery, and I'm told you can pick your wood on the Internet. Or you can just buy a gun off the shelf and have the stock bent to suit. If you are ordering a complete custom gun, you can get whatever you wish, but that can take a year, depending on engraving.

The stock also has a checkered butt, drop points aft of the sideplates, a silver oval for your initials or crest, and a fashionably long trigger tang. It's all very British and all the better for it. The tip of the forend, with its tiny Anson pushbutton bushing, is a touch bulky and not as graceful as it could be, but it's not too bad. Unfortunately, the forend on our gun was a little loose and could be

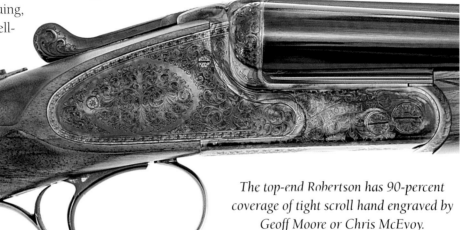

The top-end Robertson has 90-percent coverage of tight scroll hand engraved by Geoff Moore or Chris McEvoy.

moved slightly side-to-side by hand. The virtually identical setup on my 85-year-old Webley & Scott is rock solid, so it's an execution issue, not the design.

Boss lists the wood as *Juglans regia,* or European walnut. Today that can come from the US, Europe or Asia. Traditionally, it is known for its longer grain and highly contrasting colors. On our West Coast it is grafted to the native American black walnut, *Juglans nigra,* or California walnut, *Juglans hindsii.* On such a grafted tree the burl figure often depends on where on the tree the wood is taken from. Wood nearest the graft is the most highly figured.

And that can be a bit of a problem. The wood on our test gun's stock was very nicely figured, but it had a single $^{1}/_{2}$" knot in it. For $17,000 I do not wish a knot. The hand checkering had a very good feel to it. With so much mechanical checkering being used today, I almost had forgotten what the real stuff feels like. It is definitely better. But the top borders of the forend checkering weren't quite perfect, and the checkering on the butt was mediocre. I wouldn't be so critical on a $5,000 gun, but the Robertson should be held to a higher standard considering the price and provenance.

The stock was beautifully oil finished, and the drop points remained sharply cut, not sanded over. This shows extra care by a skilled finisher. Wood-to-metal fit was very nice indeed.

As to the actual shooting, I have a confession. My gun reviews are a little bit rigged. I make a real effort to select review guns that will be shooters. Not all are, but I try. Why waste your time and mine on something with sewer-pipe barrels that handles with the grace of a wallowing sow? I really like guns that handle, and the classic English side-by-side field gun is the paradigm.

And it doesn't have to be a best gun either. I'm not particularly overawed by glitz. As a certified Luddite whose main criterion is performance, I am perfectly happy with a boxlock as opposed to a sidelock. Boxlocks are mechanically simpler and more reliable when built to the same standards. I only get picky about the looks when I'm being charged extra for them.

So how does the Robertson fare where it really counts? There is no question that the Robertson side by-side is a good-looking gun, but the best part is that it handles well. At just a touch less than 6 pounds 8 ounces, the weight is at the upper end of OK for a responsive 30" 20-bore with 3" magnum capability. It is light enough to carry easily but has just enough *gravitas* to deal with the occasional heavy load and still produce a smooth swing. The balance point was $1/2$" in front of the hinge. The moment of inertia felt a little more front-biased than the classic center-weighted English standard. If you shoot your birds feet away instead of yards away, you'll want shorter, lighter barrels. For shots in the 25- to 35-yard range, the handling speed is perfect. I might not pick this particular configuration for grouse or quail, but for pheasants it would be the berries.

The Modified/Full chokes, in spite of (or perhaps because of) their conical design, handled a variety of factory shells well. It not being hunting season, breaks on clays showed surprisingly well-distributed patterns with good fringes. It is harder to get good patterns out of a 20 than a 12, 16 or 28, so Robertson must be doing something right.

The single trigger worked perfectly. The safety was easy to put on and take off, which is just as important as trigger pull in a field gun. The selective ejectors ejected reliably, but their timing was slightly off. Someone somewhere should have spent the extra time tuning them properly.

And that's the problem with this particular Robertson sample. For $17,000 we got a good-handling, solidly designed, exquisitely engraved gun that left the shop one day too soon. The flaws in the ejectors, checkering, screw indexing and forend are simple to fix but, like the knotted stock, are inappropriate on a gun of this price. Fix these little things and you would have a first-class gun.

Ruger Gold Label

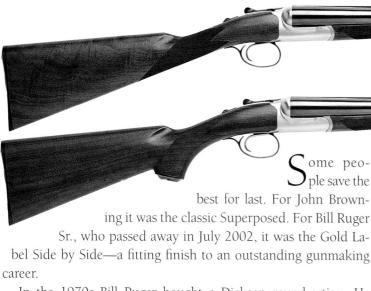

Some people save the best for last. For John Browning it was the classic Superposed. For Bill Ruger Sr., who passed away in July 2002, it was the Gold Label Side by Side—a fitting finish to an outstanding gunmaking career.

In the 1970s Bill Ruger bought a Dickson round-action. He loved the grace of the Scottish gun and wanted to build one like it, but more pressing business kept cropping up. The project briefly got traction in the early '80s but then slipped off again. Then came the Vintagers and similar groups in the mid-'90s, and Ruger saw the renewed enthusiasm for the side-by-side. In 1998 Ruger sent his Dickson to his facility in Arizona and requested that the design team, headed by Jim McGarry, come up with a gun that looked like the Dickson but—the reality of mass production being what it was (and still is)—used as many Ruger parts as possible. A year or so later the prototype and drawings were sent to Ruger's Newport, New Hampshire, plant, where the gun would be made. Design and manufacturing personnel worked to see what changes were needed to build several thousand per year.

The basic gun was never really a problem. It worked pretty well from the start. It was the cosmetics and man-hour issues that caused the company to delay production again and again during the next three years. The barrels, not the action, are the heart and soul of any shotgun. Barrels give the gun that all-important feel. Ruger built one of Don Amos's moment-of-inertia-testing turntables and measured the weight distribution of two dozen other side-by-sides to make sure the Gold Label would have excellent dynamics. That meant light barrels. Light barrels have thin barrel walls. That meant soft solder, because the high heat of silver brazing can warp thin barrel walls. Soft solder meant rust-bluing, because the chemicals used in hot-bluing are incompatible with soft solder. Thin barrels also meant thin-wall chokes so there wouldn't be any unsightly bulges at the muzzles. Ruger wasn't set up to soft-solder or rust-blue or install thinwall chokes. All of these are relatively easy to do on a hand-made, small-shop basis, but setting up a real production line is something else.

When I visited the Ruger plant, I was shown the special rust-bluing room that had been built just for the Gold. It has two tanks so that two men can work in parallel. Each barrel is polished and dipped six times. The process is time-consuming, but there's no way around it.

The soft-soldering of the ribs required rethinking. Usually ribs are wired onto the barrels and then placed in an oven to set the solder. Ruger devised a new approach: Ribs are held in place on the barrels with a jig, and then the solder is melted by blowing hot air through the barrels. It's something like a mega-hair-dryer, and you don't want to stand too close to the muzzle ends where the heated air comes out. Trust me on that. It only takes a few minutes to melt the solder, and it works like a charm.

Cleaning excess solder from along the ribs proved to be more time-consuming than anticipated. I watched as each barrel was painstakingly cleaned by hand. In fact, I was surprised by the amount of handwork that goes into the gun. I thought that Ruger would be fully automated, but there are some things that people just do better than machines. I was particularly impressed by the number of inspections I saw at each step of the process. Before bluing, the two quality-control ladies used a red marker to circle the tiniest imperfections on each gun, which was then sent back to be fixed or scrapped. Ruger is obviously very serious about getting this gun right.

The above issues —and others— caused a delay of several years in the introduction of the Gold Label. Unfortunately, advertising was not delayed and continued to trumpet a gun that did not yet exist beyond the prototype stage. After so much "vaporware"

The Ruger Gold Label, based on the Dickson round-action, is a blend of high-tech and handwork.

advertising, I felt that I had to visit the factory to ensure that the gun was actually in production before writing about it. Well, I've seen it in production. The Ruger Gold Label is very real. The gun has an SRP of $1,950. Expect a slightly lower street price once larger numbers of guns hit the pipeline. The first run of guns are all 12-gauges, with 3" chambers, 28" barrels and five Briley steel-proof Thin Wall screw-in chokes. In the future Ruger is considering introducing a "heavy" 12-gauge Gold for waterfowl and sporting clays or a 20-gauge for upland use.

The Gold's triggerplate action is unique in my experience. Ruger's engineers described it to me as basically a Dickson round-action from the opening lever forward and a Ruger Red Label 28-gauge over/under from the lever back. That certainly would be in keeping with the mandate to use as many existing Ruger parts as possible.

The action is attractive, with its broad 12-gauge shoulders and diminutive Dickson Victorian wasp waist. In reality it's about the same size as a standard Webley & Scott Anson & Deeley 12-gauge boxlock action. Both are 2 1/4" across at the breech face and 2" deep. The Gold's action is about 1/4" longer than the Webley's. The Gold has 1/16" less width at the rear of the receiver and is a full 1/4" narrower and very much more rounded at the front. This seemingly small difference gives the Gold's receiver an entirely different look. It's gorgeous. There are no exposed screw heads to break the smooth flow of the brushed stainless-steel receiver. The action starts as two castings that are CNC'd and then TIG-welded together. It looks simply awful at first, but when the weld is filled and flawlessly ground and polished, it comes to life like a butterfly out of a cocoon.

The action locks via a single bite on the rear of the two monoblock lumps. This differs from the traditional Purdey double underbite, which locks on both lumps. The Gold's front lump is quite long, whereas the rear lump is short. They were the same length in the initial Gold design, but it was found that, due to the Dickson's wider-than-normal gape, the rear lug didn't bear between the receiver bolsters when the gun was open. The front lug was lengthened to increase barrel stability with an open gun. Ruger also added carefully machined pads on the sides of the receiver relief to bear on the front lump to further stabilize the action. The engineers told me that a little change like that cost Ruger six months, because the company had to rebuild the die for the casting, redo the machining process and then test everything. The hinge pin is hardened steel, but it is not replaceable. In that respect it is just like the Webley

& Scott A&D non-replaceable pin, one that is known to be very long lived. CNC machining doesn't do everything either. The barrel lumps and breech end of the monoblock come off slightly oversized so that a file stroke or two is required to mate them correctly to the action.

The interior of the action appears very busy, with a plethora of cast parts that Ruger makes in its Pine Tree casting plant next door. It's a little tricky to disassemble. A conventional A&D action is a piece of cake by comparison. Still, the Ruger Red Label 28-gauge O/U, from which many of these parts come, is a proven gun, and that bodes well for the Gold.

The Gold is currently available only with a single trigger. It is mechanical but also has an inertia block. Under recoil the inertia block movement delays engagement of the second sear for a moment, to prevent doubling. Because it is mechanical, it does not require any recoil to shift from the first sear to the second; it will fire the second barrel if the first shell is a dud. The ultra-narrow action front has a single central cocking bar rather than two separate cocking rods.

Love it or loathe it, the top tang-mounted safety/barrel selector is straight from the Red Label O/U. The safety is automatic. It is easily converted to manual operation, although Ruger requests that you return it for this operation (at minimal charge). The rear of the safety switch toggles left and right for barrel selection. The selector seems reversed: Pushing the selector to the left activates the right barrel. That's due to the safety selector mechanism coming from Ruger's O/Us. Trigger pulls on our test gun were 4 1/4 pounds for the right barrel and 3 3/4 for the left. There was a little take-up but minimal creep and over-travel. All in all, it's a nice trigger.

The selective ejectors on our gun were adequate but not overpowering. They tossed most factory loads just fine, but they balked once or twice on my grotty reloads. (Perhaps the gun is just discerning.) As on most Dicksons, the Gold's ejector mechanism is located entirely within the receiver, with the ejector hammers at the front of the water table. There is no ejector machinery in the forend.

Cosmetically, the receiver is polished and brushed cast stainless steel. It's smooth and clean, with no visible screws or pins. The only engraving is the Ruger eagle in gold and the company name and address on the underside of the diminutive rounded receiver. This engraving is one of the few production processes that Ruger has done by an outside contractor.

Stocks on the Golds are either English or modest pistol grips, both with petite splinter forends. Either suits the gun well. The nicely figured American walnut English stock on our test gun measured 14¼" to a plastic buttplate, with 1½" drop at nose, 2¼" drop at heel, 2" pitch

The Gold's action has been described as a Dickson round action from the opening lever forward and a Red Label 28-gauge O/U from the lever back.

and zero cast. As befits the diminutive action, the wrist is very slender. The aggressive and clean 22-lpi machine checkering is helpful in maintaining a grip on the thin wrist. The buttstock is coated with a perfectly acceptable sprayed-on poly finish, but the grain on our gun was not quite filled. Ruger intends to use fancier wood on the Golds than on its Red Labels, although that's always a lottery. Wood-to-metal fit was good on the forend, but there was a noticeable gap between the wood and the top tang of the receiver. Wood

also was proud where the buttstock joined the triggerplate and receiver shoulders.

I loaned the Gold Label to numerous shooters to get their input. Many wanted more stock length and some more stock height. The factory dimensions read well, but the English stock feels small. The pistol grip stock feels a bit bigger. Ruger, Ithaca Gun Co. and Remington still make stocks sized for our grandparents, not today's super-sized hunters. Ruger did cut the butt flat where the buttplate screws on, so the addition of a pad will be easy. Still, it's always easier to cut a stock shorter than to wait for the wood to grow longer.

From the stack of scrapped experimental barrels I saw at the factory, it's obvious that Ruger put a lot of time and effort into getting the barrels just right. Although not featherlight, the Gold's barrels are no more than light middleweight. They weigh 5 oz more than the 28" barrels on my 2½"-chambered Webley & Scott boxlock, but this is appropriate, because the Gold Label is chambered for 3" shells and built to withstand far-higher pressures. Some clueless marketing or legal wonk must have insisted on the 3" chambers, because they are superfluous in a light game gun like this. The 6½-pound Gold was extensively tested by Ruger with 3" steel loads. The gun will take it, but I tip my cap to the man who pulled the trigger.

I was told that the forcing cones are slightly longer than usual, but to me they appeared to be of conventional length. The barrels are overbored, at .743", like those on Red Label 12s. When I asked why the overbore and longer cones, the vague answer was, "I'm told it's recoil." More on this later. The gun has Briley's special VX-series high-quality Thin Wall flush chokes built for steel shot. Two Skeet plus an Improved Cylinder, Modified and Full are included. That's pretty generous, considering that Briley retails these for $65 each. One of the Ruger engineers told me, "Our constrictions are a little less, to guarantee it for steel shot. Our Full is only .022" choke. Modified is .015" and Improved Cylinder runs around .007". More than .022" for any steel shot becomes an issue." Just remember this when setting up to shoot lead and you'll be fine. Most people over-choke their 12s for gamebirds anyway.

One of the main reasons for using the excellent and expensive Briley Thin Wall chokes was to avoid jugging the barrels, which Ruger would have had to do if it had used the thicker, heavier chokes found on the company's O/Us. Not only would this have ruined the lines of this svelte side-by-side, but the added weight up front would have interfered with responsive field handling. Ruger took the high road here.

The barrel tubes themselves are hammer-forged and polished inside, not chrome-lined. Outside they have the marvelous rust blue mentioned earlier. It really looks classy—in keeping with the gun. If you hold the barrels up to the light and look down the sides, you can see a slight swelling where the tubes join the monoblock and an almost immeasurable bit of rippling. It's not noticeable unless you get the light exactly right. In a side-by-side retailing for less than $2,000, it's a reasonable compromise of cosmetics versus price. In fact, all through the testing I had to keep reminding myself that this gun costs less than two grand. It looks and feels as though it costs more, especially when you try to find other side-by-side guns in the same price range.

The top rib is raised and flat, machined from a piece of $7/16$" stock that is ground and hollowed. It is more in the American genre than the more graceful swamped game rib would be, but when I asked, no one seemed to know who made the decision to go with one rib rather than the other. There is a tasteful small single brass bead up front, just the way it should be. One of the best surprises was that there is no verbiage stamped for eternity on the outside of the barrels advising us to read manuals or send away for free ones. The only thing stamped on the barrels is "12 ga 3" chambers." That's it. No great American novel. No paean to a berserk legal system.

Our test gun balanced about an inch in front of the hinge pin, but the weight was distributed along the barrels. The balance was a tribute to the development time spent with the MOI machine. The Gold had a surprising smoothness for a $6^{1}/_{2}$-pound gun. Most field 12s weigh $^{1}/_{4}$ to $^{3}/_{4}$ of a pound more. This gun felt responsive but not whippy. It was cooperative. I never had to fight it. Personally, I'd have preferred it with just a touch more weight in the butt, but for me that's a self-fulfilling prophesy because I would have to lengthen the stock with a pad and that would add about the right amount of weight. Other shooters will have their own preferences. One size does not fit all; that's for sure.

Point of impact was a flat 50/50 and appropriate for a game gun. If you want a higher POI, bend up the stock. Barrel convergence was spot-on perfect. That's not surprising, as every one of the early production guns was test-fired for convergence. The barrels that failed were scrapped, not re-regulated. The crisp trigger pulls made timing the shots easy. Everything worked as it should have. The gun had no misfires and ejected decently, although the right ejector was the tiniest bit stronger than the left. The safety worked smoothly as well, and I even started to get used to the barrel selector. Because of the fine threads, installing and removing the screw chokes took a lot of turning, but the excellent Briley "fishing reel handle" wrench was a delight to use compared to the wretched excuses for wrenches some gun companies give you. When the gun was open, there was just a little bit of wobble at the hinge. Ruger might set its CNC mill to add another thou to the receiver pads that bear against the sides of the front lump, but this looseness was mostly superficial. The gun was rock-solid when closed, and that's what counts.

A number of shooters tried the gun. Everyone commented on the svelte receiver. The gun really does look more like a 20 than a 12. Many felt that recoil was noticeably less than they expected from such a light gun. It's all subjective, but perhaps there's something to that backboring, even though the recoil formulae don't bear it out. One of the things I like best about the Gold Label is its "carry." That dainty little rounded receiver feels so very comfortable when held in one hand. It definitely doesn't feel like a 12.

Though I prefer the looks of the English stock, I think the pistol-grip stock would make the gun even nicer to shoot, especially considering the single trigger. The bottom line is that this was an easy gun to shoot. That's just the way it is with some guns.

I'm often asked how a gun will hold up. You can't really tell with a completely new gun, because there's no track record. Just about any decent gun will outlast several hunters' lifetimes, and the Gold is certainly better than decent. Also Ruger's service is highly thought of in an industry where good service is the exception, not the rule.

Ruger gets real credit for staying the course with the Gold Label in spite of the production hurdles and delays. As his last gun, it's a fitting memorial to Bill Ruger Sr. Like his first .22-caliber Red Eagle semi-auto pistol in 1949, the Gold Label is attractive, functional, innovative and affordable. It took a lot more work than Ruger bargained for, but for the price it will be a lot more gun than you bargained for.

POST MORTEM

Technically, the Ruger Gold Label was produced from 2002 to 2008, but it got off to a slow start and was also a scarce commodity in its last three years of production. The company never did produce the promised heavy 12 or upland 20. Demand wasn't the problem. Manufacturing was. Ruger just wasn't set up to produce the gun economically. More's the pity. Used values of Golds have held up quite well. The guns may be gone, but they are not forgotten. It was a good try.

Smith & Wesson Elite Gold

As I write this in 2007, the euro has just reached a record high against the US dollar. It's small wonder that non-euro gun producers like our NATO ally Turkey are getting more work. When Smith & Wesson announced that it was reentering the shotgun business a year ago, it should not have come as a surprise that the company would make its guns in Turkey.

S&W's last effort at shotguns was from 1972 to 1984, when the company imported a line of pumps and autoloaders from Howa in Japan. Today production in Japan is far more costly, whereas Turkey offers an enviable combination of gunmaking skills and moderate production costs.

If joining DeHaan, CZ, Kimber, Savage, Hatfield and others in importing guns from Turkey does not come as a surprise, the extent of S&W's commitment might. S&W is not rebranding an existing line of guns. S&W told me that it has teamed with an experienced Turkish gunmaking partner, UTAS, to build two entirely new plants near the village of Uzmulu, in the Taurus Mountains. Among the principals of UTAS is Ted Hatfield, whose completely separate plant elsewhere in Turkey produces the Kimber Marias and Valier shotguns.

The S&W plants make only S&W products. The plant for the 1000 Series gas-operated semi-auto has 360 workers and 75,000 square feet. The Elite Silver over/under and Elite Gold side-by-side guns are made in a separate 41,000-square-foot two-building facility with 230 craftsmen.

Our test gun was the S&W Elite Gold Grade 1 side-by-side. Currently it comes only in 20 gauge with a single trigger and fixed Improved Cylinder/Modified chokes. The options right now are limited to 26" or 28" barrels and English or Prince of Wales stocks. Our gun had the longer barrels and a stock with a Prince of Wales grip. List price is $2,350.

At a glance, the action of the gun appears to be the usual box-lock. But it is not. This is a true triggerplate gun, with the hammers, sears, springs, trigger, inertia block and other bits on the trigger-plate. The leaf springs are curved up behind the hammers. This triggerplate has some rigidity and alignment advantages over the standard Anson & Deeley boxlock action. It also permits more aggressive rounding of the bottom of the action. S&W has patented this particular design.

This round action is what gives the gun its delightful one-hand carry. Your hand just curves around the receiver. The "rounded" action (as opposed to "round" action) popular today on some side-locks and boxlocks is, in its crudest terms, simply a grinding away of excess metals on the lower edges of a conventional receiver. A round-action gun, like S&W's triggerplate version, has the important action internals located higher and more toward the inside of the action on the triggerplate, permitting an even greater rounding. The difference is one that you feel more than see. It's a Scottish thing, with James MacNaughton starting it 125 years ago, John Dickson & Son popularizing it, and today's McKay Brown continuing the tradition. There are also some similarities with the design of the diminutive Ruger Gold Label round-action.

Lockup is by the proven Purdey double underbolt. Neither locking lug pierces through the triggerplate on the bottom of the

The triggerplate action, single trigger, scalloped receiver and subdued case colors all offer good value at a relatively low price.

receiver, giving the gun cleaner-looking mechanics and less likeli-hood of picking up grit than most A&D boxlocks. The locking tongue is polished to a high finish, as are all of the other inter-nal action parts. The firing pins are not bushed, but the standing breech does have shallow gas-escape channels in case of a pierced primer. Unlike the Webley & Scott A&D boxlock, the S&W's hinge pin is factory replaceable.

The Elite Gold's standard single trigger is mechanical and relies on the usual inertia block to prevent doubling. Sears are specially hardened. The trigger is not selective, so the right barrel will always fire first. This saves complexity and cost at the ex-pense of flexibility. The gun also has a manual safety, again a saving in com-plexity and cost. Single triggers on side-by-side guns are normally an extra-cost option, but it is easier to make one on a triggerplate action.

Ejectors are the tried-and-true automatic selective Southgates. Because of the rounded receiver, the cutouts for the cocking rods come perilously close to the lower edge of the receiver, but you can't see daylight through the metal, so it must be OK. The triggerplate incorporates the entire bottom of the action as a single part instead of the two separate pieces on the bottom of the A&D action. The metal-to-metal seams on our S&W plate were perfect, although they were easy to see due to the differences in the way the triggerplate and the receiver body took the case coloring. I could find no cosmetic metal flaws.

S&W uses traditional charcoal case coloring. I was told that Doug

Turnbull, the American master of case coloring, was consulted on the project. Our example had subdued blues and beiges but none of the flashier purples, reds and yellows that some makers produce. It's really a matter of taste, not quality.

The receiver has minimal 10-percent-coverage engraving. It is hand cut in a simple pattern but well executed. Scalloping the rear edge of the receiver avoids that brutally straight line common to basic boxlocks and kicks things up a notch.

Our gun came with 28" barrels, and they appeared to be well struck, with no visible ripples or blemishes. The barrels are rust blued, but the glossy blue-black finish might look like hot bluing. S&W said that the rust bluing involves seven baths and cardings over a week's time. The repeated carding between rounds of barrel-wetting combined with shorter periods of oxidization is what gives the barrels their high-blue shine instead of the traditional rust-blue matte.

All the barrel-rib solder work was neat, with no evidence of blush or gaps. It is traditional soft solder but is applied by machine. The often-awkward stub rib that incorporates the forend hook was exceptionally clean—much nicer than those on some other more expensive side-by-side barrels I've seen. The barrel flats are engine turned. The barrel jointing uses hooks integral to a bottom plate, which is brazed to the two drilled barrel tubes. S&W calls this a "semi-chopper-lump" configuration. Steven Skrubis, S&W's long-gun project manager, says that he prefers this to traditional

The Elite Gold is of excellent quality and has classically restrained cosmetics.

chopper-lump construction because the company can produce the bottom plate out of 4140 steel and heat treat it for strength. The work appeared flawless.

Currently the Elite Gold Grade 1 comes with fixed chokes. In the near future screw chokes will be available for those who insist on them (and the extra muzzle weight they might add). Our fixed chokes were marked IC and M. They measured .011" and .017", which is in the ballpark for a 20. The chokes are about 3" long and conical—not conical parallel—to a slight flare. These chokes ought to be just about perfect for the vast majority of upland hunting for which a 20-gauge is suitable. The chromed barrel bores were not quite identical, at .630" right and .628" left. This is an overbore of the .615" 20-gauge standard. The barrels are approved for steel shot.

Chambers are 3", which offers a little more flexibility when it comes to shell selection. Don't overlook the buffered Remington 3" Nitro-Mag shells if you think that all 3" 20s produce poor patterns. You might be surprised. Forcing cones are standard length.

The rib is one of those flat-filed raised things that some people like. Many feel that the raised rib gives a slight peripheral sighting aid. I wish S&W had offered the classic English swamped game rib. It's lighter and gives a cleaner look to the gun. It is the classic game rib for a reason.

The raised rib has been inflicted with a Bradley-style white bead on a block more fitting to a target gun. S&W also threatens to put a center bead on future guns. I guess those things are meant for hunters who like to aim really hard. It must be a carryover from the S&W target-pistol mentality. A simple brass front bead and no middle bead would be so much nicer.

The Turkish walnut on our Elite Gold Grade 1 was, well, grade one. S&W optimistically calls it AAA Grade III. Perhaps other samples are AAA, but the grain patterns on the three Elite Golds I saw were modest. Certainly not featureless, but they had a subdued straight grain. Of course straight-grained wood is strong, but it's certainly not going to make onlookers gasp. That said, others have reported seeing better wood on some Elite Golds, so perhaps it is the luck of the draw.

The finish seems like a sprayed-on high-gloss synthetic of some sort. S&W calls it a "proprietary catalytic finish." The wood grain is fully filled, and the checkering is appropriately cut and then oiled after the finish has been applied. The insides of the forend and stock head are also properly coated. The finish does not appear to penetrate the wood. Our test sample had made the rounds of my fellow journalists and had a couple of chips in the finish that showed bare wood underneath. The finish does appear to be chemically resistant, as it was unfazed by my favorite sunscreen lotion—a serious candidate for the universal solvent.

Checkering is listed as being hand cut at 24 lpi. Some diamond

A checkered wood panel must be removed to access the drawbolt that holds the stock to the receiver.

areas on our gun were a little flat, but nothing major. Overall it was of pretty good quality, certainly more than adequate. It's a simple, no-risk pattern with a single deep border. It goes with the subdued, tasteful appearance of the gun.

As befits a classic field side-by-side, the Elite Gold comes with a checkered butt. The pluses to that are classic good looks, ease of mounting, low weight and easy lengthening via a pad if necessary. The downsides are that it is easily marred when stored butt down, offers no recoil absorption and sooner or later will slip when carelessly propped against a wall.

The butt shows a checkered wood panel held in place with two indexed screws. The panel must be removed to access the drawbolt that holds the stock to the receiver. The insert is a tight fit and is a real pain to remove, but you'll have to do it if you want to get into the receiver. The drawbolt, an off-the-shelf aftermarket item, was the only piece of ordinary-quality metal I saw in the gun. Everything else was nice.

As mentioned, our stock had the nicely shaped, relaxed rounded pistol grip, and it complemented the single trigger. Stock dimensions were 14$^{1}/_{2}$" x 1$^{3}/_{8}$" x 2$^{1}/_{8}$". There was a very slight cast-off at the toe. The nominal factory dimensions are $^{1}/_{8}$" lower with zero cast, so our sample was a little higher and had a little more cast than normal. Pitch was 1$^{1}/_{2}$" stand-off at the muzzle. The stocks are deliciously slender through the wrist, but the cross-section is oval to provide good control.

The splinter forend is good looking but somewhat unusual. It uses a central Deeley underlatch in the middle rather than the more common Anson pushbutton at the tip. The construction of the Deeley latch necessitates a slightly deeper forend. This forces the bottom line of the forend to run closer to parallel with the barrels, resulting in the S&W's forend being about 2" longer than the English paradigm. Even then it doesn't meet the barrel in front, so S&W has given the nose of the forend a sort of gape rather than just giving up and rounding it bluntly. The Huglu side-by-side has the same open space, but the company chose to use a slight Schnabel tip to hide it. S&W's approach is the better compromise in light of the design constraints, and it makes the forend look slimmer than it really is. The downside is that if you hunt in heavy cover, the gap between the forend front and the barrel is going to pick up a veritable salad of local flora.

Other than that intentional forend opening, wood-to-metal fit was very nice indeed. There were no gaps or excessively proud wood. The complicated area at the rear of the scalloped receiver was properly inletted. Top and bottom tangs were snugly fit to the wood. It was a good job.

Like the Krieghoff Essencia 20-gauge side-by-side I reviewed earlier, the S&W Elite Gold was one of those guns that seemed to fit everyone. The slightly higher stock was a big help. I hope future production will stay that way. Side-by-sides need higher stocks than over/unders because they tend to shoot flatter.

The weight of 6 pounds 6.6 ounces is fine for a 3" 20 capable of shooting 1¼-oz shells. Of course balance and feel are more important than pure weight. In the hands, the Elite Gold really feels good. That's not particularly revealing, but describing gun handling is like trying to describe color to a blind person. Guns either feel right or they don't, and this one feels right.

The balance point is on the knuckle—½" in front of the hinge pin and 5¼" in front of the trigger. The gun definitely has more weight up front than my whippy 20-gauge Webley & Scott, but it's the kind of weight that gives the S&W better handling. There is nothing porcine about the gun. It is easy to move. There's no doubt that it would be very comfortable to use in the uplands.

The manual safety had just the right amount of resistance for the field, yet it didn't pester me when I practiced on clays. The ejectors worked well and were perfectly timed. The pair of empties touched as they flew about 10 feet through the air. There were nice uniform dents in the primers with no drag marks. The gun opened and closed properly. It felt tight. It felt right. Barrel convergence seemed correct.

I don't pattern test guns due to the variances caused by shells, but the S&W's fixed chokes measured correctly for their designations. The big Bradley bead isn't my favorite for a field gun, but it's easy enough to exorcise. The raised flat rib isn't a personal favorite either, but it didn't hamper the shooting. The nicely rounded receiver made the gun a delight to carry. The checkered butt slipped into the shoulder nicely without hanging up.

It really would have been a pleasure shooting the gun if it hadn't been for the 10-pound trigger pulls. Well, that's my guesstimate. My trigger scale stops at eight pounds, and these went off the scale. If it were my gun, it would go back to S&W repair to be straightened out. It shouldn't be a big deal. Another Elite Gold that I shot on the journalists' play day just before the SHOT Show had normal trigger pulls, so this is probably an anomaly. After making a gazillion target pistols, S&W certainly knows how to cut a sear.

One of the big problems when outsourcing a gun from Turkey is convincing buyers that they aren't taking a risk buying it. Like many gunmaking countries when they first target an American market (Belgium and Spain particularly come to mind), early Turkish production was often of suspect quality to meet a price point. Smith & Wesson has addressed the concern of quality and durability with a most interesting guarantee.

It's called the Smith & Wesson "Heirloom Warranty." Basically, it's a lifetime guarantee on the Elite series side-by-side and over/under guns. Here's the big print: "The Smith & Wesson Corp. proudly warrants your Smith & Wesson Elite Series shotgun to be free from defects in materials and workmanship for the life of the original purchaser and continuing for the lifetime of their registered heir— subject to the conditions stated on the reverse . . . ." Including one stipulated heir under the warranty is a nice PR touch.

As I learned in contracts class, the big print giveth and the small print taketh away. The fine print says that wood is not covered, nor are defects resulting from careless handling or modifications, defec-

A slight "gape" makes the Elite's forend nose look slimmer than it really is.

tive ammo, "ordinary wear and tear, or unreasonable use." Obviously S&W has left itself with some wiggle room, but the 154-year-old company has earned a good reputation, so there is no reason to be overly suspicious.

Other than by the trigger pulls, I was surprised that this early production gun got just about everything else right in terms of quality control. New-gun production from new factories generally takes a little settling-in time, as we saw with the excellent Galazan RBL. UTAS obviously knows what it is doing, and the S&W-patented action seems to be a good design.

I really liked this gun. It has the "feel." The cosmetics are classically restrained but mostly quite nice. Construction seems very

good. The $2,350 price is certainly right, falling between the Kimber at the Turkish high end and the Huglu on the less-expensive side. The quality is excellent. S&W's lifetime guarantee is an added bonus.

The future holds a number of additions: 30" barrels, optional choke tubes, fancier grades, double triggers, and 28 and even 16 gauges on the near horizon. But first S&W has to get through the current backorder situation. You see, the S&W Elite Gold already has been discovered. This will be a popular gun and deservedly so. The line forms on the right.

UPDATE:

S&W marketed its Elite Gold from 2007 to 2009. In 2009 the company offered the gun with double triggers. Gauges other than the 20, 30" barrels, screw chokes and fancier grades never materialized. With pistol and black-rifle sales exploding in 2009, S&W got out of the shotgun business entirely. Of the roughly 3,000 Elite Golds made, all those that were unsold were remaindered out to resellers such as CDNN Sports and others and were sold at prices from $1,200 up.

Some things gain the fame in death that eluded them in life. The S&W Elite Gold was a case in point. The low price encouraged buyers. These buyers quickly found out that the S&W was a heck of a gun and an extraordinary bargain. I bought one with 28" barrels, English stock and properly tuned double triggers. As I write this, I have more than 5,000 logged rounds through it with no problems of any kind. The gun feels as tight as new. Locally, a dozen or so of my shooting friends have purchased these guns, and no one has reported any kind of quality issue. They all seem to love their guns and, surprisingly, all shoot them well. It's just one of those fortunate guns.

Nothing this good should be allowed to rest in peace. And it doesn't appear that it will. The Turkish marketing firm Commando Arms (www.commando-arms.com) distributes many UTAS-made guns in Europe and the Near East, though not yet in the US. The firm shows the gun in its catalog as the Estate model in 12 and 20 gauge. It also shows the gun as the S&W Elite Gold at the back of the catalog and again as a Webley & Scott complete with gold lettering attesting to the fact. I did not see the gun listed as a Webley & Scott on Webley's site. It will be interesting to see where this excellent gun goes. Only time will tell.

Verney-Carron Azur Eloge .410

The Verney-Carron Azur Eloge Side by Side .410 is French. *Really, really* French. The price is more Lafite Rothschild than *vin ordinaire*, but if you are intrigued by something that is not only different but also well done, you might enjoy looking at one of these.

The Verney-Carron firm has been making guns since 1820 in the French gun center of St. Etienne. In the US the guns currently are imported, distributed and retailed by Kebco LLC, headed up by Ken Buch. Griffin & Howe also sells the guns as a retailer.

Verney-Carron claims to be the leading French producer of hunting firearms, with a range that includes an inexpensive break-open single-barrel .410, full lines of bolt-action and autoloading rifles, the moderately priced Sagittaire and Super 9 over/unders, and shotguns and double rifles up to $40,000 before options. This latter group of elite guns is from the firm's custom shop, L'Atelier Verney-Carron. Shotguns from L'Atelier, whether side-by-side or over/under, start around $9,000 and escalate with every option you check on the order form. Our test gun was fairly well up the scale at about $23,000.

Before getting into the details, I want to emphasize that in L'Atelier Verney-Carron, everything is negotiable. Each gun is made to order, so if something on the review gun is not to your taste, simply specify what you want when you order yours.

The action of the Verney-Carron Azur is unique. Well, at least the lockup is. The trigger/sear/cocking mechanism is that of a conventional modern double-trigger boxlock. The sears are suspended from the top strap. The hammers pivot from below and are driven by coil springs braced at the rear. It really looks more like a modern boxlock O/U arrangement than that of a side-by-side. The company states that all of the internals are fully hand-polished.

The receiver itself is tripartite. The top tang is integral with the main receiver. The bottom triggerplate is separate and secured by a screw in the action floor and another in the separate rear vertical support. This is all pretty standard practice. There is the normal full-width, replaceable hinge pin at the front of the action. The ejector system is the proven and reliable Southgate pattern, with the ejector hammers and springs set in the forend. The disk-set strikers add a classy touch.

What isn't standard is the lockup. Again, more like an over/under than a side-by-side, the Azur employs a single, wide, locking tongue emerging from the bottom of the standing breech face and engaging a slot in the monoblock just below the barrels. This is more like John Browning's Superposed than the usual Purdey double bite you see on most side-by-side guns.

But that's just the start. Whereas most side-by-sides have two lugs on the bottom of the monoblock or chopper lumps, the Azur has six—count 'em, six. The bottom of the receiver is relieved to engage them, but the lugs do not completely penetrate the floor of the receiver. This keeps the exterior smooth and the interior grit-free, but it would be a bear to clean all those nooks and crannies. There is also a crossbar in the middle of the receiver floor to relieve the hinge pin and treble hooks from some of the burden of restraining fore-and-aft movement. The company calls this the "triple parallel lumps breeching system." Something has been lost in translation.

One might think that on a .410 this tremendously strong action is more than is needed, and it probably is. But it shows the double-rifle heritage of this shotgun. Besides, it looks really neat.

The barrels on our test gun were 26" long, but any reasonable length is available. The rust bluing was flawless. There were no ripples of any kind on the exterior. The solder seams had no blem-

ishes, gaps or run-overs. Verney-Carron makes barrels for a number of the big-name makers, and I can see why.

The .410 chambers on our gun were 3", and the fixed chokes measured .010" and .030". On Briley's screw-choke scale of things, .010" in .410 is Light Modified and .030" is off-the-charts tight. Extra Full is listed at .020". Of course, this was just the sample gun, and you can order whatever constrictions please you.

The under rib was conventional, with the usual forend-iron hook integral with a separate short rib section, but the top rib(s)

Lockup of the tremendously strong action is via six lugs —belying the double-rifle heritage of the gun.

sure were different. The gun had a very low swamped game rib nestled between the barrels, which is fairly common on French guns. But at the breech end there was a second, 5" tapered express-rifle-type stub rib laid on top. I've never seen anything like it on a shotgun. You don't really see any of it when you mount the gun, so it is there for a unique cosmetic effect. It certainly gives things a different look, and it is not at all unpleasing.

At the muzzle the Azur Eloge's barrels are 1¼" wide from outside to outside, with a fairly wide spacer dividing them. This width avoids the "toy gun" look that some .410s have.

I won't go into the configuration of the stock or forend too much, because each customer will order what he wishes. Our sample came with an English stock and a dainty beavertail forend. The forend was attached with a nicely machined Anson pushbutton latch.

The English stock, finished in hand-rubbed oil, was made of Turkish walnut befitting a $23,000 gun. It was fitted with a long, ornate trigger-guard tang and an absolutely exquisite engraved skeleton buttplate that was beautifully inletted and surrounded finely checkered wood. In fact, all the exterior metalwork on the gun was both artistic and well executed.

Checkering on the wrist and forend was so fine that I simply didn't have the patience to count the lines per inch. It felt like sharkskin. The checkering borders were finely beaded in an attractive treatment I'd rarely seen before. The rear of the boxlock receiver was heavily scalloped, and the heading up of the stock was flawless. If I were an anal-retentive gun writer, I'd mention that the wood surrounded by the skeleton buttplate was a tiny bit proud, but that could have been intentional to allow for re-checkering as the wood wears.

The inletting of the engraved forend Anson rod guide and screw shield midway back were perfect. The sides of the head of the stock eschewed teardrops for a more fittingly subtle double-cheek presentation. The detail work on this gun was first class.

The receiver got very special treatment. The action size is petite, as befits the .410. The action was scaled down from a 20-gauge receiver, but it certainly is in correct proportion for the .410. The resizing was very well done.

In addition to being resized from a 20-gauge, the fences were deeply relieved and quite intricate. Each side of the receiver sports what Verney-Carron calls a raised "moustache" line—an action bolster—standing proud of the main metal. When you think about the machining steps required to do this, you realize that they had to remove a great deal of metal on the entire remainder of the action just to obtain this effect. The receiver is also slightly rounded for a comfortable one-hand carry afield. It is truly a sculpted piece of art, and it altered my perception of boxlock cosmetics.

The receiver and forend metal's bright finish received 100-percent hand-engraving coverage signed by the respected G. Ripamonti. It was a tight, fine foliate theme that displayed nicely on the small re-

The Azur Eloge boasts wonderful cosmetics, with a scalloped receiver, raised action bolster and first-class detail work.

ceiver. It was in good taste, just like the rest of the gun.

One of the problems with a gun like this is that you eventually have to take it off the velvet cushion in the glass case and subject it to the real world. A dainty little tidbit of a gun like this looks as though it was built to shoot butterflies, but I had other things in mind.

Shooting reality doesn't care about cosmetics. What matters is weight, balance and mechanical function. Our gun weighed 6 pounds 1 ounce. That's a nice weight for a .410. Much lighter and things become whippy. Much heavier and the gun becomes a piglet. The gun felt well balanced, and I was surprised to find that the balance point was ³/₄" aft of the hinge pin. I thought that a rearward bias like that would make the gun skittish, but it didn't. Of course, that's with 26" barrels. You could just as easily order longer barrels or simply ask for a more forward balance.

Although the stock wasn't to my dimensions, the temporary addition of a strap-on butt pad got things close enough so that I could deal with it pretty well. The gun came up nicely, and the side-by-side .410 barrels weren't the slightest bit disconcerting. In fact, I felt more comfortable with them than with the broader plane of a 12-gauge side-by-side.

I took the gun to the 5 Stand field, loaded up and called for a bird. Then it happened. I just about fell over in a vain attempt to pull the front trigger. For reasons totally unclear to me or any other sentient soul, this perfect little jewel of a gun had a monstrous 8-pound front-trigger pull. It was scratchy too. The rear trigger wasn't much better at 7 pounds. You know that you're in trouble when the trigger pulls are heavier than the gun.

How could this be? Coming from a custom shop known for its double rifles, the best part of this gun should have been the triggers. I don't have a clue how this *faux pas* escaped final inspection. The rest of the Azur Eloge was absolutely first quality. Well, Mrs. Lincoln, other than that, how did you enjoy the play?

The trigger pulls easily could be remedied in an hour's shop time. The gun comes with a five-year guarantee, and Kebco uses qualified US gunsmiths. But as the triggers were, they made testing the gun a trial. By using a tighter grip than usual and employing the slightly lighter and smoother rear trigger first (with that ultra-tight .030"-choke barrel), I shot some clays. The gun was dynamic yet steady enough. In spite of the rearward balance, it handled much better than I thought it would. Quite nicely, in fact. With decent triggers, perhaps an extra two inches of barrel, and a little more hollowing inside the stock for those who prefer a more weight-forward

bias (all of which you could specify on ordering), this gun would be a heck of a shooter. It felt like a real gun, not a toy.

To be perfectly fair, as I got into my second flat of shells the triggers started to lighten up. The front trigger now wandered between 5¹/₂ and 7 pounds and was still devilishly catchy. The rear trigger was smoother and at least consistent at a heavy 6¹/₂ pounds. Not good, but not totally debilitating either. Overall, the gun felt bigger than it was. The powerful ejectors certainly would feel at home with metallic rifle cartridges. There were no mechanical malfunctions.

I brought the gun along when I went to the *Shooting Sportsman* Readers & Writers hunt at Quail Country Plantation, in Georgia. This was a great chance to show the gun to some knowledgeable hunters and try it out in the field. It also would give me a break from the manual labor involved with my usual Winchester Model 42 quail gun.

Between the triggers and the gunfit, I struggled and the quail rejoiced. Until, that is, I loaned it to Karl Kindig, one of our readers on the trip. After a hesitant start, he adapted to the gun and took a few quail at the usual distances. He then proceeded to make two left-barrel shots at a bit more than 40 yards each. Honest. I was there and saw it. That 30-thou choke must have been like a laser beam in that little .410. Set up as it was, Karl felt that the gun was more of a precision shooter than an instinctive one. Comments from other *SSM* readers at Quail Country were universally appreciative of the cosmetics. Most could not recall having seen a boxlock of this quality.

I think that the heavy triggers were an aberration and certainly would be easy enough to remedy. The rest of the gun was a delight. Those who feel that classy guns are always made as sidelocks might want to reconsider after seeing the Azur Eloge. A blend of French artistry and practical design, it would be equally attractive to use in the field or to show off afterward when you celebrate with a snifter of Courvoisier. *Vive la France!*

Webley & Scott Boxlock

A 1957 Webley & Scott Model 700 12-gauge in 95-percent condition.

(Seth Goltzer)

Want a side-by-side that is sweet-handling, durable and affordable? Don't we all. It's relatively easy to find a gun with two out of the three criteria, but the trifecta is a toughie. For many shooters the 20th Century English Anson & Deeley boxlock fills the bill. And if you had to pick one marque to represent that genre, it has to be the ubiquitous Webley & Scott.

This is a review of a working gun for today's hunter, not a historical reminiscence for collectors. Webley & Scott shotguns, along with a lot of other English boxlocks, are out of production—victims of changing times, labor costs and foreign competition. Still, Webley & Scott's large production, both for itself and the trade, assures a broad availability in today's used market. These guns are viable alternatives to the current Spanish sidelocks and might save you a little money, too.

It all started with William Scott. In the early 19th Century he worked as a gunmaker in Birmingham. In 1840 he joined his brother, Charles, to form W&C Scott. Later two of William's sons joined

the firm, and in 1865 it became W&C Scott & Son. As the Industrial Revolution burgeoned, so did the company, with the addition of offices in London and Turin. The firm also did a large business in America after our Civil War. In 1897 W&C Scott & Son merged with P. Webley & Son, a large Birmingham maker of rifles and pistols, to form Webley & Scott Revolver & Arms Co., Ltd. In 1906 the name was shortened to Webley & Scott, Ltd.

Things at Webley & Scott jolted along the bumpy road of gunmaking through two world wars, the Great Depression and into the 1970s. W&C Scott & Son guns were marketed right along with Webley & Scott guns, though in smaller numbers. The guns ranged from basic boxlocks through excellent sidelocks. Webley & Scott reserved separate serial-number ranges for the W&C Scotts, but all the guns came from the same factory. In 1979, after declining sales in the slumping English gun trade, Webley & Scott, Ltd., closed its shotgun facilities and concentrated on the air guns the company is known for today. In 1980 W&C Scott rose from the ashes with some new financing. Holland & Holland bought W&C Scott in 1985

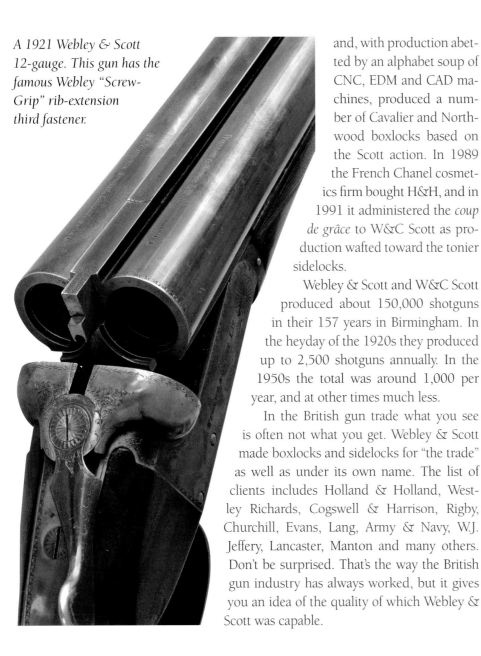

A 1921 Webley & Scott 12-gauge. This gun has the famous Webley "Screw-Grip" rib-extension third fastener.

and, with production abetted by an alphabet soup of CNC, EDM and CAD machines, produced a number of Cavalier and Northwood boxlocks based on the Scott action. In 1989 the French Chanel cosmetics firm bought H&H, and in 1991 it administered the *coup de grâce* to W&C Scott as production wafted toward the tonier sidelocks.

Webley & Scott and W&C Scott produced about 150,000 shotguns in their 157 years in Birmingham. In the heyday of the 1920s they produced up to 2,500 shotguns annually. In the 1950s the total was around 1,000 per year, and at other times much less.

In the British gun trade what you see is often not what you get. Webley & Scott made boxlocks and sidelocks for "the trade" as well as under its own name. The list of clients includes Holland & Holland, Westley Richards, Cogswell & Harrison, Rigby, Churchill, Evans, Lang, Army & Navy, W.J. Jeffery, Lancaster, Manton and many others. Don't be surprised. That's the way the British gun industry has always worked, but it gives you an idea of the quality of which Webley & Scott was capable.

The building block of all Scott boxlocks is the Anson & Deeley action, invented at Westley Richards in 1875. W&C Scott started using the design in 1890, before it joined Webley's. Because of its simplicity of manufacture and reliability, the A&D action has become the paradigm of boxlock designs. When you say "British boxlock," you are saying A&D. The action is compact, with a very short water table of about $1^5/8"$, compared to 2" for the typical London sidelock. There's a Purdey double underbolt, with the front lump anchored through the bottom of the action just in front of the removable bottom plate. One notable feature of 20th Century Scott boxlocks is that the hinge pin is not replaceable. When the action is off the face, the front hook can be welded up or replacement metal can be dovetailed in. When Holland & Holland took over the design in the 1980s, it added a replaceable hinge pin.

Not to wade into the boxlock v. sidelock argument here, but many consider the boxlock an advancement over the sidelock. There is a good argument that, had the A&D boxlock been invented before the hammerless sidelock, the boxlock would be today's side-by-side paradigm. The A&D action is stronger, simpler, more compact, more reliable and less expensive to produce. Because of the flat rear of the action body, the stock head can be seated firmly without intricate and fragile inletting. Hammers, sears and trigger bits are securely suspended between top and bottom receiver tangs—unlike on sidelocks, where they

gun has been limited to 1-oz shells, just to be on the safe side. It was originally choked Cylinder and .038" Full. One barrel flat is stamped "choke"; the other has no such marking. This extreme spread in chokes was common in older guns because the soft shot and fiber wads of the time produced less-reliable Full-choke patterns. With tighter-patterning modern shells, the choke side

bear partly on wood. Of course, there isn't much of an engraver's canvas on the boxlock, which will please some and disappoint others.

I have three Webley & Scott boxlocks in front of me as I write this. They are typical of what's on the used market today. The first is a 1921 gun serialized in the 95,000 range. It's either a Model 400 or 500. I confess I don't know for sure. (It's only a few serial numbers away from Percy Stanbury's famous Webley & Scott, which one of my sources indicates was a Model 400 and another says was a 500. Stanbury was probably the best British clay shooter from the 1920s through the '50s as well as a noted West London shooting coach, author and inventor of the "Stanbury Method" of shooting.) Both the 400 and 500 have the famous Webley "Screw-Grip" rib-extension third fastener, invented by T.W. Webley in 1882.

The 1921 gun is a 12-gauge, 1⅛-oz Birmingham proof, but with 2¾" chambers. A previous owner had the chambers lengthened from 2½" in the US, as the gun bears no British reproof marks. The

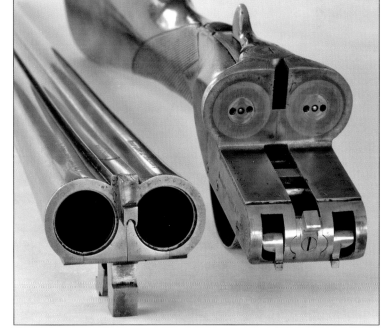

This 1921 W&S 12-gauge has bushed firing pins, a stock with a "diamond" wrist, 28" barrels with a swamped game rib, and excellent handling characteristics.

was opened to .018" (Modified) to give a 10-yard separation between barrels.

It has 28" tubes and weighed slightly more than 6 pounds before its checkered butt was replaced by a recoil pad to gain length. It has a swamped game rib, splinter forend and English stock. The double triggers are as crisp as a match pistol's. The firing pins are bushed as a little extra touch. The bluing on the barrels is turning purple, and the case coloring is mostly gone. The stock has an extremely slender "diamond" wrist rather than the usual oval cross-section. This was done to give a better grip while maintaining slimness. You can feel the stock flex in the wrist when the gun fires. The checkering isn't; it's "flat lining," not the usual diamonds. I thought it had been worn off, but that's the way it came from the factory. The 2½" 12-gauge game gun is what the English do better than anyone. Light but not whippy, this example handles as well as any English "best" I've ever shot.

I bought this gun in 1986, when it was already 65 years old and well used. It's been my grouse gun ever since. Grouse and woodcock being what they are, most of its 1,000 rounds per year have been at clays in preparation for the season. In the 17 years I've owned it the gun has broken two leaf springs and one hammer. The stock head required interior reinforcement 10 years ago, and recently the safety button had to be recheckered. There have been a few other little things, but considering its age and usage, it rates as quite reliable for a light game gun. A gun like this and with this mileage might be had today for something south of $2,000.

I also have at hand a newer example: a little 1969 Webley & Scott 20-gauge in the 140,000 serial-number range. This gun appears to be a standard Model 700. The 700 line, introduced in 1947, simplified the action by abandoning the screw-grip and making several other small changes. It has slightly more engraving than the 1921 Model 400, but it is barely 50-percent coverage. Although minimal, the hand-engraving on all the Webleys I've seen has been

good quality. (Unfortunately, the name "Webley & Scott" is crudely stamped on the receiver side of all three guns, like the stigmata of cheapness.) This 20 is in "as new" unaltered condition. The case coloring is vivid and still remains on the standing breech, and the barrels retain all their soft rust blue. It's a good example of how the gun came from the factory.

Like most Webley 20s, this gun's true 20-gauge action is fitted with 26" barrels. With its center balance and 6-pound weight, it is easy to carry and very fast. It requires discipline to shoot well. The English never understood something that the Italians know instinctively: You don't balance a sub-gauge side-by-side game gun the same way you balance a 12, because centrally balanced lightweight smallbores become whippy. This gun has a raised flat rib, but an equal number will have swamped game ribs. Unlike most Webleys, this gun lucked out in the wood lottery and got a snappy chunk of lumber for its straight-grip stock. Checkering on the forend, stock and butt is well executed and pointed up. Chambers are 3" and proofed at 3½ tons, and the chokes are snug at Improved Cylinder and Improved Modified. Mechanically, this gun appears nearly identical to the 1921 gun, lacking only the screw-grip third fastener and bushed firing pins. Twenties were a small part of Webley's production and now will command a premium price of $3,500 and up in 100-percent condition.

The final gun of this trio is the most common and the best bargain. It's a 1957 125,000 serial-number-range Model 700 12-gauge. It was sold by Abercrombie & Fitch in New York and is so engraved on the swamped game rib. Like the 20, there is no third fastener or bushed pins. The engraving and case coloring compare to that on the other two guns in amount, style and execution. It has 30" barrels chambered 2¾" and proofed at 3¼ tons. This gun came with Modified and Full chokes. The wood is very plain—typical of many Model 700 12s. The checkering was cut with intentionally flat diamonds. The forend is a splinter, but the buttstock has a relaxed Prince of Wales grip that was quite common on the 12-gauge 700s. The current owner replaced the checkered butt with a wooden stock extension and pad, but the gun still weighs only 6¾ pounds and balances on the hinge. This 700 is appropriately slower and steadier to shoot than the lighter 2½" gun, but it remains responsive and is an ideal all-around gun with modern ammunition. This gun is in 95-percent condition, and the owner has experienced no mechanical problems with it. The rear trigger is developing some creep and soon will need attention. Guns like this often sell for around $2,500.

The three models discussed are just the tip of the iceberg. As Geoffrey Boothroyd said in his book *Sidelocks & Boxlocks*, "The vast range of Scott, Webley and later Webley & Scott guns which were manufactured, most in a bewildering variety of styles and options, must have been the very devil for the factory to keep track of over the years." In the company's 700 boxlock series, the 700 was the base grade and the 701 was the high grade. W&S also made a medium-upgrade boxlock Model 712 (12 gauge), 720

A 1969 Webley & Scott 20-gauge in "as new" condition, with vivid case colors and good quality—though minimal—hand engraving. (Seth Goltzer)

(20 gauge) and 728 (28 gauge) for the US market.

So what are you going to find when you look for one of these guns to buy? Far more boxlocks were produced under the Webley & Scott brand than under the W&C Scott brand. You'll most probably see Webley & Scott Model 700 boxlocks. The company made about 25,000 of them between 1947 and 1979. As with any used gun, they are where you find them. Be proactive and contact the dealers in your favorite (ahem) magazines. Don't forget the various Internet search engines and auction sites like www.GunsAmerica.com and www.GunBroker.com. Make sure to include vendors in the UK. Most will arrange US importation for you.

A little time spent with these sources will give you a good feel for the market. Prices vary wildly, so do your homework. (Prices in the *Blue Book of Gun Values* seem a bit under what I've been seeing.) The Birmingham boxlocks aren't collectors' items like some of the American Parker and Fox boxlocks; you'll be buying a shooter, not a wallhanger. I've seen prices between $1,500 and $4,000 for virtually identical guns, so keep a hand on your wallet.

Although our three review guns are very different in configuration and date of manufacture, all exhibit the same excellent quality that typifies every W&S I've seen. Barrel surfaces are perfect, all metal parts fit correctly and wood-to-metal is good. What engraving there is is of good quality, as is the checkering. The guns clearly were built to a high standard. They just don't have many extras. As Douglas Tate said in his book *Birmingham Gunmakers*, "Perhaps because so many were made, or perhaps because machines assisted in their manufacture, Webley & Scott guns continue to be undervalued."

A used British boxlock like the Webley & Scott has a great deal to recommend it. There are enough out there so you have a fair chance of finding what you want. Their durability is undisputed, their quality is high, they handle well, their prices are usually sane and they have excellent resale value. Of course they won't be new, but maybe the previous owner used up all the misses in the gun. That would be nice.

POSTSCRIPT

Holland & Holland-owned Webley & Scott ceased shotgun production in 1991. In 2006 Webley & Scott was purchased by AGS. Webley stayed in the air-gun business, but it also reentered the shotgun market, importing guns from Turkey. In 2007 and '08 the company marketed a 700 Series side-by-side through Legacy Sports. As of this writing, the W&S Website (www.webley.co.uk) shows a 3000 Series Premium side-by-side sidelock that looks exactly like the discontinued Kimber Valier. Turkish distributor Commando Arms' Website (www.commando-arms.com) shows an O/U and a side-by-side Premium 3000 Series inscribed with "Webley & Scott" in gold. The O/U looks like the Kimber Marias and the side-by-side like the Kimber Valier. In Commando's Premium 2000 Series, the boxlock side-by-side marked "Webley & Scott" looks exactly like the S&W Elite Gold.

Winchester Model 42

Shooting Sportsman is devoted to "wingshooting & fine guns." So what was a little shucker like the Winchester Model 42 .410 pump doing in those hallowed pages? It was certainly well made but never remotely "fine." As for suitability for wingshooting, that's an ongoing debate. On the plus side it is a "magazine" gun after all. But most important, the 42 was absolutely wonderful. It still is wonderful. If you define "classic" as something that sets the standard for the genre, the Winchester M-42 meets that criterion. It's everyone's idea of what a .410 really ought to be. Better yet, you can still find plenty of them on the used market, some even at sane prices.

It all started in 1933, when Winchester's William Roemer, who had worked under Model 12 designer T.C. Johnson, submitted patent papers and Winchester began production. Though the 42 could have debuted the previous year, John Olin held up production on this $30 pump to coincide with Winchester's introduction of the new 3" .410 shell. Winchester often named its models after the year of introduction, so I don't have the vaguest idea why the gun was named the Model 42. After 30 years and approximately 160,000 guns, the M-42 died in the 1964 Winchester massacre.

The story definitely doesn't end there, but this isn't going to be a history lesson. If you want to know the biography of the Model 42, Ned Schwing's *The Winchester Model 42* (Krause Publications, 1990) is definitive. Schwing goes into great detail about its development and endless variations. With Schwing's book covering the history, I'll tell you what the little gun is like to buy, shoot and maintain today. I must confess that this will not be a neutral review. I have always admired the Model 42. It makes me smile.

The 42 was made only in .410 caliber—or 67 bore if you do the math. Most were bored for 3" shells, but some skeet guns came with 2½" chambers. Barrels were 26" or 28". It's a baby Model 12 on its own little frame, but not mechanically identical. Like its big brother, the 42 breaks down into two pieces with a twist of the wrist. Most of the production was plain-barreled field guns with uncheckered and unremarkable wood, but there were a number of ribbed target guns with fancy target stocks. Due to the scarcity of ribbed guns, many plain field guns were later upgraded with the addition of a Simmons rib and snappy Bishop or Fajen wood. The guns are entirely steel and walnut. Everything inside is machined. Components are finished where it was necessary and left with raw machining marks where it wasn't. The trigger on every 42 I've ever shot has been excellent. I don't know if it's because of design or a bit of extra handwork.

Shooting the 42 is an absolute hoot. It's guaranteed to make you grin. In target dress it weighs around 6¾ pounds and feels like a real gun. In plain-barreled field trim it's closer to 6¼ pounds, and some find the gun a little whippy. Others don't. The magazine holds six 2½" shells, so there is plenty of room for a little extra weight in there if you want a steadier gun.

Many of the skeet versions had factory or aftermarket Cutts Compensators. These were a great help in stabilizing the plain-barreled versions, though the look takes a bit of getting used to. Balance point on the ribbed target guns that I've used is around 5½" in front of the trigger. This is neither loady nor whippy. The weight-forward aspect works on clay targets, whereas the overall relatively light weight makes the gun suitable for some feathered targets.

I can hear the groans now. Bird hunting with a .410? Well, yes and no. As Dirty Harry said, "A man's got to know his limitations." Skeet with a .410 is shot with a 2½" shell containing a minuscule ½ oz of shot. The 3" .410, for which the vast majority of 42s are chambered, offers ¹¹/₁₆ oz of shot and puts the shell into a different category. But doesn't the 3" .410 have a shotstring so long that a pig could waltz through it? Maybe, but if you limit your range to no more than about 30 yards, the short distance makes the shotstring far less of an issue, as it has less time to develop. It is critical to use absolutely the best-quality shells with the hardest shot for .410 hunting. Within proper distances, the .410 is perfectly adequate on small birds like doves, quail, woodcock and rail.

After much patterning, a pen pal of mine concluded that the much-maligned 3" shell was clearly superior to the 2½", putting more pellets on target. That's no surprise, but what did surprise was that the pattern percentages from both were very close to the same. As Marshall Williams wrote on www.fourten.org.uk (a UK Website devoted to the .410), the 3" shell gives the gun an extra five yards compared to the 2½".

As to .410 chokes for hunting with 3" shells, Williams argues for constrictions in the Skeet (.005") to Modified (.012") range. Winchester's .410 Full was .018". He says a .410 Full makes the close shots for which the gun is suitable too difficult. I've had good luck with a Full-choked 42 in the 20- to 30-yard range, so maybe it's an individual thing. If you shoot quickly, I'm sure he's right. The original 42 came in all the choke designations. You'll learn to love whichever constriction your gun comes with.

Still, you do have to face reality. Bob Brister was right when he said that the 3" .410 can't hold a candle to the 28 gauge. But that's another story.

With so many Model 42s made, plus the fact that they last forever, there is an active trade in used guns. The market is in two segments: collectors and shooters. If you just want a 42 to shoot, you don't want to bid against collectors. If a version of the gun is particularly rare, dealers will add on zeros faster than a tort lawyer who tripped on your sidewalk. I saw a unique 42 advertised for a hopeful $15,000. Closer to reality, you ought to be able to get an original Standard Grade 42 plain-barreled field gun in good shooting shape for less than $1,500. Expect to more than double that for an original Skeet Grade gun with a rib and target wood.

Or you can pull an end run. I have a couple of 42s that are "made up" guns. They are ordinary ribless field guns that had Simmons vent ribs and aftermarket target wood added by previous owners. As modified guns, they have little collector value, but I think they are better shooters than they were in their original condition. Either way, you can assure your wife that these guns appreciate in value to a surprising degree and you won't have to look down at your shoes while you say it. Simmons Gun Specialties, in Olathe, Kansas, is still one of the best places to repair and upgrade your 42. Since 1945 the company has been putting ribs on Winchester pumps. Even today it adds ribs to many 42s each year. Simmons also has all the parts needed to keep your 42 running. For fancy custom 42 wood, a good bet is Wenig Custom Gunstocks, in Lincoln, Missouri. Don't be afraid to shoot your little gun. You aren't going to wear it out.

This is a good place to mention the Browning and Winchester Model 42 reproductions. From 1991 to 1993 Miroku, in Japan, made a copy of the M-42. These guns were popular—12,000 were sold in the US by Browning in Grades I and V and 850 by Winchester as the deluxe Model 42 High Grade Limited Edition. Newly made on computerized machinery, they were a lot cleaner inside than the original M-42s. They had 26" vent-rib barrels and often very nice wood. They were well-made guns.

Unfortunately, all was not perfect in reproland. If there is any enduring feature about an original Model 42, it is that it's so effortless and slick to pump. It's noticeably faster than most gas-operated autos. Except for the repros. Perhaps the developers of the repro 42 thought that the original was more fun than the law allowed. To save you from yourself, the repros were "improved" by the addition of a trigger disconnector. It drove me mad. Unlike the 12 and 20 gauge, the .410 doesn't have enough recoil to effectively give the forehand a little push to unlatch a disconnector. If you hold some back pressure with the forehand as you pull the trigger, the darn thing just sticks there. After shooting the effortless original, this hitch in the repro's giddyup took all the fun out of the gun. I had to concentrate on not pumping too soon after firing. With a real disconnector-less 42, you can hold the trigger back and pump like hell, just like Herb Parsons did in those Winchester shooting demos. Used Grade 1 repros sell for around $900 in excellent condition. They are good guns if you don't have the need for speed.

This M-42 started life as a standard field gun; the rib and upgraded wood were later add-ons.

Today there are few .410 pumps out there. Remington's 870 has always been a good gun and may become even more interesting if Remington migrates the new 27" barrel from the .410 1100 auto to the pump. Mossberg's Model 500 .410 has been a popular starter gun. These days Winchester is out of the .410 pumpgun business. Even if you count the unique lever-action .410 Model 9410, based on the Model 94 rifle action, that only lasted from 2001 to 2006. Still, even now, 80 years after its birth, the Winchester Model 42 is the king of the Lilliputians. It was the best. It still is the best. It will make you smile, too.

SLIDE-ACTION SERENDIPITY

Some guns just have good karma. The Winchester Model 42 is one of these. In the late 1970s I bought one with particularly high mileage. Someone else had obviously enjoyed it a great deal. I happily shot it for a month or so before the action got sticky. My heart sank when I pulled off the sideplate and took it apart. The bolt had cracked on the left side where it is very thin. I had no idea how to get parts back then. Marooned! My little broken 42 languished in the back of the cabinet.

A number of years later I was shooting at Remington's Lordship complex in Stratford, Connecticut. A gunsmith on my squad mentioned 42s, and I told him that I had one awaiting a transplant. He smiled and said he might be able to help. Years previously a client had ordered a large supply of spare parts for a Model 42 but had never picked them up. The gunsmith didn't know exactly what was in the package, as it was still unopened. If I felt like taking a gamble, he said I could have whatever it was for the invoice price. It turned out to be a treasure trove of parts—three complete bolts, action bars, extractor claws, springs, adjustment rings and about a pound of other bits and pieces. I was back in slide action!

I took the gun and my treasure trove of parts to a retired Winchester custom-shop worker I'd heard of. He completely rebuilt and timed the gun. He also replaced the barrel-adjustment ring because the gun had been disassembled so many times that the barrel wobbled in the receiver. When I asked him what the charge was, he said, "Are you a shooter or a collector?" I told him that I was going to shoot the gun until it was worn out again. "Then there's no charge," he said. "The Model 42 deserves to be shot and appreciated, not squirreled away in some safe."

To this day I've kept my part of the bargain.

Zoli Z Expedition

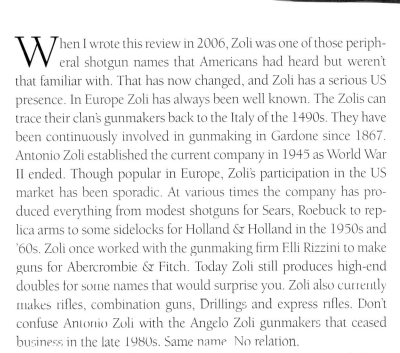

When I wrote this review in 2006, Zoli was one of those peripheral shotgun names that Americans had heard but weren't that familiar with. That has now changed, and Zoli has a serious US presence. In Europe Zoli has always been well known. The Zolis can trace their clan's gunmakers back to the Italy of the 1490s. They have been continuously involved in gunmaking in Gardone since 1867. Antonio Zoli established the current company in 1945 as World War II ended. Though popular in Europe, Zoli's participation in the US market has been sporadic. At various times the company has produced everything from modest shotguns for Sears, Roebuck to replica arms to some sidelocks for Holland & Holland in the 1950s and '60s. Zoli once worked with the gunmaking firm F.lli Rizzini to make guns for Abercrombie & Fitch. Today Zoli still produces high-end doubles for some names that would surprise you. Zoli also currently makes rifles, combination guns, Drillings and express rifles. Don't confuse Antonio Zoli with the Angelo Zoli gunmakers that ceased business in the late 1980s. Same name. No relation.

I met the personable Paolo Zoli, the third-generation head of the company, at the 2006 SHOT Show, and we discussed the maker's then-new Z Guns and Antonio Zoli's new North American organization. Steve Lamboy, one of the more knowledgeable double-gun people in the business, runs the US-sales side. The well-respected Rich Cole (Cole Gunsmithing, www.colegun.com) handles repairs, warrantee, extra barrels and custom wood. This is an all-star lineup. They intend to sell up to 800 guns each year in the US market.

The gun they introduced to the American market was the Z Gun, a detachable-trigger over/under. It is similar, but by no means identical, to the less-expensive Kronos and Columbus models that Zoli sells in Europe and now in the US. It is of a more refined quality than the Verona LX980 that Carlo Fiocchi sold through BC Outdoors in the US some years ago. Lamboy emphasized that the Z Gun has undergone many modifications exclusively aimed at the American market and is built to a higher level of fit and finish than was the Verona. The bulk of the Z Guns to arrive in the US are 12-gauge clays guns, but the company's field gun is so interesting that I chose to review it instead.

Our test gun was a 28" standard-grade 20-gauge Expedition model. It retailed for $4,500 in 2006. In 2011 the standard Expedition does not appear in the Zoli catalog. It has been replaced by the Expedition EL for $5,000. The Expedition EL appears to be the same gun, only now with an engraved French gray receiver and gold gamebirds, which move it up a notch. The Expedition EL is available in 12, 20 and 28 gauge. As with all Z Guns, the Expedition has a very strong boxlock action with a detachable trigger group. Like Dick Cheney's Perazzi field gun, the Expedition is one of the few hunting guns with direct competition-gun heritage. Usually it is the other way around, with economics requiring that the competition gun be made from a re-badged field gun.

The receiver on the 20-gauge is roughly the same size as that of a Perazzi 20-gauge MX8/20 and very slightly larger than that of a 20-gauge Beretta. Locking is by a split bolt emerging halfway up the standing breech and engaging monoblock extensions. It looks very similar to the Perazzi. Unlike the Perazzi, which uses side bolsters, the Zoli monoblock has four shallow blocks on the bottom that engage EDM-cut recesses on the floor of the receiver. The floor is solid, as the recesses do not fully penetrate. The stub hinges on the sides of the receiver also are similar to Perazzi's and engage half-moon recesses on the lower front of the monoblock. The receiver is forged from steel as a single piece. Final shaping is done by spark-erosion EDM, which can hold incredibly fine tolerances. Much is made of the gun not using any metal castings, but the opening lever sure looked like a casting to me.

The centerpiece of the action, literally, is the detachable inertia trigger. In this the Z Gun joins the Perazzi MX8, Beretta ASE/DT10 and some others. I don't really see the necessity of a detachable trigger in a field gun, but it's sort of neat to yank out and show people. Unlike Perazzi, Zoli has managed to incorporate a trouble-free barrel selector working off of a Beretta-style safety.

The trigger-group housing is obviously carefully machined and fits properly in the frame. It is not hand-detachable like those on the Perazzi and Beretta; removal requires a few turns of an included Allen wrench. Zoli feels that this method is more secure and less troublesome. With the trigger group removed, you'll immediately notice that the hammers, sears, cocking cams and inertia block are gold colored. This is a titanium nitride (TiN) hard coating similar to what you see on better drill bits. It is intended to increase surface hardness and reduce wear. Hammers are driven by reliable coil springs that have been coated with blue titanium. Ostensibly, that's to forestall corrosion, but I think it's for looks too. The hammer springs are captive on rods, so they still will work if broken.

The trigger blade is moveable fore and aft in three positions over a total of about $5/16$". It seems to lock securely in place. There are also two tiny Allen screws behind the trigger blade to adjust creep and pull weight. It was urged upon me that these were the province of only factory-trained gunsmiths. Zoli says the triggers are normally set at 4 pounds, but our sample was 5 pounds to $5\frac{3}{8}$ pounds on the bottom and $5\frac{3}{4}$ pounds on the top. Perhaps this could be adjusted if I had the required itsy-bitsy little Allen wrench, which Zoli intentionally does not include. The important thing is that there was zero creep. None at all. I'd rate a Krieghoff K-80 and a tuned Perazzi better, but this Zoli trigger was very, very nice indeed.

The firing pins nestle in their own detachable sleeves inserted into the breech to ensure frictionless travel. It's not something you can readily see, but Zoli went to a lot of trouble to do it that way rather than just drop the pins and return springs into a couple of holes in the receiver. The hammers are not rebounding, so the opening lever was designed to move both hammers back a touch on opening. The return springs can then retract the pins to prevent primer drag.

The ejector system is pretty standard stuff. Ejector springs are housed in the monoblock behind the ejectors and are compressed when the gun is closed. Sears in the forend hold the ejectors in place; when the gun is opened, they are tripped by wire ejector rods protruding from the knuckle. The ejectors on our gun worked reliably, threw the hulls together a medium distance and were almost, but not quite, perfectly timed. I noted that the forend iron was a slightly different blue color than the receiver, so I tested it with a magnet. Sure enough—non-ferrous and probably aluminum. This is no doubt done to reduce forend weight. All the stressed parts, including the pull-down Deeley latch, in the forend are steel.

Engraving on the nicely blued receiver is minimal, restrained and tasteful. There is a chained border with "Z GUN" on the sides and a tasteful logo plus "Expedition" in gold on the bottom. Our standard Expedition field model was also available in French gray. The current Z Expedition EL's engraved gray receiver is far more ornate with full scroll coverage plus a gold deep-relief partridge on one side and woodcock on the other. Engraving is by laser and is well done. The Z Ambassador EL ($10,500) and Super Luxus RB ($13,000) have increasingly more exotic hand engraving and custom options. The engraving is outsourced to Giovanelli Studios and others. There is now also a Columbus Gold game series starting at $3,600 that is mechanically similar to the Expedition but with slightly plainer cosmetics and wood. Additionally, Z Guns come in an extensive line of clay competition models in the same price ranges. The Z Sport clays guns have an excellent reputation in sporting clays. Brad Kidd used one to win the NSCA national championship in 2010.

Unlike most manufacturers, Zoli makes its own barrels, and the company is justly proud of them. Wall thickness is adjusted to regulate weight depending on the application. This allows Zoli to build long, light tubes if required. Many lower-priced makers simply have one tube thickness that they cut longer or shorter as needed, so the longer the barrels are, the heavier they get. The test gun's barrels were 28" long, but they also come in 29½" and 32" lengths.

Barrel convergence is a serious issue for any double-barreled shotgun. Zoli has vast experience in this area because of the company's manufacture of double rifles, where convergence is critical. The firm knows how to get both barrels to shoot to the same point of impact. Lamboy told me that Zoli ensures

The detachable trigger group gives ready access to the Z Gun's well-made internal workings.

proper convergence by using different monoblocks and ribs, depending on the lengths of the barrels. This allows the maker to get the angles just right. Our test sample was spot on.

Our Expedition's 20-gauge barrels were chambered for 3" shells. They were chrome lined for durability, ease of cleaning and rust resistance. Bores were slightly overbore at .622" versus a nominal .615", and the forcing cones were definitely longish at slightly more than 1". Side ribs are solid all the way back to the monoblock. The top rib is vented and slightly tapered from .275" at the breech to .200" just under the steel front bead. A replacement brass front bead is also included. Although narrow as befits a field gun, the rib is also just slightly thicker than some of the Beretta field ribs I've seen. That means it's heavier but also more resistant to the inevitable field dents and dings. One noticeable flaw is that the top of the receiver face on our test gun was considerably wider than the rear of the rib. It looks as though the receiver was made for a rib that was 1/4" wider. This was out of place on a gun of this obvious quality and should be addressed on current production.

The barrel ribs are brazed in place, and the factory pays great attention to alignment. The joining process slowly heats, cools and heats again to avoid warpage. Though I can find no reference to it, the barrels appear to be hot blued, with the telltale bright blue-black color. The finish on our gun, both inside and out, was flawless. The barrel muzzles are jugged out .08" to accept the chokes, but the taper is so gradual that it is hard to see with the naked eye.

The barrels are screw-choked and proofed for steel shot. Five titanium-nitride-coated chokes (Cylinder, Improved Cylinder, Modified, Improved Modified and Full) come in the package. Each choke is about .010" apart, but other constrictions are available on request. The chokes are flush mounted and conventional in appearance, with threading to the rear and choke-wrench notches in front as well as notches to designate constriction. The chokes are relatively short, at a little more than 1.5" long. That's not much room for long tapers or stabilizing parallels, where fixed chokes excel. The choke tubes open to about .010" overbore at the rear for safety, so there is a little bore-to-choke jump. All in all, they are adequate and unremarkable. On the plus side, they stayed put and were not difficult to change with the wrench Zoli supplied.

The wood on our Expedition was exceptional. By that I include both the figure and the configuration. Dimensions of the field stock were 14 3/4" x 1 3/8" x 2 3/16", with about 2" pitch, 1/8" cast at heel and 1/4" cast at toe. Compared to Remingtons, Rugers and some others, that sounds long and high, but it's a lot easier to cut a little bit off than wait for the wood to grow. The stock doesn't feel as long as it measures, because the flat-bottomed pistol grip is somewhat relaxed though a bit thicker than many. It's not quite a Prince of Wales, but it does allow more flexible positioning of the hand than a more vertical grip. If you wish a custom stock, Zoli ships headed but unshaped stocks to Rich Cole for custom finishing on Cole's state-of-the-art CNC stockmaking machine. It takes 45 days and costs $1,500 extra, but you can have anything within reason.

The small, smooth conventional forend is in perfect proportion to the rest of the gun. It's about as small as you can make and yet retain adequate wood thickness and appropriate length. It's just perfect. The lack of a Schnabel beak will no doubt discommode the Philistines, but the gun is more attractive for its absence.

The wood holds an oil finish of average quality. Grain was not completely filled on the sides of our stock, but it was elsewhere. The oil finish does not appear to be resistant to sunscreen, as it thinned on the stock comb where my cheek rested. The interior of the forend was properly coated to deter oil seepage, but the stock head interior had some unfinished areas that should have been addressed.

Like the finish, the wood-to-metal fit on this particular gun was also average. The wood, which is outsourced, is generally proud enough to allow one refinishing without going below metal, but it was too high on the left side of the stock head of our sample. There was also a noticeable wood-to-metal gap alongside the trigger group underneath. The forend latch was just enough below the wood surface so that you wouldn't burn your hand if things got really hot.

The checkering is laser cut in a conventional pattern and seems to be about 26 lpi to a fine double-line border. I have not seen laser checkering this fine before. Some of the diamonds near the edges were flattened, probably during finishing. The Expedition is fitted with a walnut buttplate similar in grain to the stock. The buttplate is easily removed if you happen to have a set of Torx drivers to pull the wood screws. Removal of the buttplate reveals a hollowed stock and the standard drawbolt.

The wood on our Expedition was highly figured and really good-looking. In fact, the wood on every Z Gun I saw at the SHOT Show had high-contrasting figure typical of Turkish walnut. The unadorned blued receiver made the dark wood with black swirls stand out. Whereas the rest of the gun modestly hid its quality inside, this wood made the gun strut.

But the pretty wood requires some caution. The manual warns: "To remove the forend from the barrel, do not rotate it against the curve section of the frame, but slide it out towards the muzzle." Failure to do so "could cause the wood to break in the ejector area." Well, it does and it did for some previous user of this gun. There was a tiny crack in the wood where the front of the ejector extension pried at the rear of the forend wood when the gun was incorrectly disassembled. Manuals may be mundane, but it pays to read them.

The gun is shipped in a good-quality case along with the five choke tubes, an adequate choke wrench, Allen wrenches to move the trigger blade and remove the trigger group (but not to adjust trigger-pull weight or sear engagement), an owner's manual and an extra brass front bead. The warranty from Zoli is five years.

The penalties for hunting out of season being what they are, I shot the Expedition quite a bit at FITASC, 5 Stand and low-gun skeet. Repeatable clay targets lend themselves to helpful gun analysis. This gun is flat out a shooter. At 6½ pounds, it is at what I consider the upper weight suitable for a field 20, but that weight really pays off in steadying the gun. It was balanced with enough weight forward so that it wasn't whippy but not so much that it failed on quick reflex shots. The Expedition was fast enough for 10-yard shots and stable enough for 40-yard attempts. The balance point on our sample was ¾" in front of the hinge. That's a bit more forward than usual for the field, but the key is that the weight was distributed all along the barrels, so the gun didn't feel muzzle heavy. That's the product of careful barrel design and manufacture. So many lesser screw-choke guns carry a gobbet of weight at the snout due to cheap choke installation. The 20-gauge Expedition has a little heftier feel than a Beretta Pigeon grade. Although not quite as fast, I found it a more forgiving gun to shoot.

The stock is of the slightly long, slightly high variety more favored by European makers than American makers. It fit a surprising number of the shooters who tried it during testing. One shooter with a short neck and full face picked it up, pronounced it too long and too high, and then proceeded to inkball five targets in a row. It always seems that stocks that are a little long and high suit more people than those that are short and low.

Five thousand dollars is an awkward price point. One need only look at Beretta, B. Rizzini and Caesar Guerini to see very good field guns at lesser prices than the Expedtion. Zoli's obvious strength, durability and competition build may not be a big selling point in a field gun that is carried more than it is shot. Still, there are always those who are willing to pay more for careful design and manufacturing. On a personal note, I found the cosmetics of the Zoli to be attractive. But it's the handling that makes the Zoli so nice. For me, this gun really had "the feel." Of course, my tastes may not be yours, but I think this gun is worth a look. Perhaps you will find, as I did, that the closer you look, the more you will see. Although the Zoli is certainly good looking outside, its real value is inside. Where it belongs.

Sources

Considering the long life of books, I don't know how soon after publication you are reading this. The information listed here was current at publication, but things in the gun industry, especially among the smaller producers or single importers, can change faster than a grouse can get behind a tree. It's just that kind of business. Fortunately, you have Google on your side if all else fails.

Arrieta

Arrieta, 01134-943-74-31-50; www.arrietashotguns.com

US Distributors:
Griffin & Howe, 908-766-5171; www.griffinhowe.com
The Orvis Co., 888-235-9763; www.orvis.com
Quality Arms, 281-870-8377; www.arrieta.com
William Larkin Moore & Co., 480-951-8913; www.williamlarkin
 moore.com
Wingshooting Adventures, 616-837-9000; www.wingshootingadv.com

AyA

Aguirre y Aranzabal, 01134-943-82-04-37; www.aya-fineguns.com

US Importer:
AyA-USA, 860-388-3989; www.aya-fineguns.com

US Distributors:
Fieldsport, 231-933-0767; www.fieldsportltd.com
Kevin's of Thomasville, 229-226-7766; www.kevinscatalog.com
M.W. Reynolds, Inc., 303-761-0021; www.mwreynolds.com
Michael Murphy & Sons, 316-775-2137; www.murphyshotguns.com
New England Custom Gun Service, Ltd., 603-287-4836; www.new
 englandcustomgun.com

Baserri

Baserri Shotguns, 281-686-3544; www.baserrishotguns.com

Beretta

Beretta USA Corp., 800-929-2901; www.berettausa.com

Blaser

Blaser USA, Inc., 210-377-2527; www.blaser-usa.com

Browning

Browning, 800-333-3288; www.browning.com

Caesar Guerini

Caesar Guerini USA, Inc., 410-901-1131; www.gueriniusa.com

Commando Arms

Commando Arms, 01190-266-243-4763, www.commando-arms.com

Connecticut Shotgun Mfg. Co.

CSMC, 860-225-6581; www.connecticutshotgun.com

FAMARS

FAMARS USA, 855-326-2771; www.famars.com

Fausti

Fausti USA, 540-371-3287; www.faustiusa.com

Franchi

Franchi USA, 800-264-4962; www.franchiusa.com

Grulla

Grulla Armas, S.L., 01134-943-20-87-56; www.grullaarmas.com

Huglu

CZ-USA, 800-955-4486; www.cz-usa.com

US Dealer:
DeHaan Shotguns, 208-538-6744; www.dhshotguns.com

Ithaca

Ithaca Gun Co., 877-648-4222; www.ithacagun.com

Kimber

Kimber Marketing & Sales, 800-880-2418; www.kimberamerica.com

Kolar

Kolar Arms, 262-554-0800; www.kolararms.com

Krieghoff

Krieghoff International, Inc., 610-847-5173; www.krieghoff.com

McKay Brown

McKay Brown, 01144-1698-853727; www.mckaybrown.com

Merkel

Merkel USA, Steyr Arms, 205-655-8299; www.merkel-usa.com

Perazzi

Perazzi USA, 626-334-1234; www.perazzi.it

Remington

Remington Arms Co., Inc., 800-243-9700; www.remington.com

Rizzini

Rizzini USA, 860-225-6581; www.rizziniusa.com

Robertson

Boss & Co, Ltd., 01144-20-7493-1127; www.bossguns.co.uk

US Dealer:
Cabelas, 800-237-4444; www.cabelas.com

Ruger

Sturm, Ruger & Co., Inc., 603-865-2442; www.ruger.com

Smith & Wesson

Smith & Wesson, 800-331-0852; www.smith-wesson.com

Verney-Carron

Verney-Carron, 01133-477-7915-00; www.verney-carron.com

US Importer:
Kebco LLC, 301-460-9563; www.verney-carron.us

Webley & Scott

Webley & Scott, 775-825-9835; www.webley.co.uk

Winchester

Winchester Repeating Arms, 800-333-3288; www.winchesterguns.com

Zoli

Antonio Zoli North America, 585-394-1271; www.zoli.it